At Cuyahoga Valley Church, it is our desire to continually help everyone cu
Christ. It is especially important for those new in their faith. However, all those who follow Christ at times
to re-engage the basics of our faith for continued growth in their personal spiritual walk.

This study, titled *"Living New: Growing in the Fruit of New Life,"* was prayerfully put together to enable all believers to further cultivate their lives as disciples of Jesus and grow deeper, stronger roots to live out their new life in Christ.

Each of the 13 weeks will contain a topical lesson (e.g. Bible Intake). Included with each weekly topic is a brief, interactive personal Bible study (5 of 7 days) to reinforce the spiritual value in the lesson of a specific week.

In addition, those involved working through this study in a LifeGroup setting will have opportunity to experience Caring Community as each chapter is discussed during their Group's time together.

Also, I recommend reviewing CVC's "Essential Beliefs" in order to familiarize yourself with them and gain a basic theological understanding of who this God is who gives us new life in Christ.

May God bless your life in taking this intentional step toward spiritual growth!

LIVENEW!

Chad Allen | Lead Pastor
Cuyahoga Valley Church

Living New

Living New

GROWING IN THE FRUIT OF NEW LIFE

Richard Duncan

ISBN: 1534736565
ISBN 13: 9781534736566

CVC's Essential Beliefs

1. About God
   There is only one, Creator of all things, infinitely perfect and eternally existing in three Persons: Father, Son, and Holy Spirit. (Deuteronomy 6:4, Genesis 1-2, Psalm 145:3, John 1:1, Psalm 90:2).

2. About Jesus Christ
   The Lord Jesus Christ is fully divine and fully man. He was born of a virgin, lived a sinless life, performed authentic miracles, died in the place of sinners to pay for their sins, rose bodily from the grave, and works as mediator in heaven. (Matthew 28:18-20, John 1:1, John 1:14, Isaiah 9:6, 2 Corinthians 5:21, 1 Peter 2:21, Matthew 28:6, 1 John 2:1)

3. About the Holy Spirit
   Spiritual life given by the Holy Spirit is absolutely necessary for the salvation of man. His ministry includes indwelling the believer, enabling him to live a godly life. (John 3:5-7, Romans 8:9-11, 1 Corinthians 6:19)

4. About the Bible
   The Bible is the inspired, infallible, and authoritative Word of God without error in its original writings.
   Inspired – The Holy Scripture was given to us by God through human writers. (2 Timothy 3:16, 2 Peter 1:21)
   Infallible – The Holy Scripture is not misleading and is a sure, safe, and reliable rule and guide in all matters. (Proverbs 30:5)
   Inerrant – The Holy Scripture is free from all falsehood or mistakes and is entirely true and trustworthy in all its assertions. (Matthew 4:4, Deuteronomy 8:3, Matthew 5:17-18)

5. About Man
   Although man was created in the image of God, he sinned, causing physical death and separation from God. All human beings are born with a sinful nature, and those who reach moral responsibility exercise their sinful nature in thought, word, and deed. (Genesis 1:27, 2:17, Romans 6:23, 5:12-14, 3:23, 3:10)

6. About Marriage
   We believe that marriage, as sanctioned by God, is the joining of one man and one woman, as their gender was determined at birth, in a single, covenantal union as taught by Scripture. We believe that any other type of sexual activity, identity, or expression that lies outside this definition of marriage is contradictory to God's natural design and purpose for sexual activity (Gen. 2:24; Lev. 18:1-30; Rom. 1:26-29; 1Cor. 5:1, 6:9-10; 1 Thess. 4:1-8; Heb. 13:4).

7. About Salvation
   The sinless life, death, and resurrection of Jesus Christ, provide the only basis for the salvation of all who believe. Only those who receive Jesus Christ as Lord, exercising repentance and faith, are children of God. (1 Corinthians 15:3-6, John 14:6, Acts 4:12, John 1:12)

8. About Our Future
   The Lord Jesus Christ will return bodily to the earth to complete our salvation and establish His kingdom. All the dead will experience a bodily resurrection, the believer to eternal joy with the Lord, and the unbeliever to judgement and eternal punishment. (1 Thessalonians 4:13-18, 1 John 3:2, Daniel 12:2, Revelation 7:14) We also affirm the "Baptist Faith and Message" (1963) and the "Second London Confession" (1689).

For a more in-depth study and understanding of theological issues, we recommend Wayne Grudem's *Systematic Theology*. You can purchase the book or download the free podcast. (https://itunes.apple.com/us/podcast/wayne-grudems-systematic-theology/id322844869?mt=2)

TABLE OF CONTENTS

Unless otherwise indicated, all Scriptures used in this study are taken from the English Standard Version (ESV) of the Holy Bible.

ACKNOWLEDGMENTS

So many people have made possible the book you now hold in your hands.

Thanks to my dad, Vern, and my mother, Lena, for demonstrating radical, trusting obedience and for giving me a solid foundation in the Lord. Thanks to my wife, Maryanne, and my sons, Alan, Ryan, and Evan, for all the ways that you have helped me grow in my discipleship journey. Your grace and unconditional love have given me fuel for my discipleship journey. Thanks to our daughter-in-law, Joanna, and to our two grandchildren, Ethan and Caleb. I am still learning more and more about joyful living with you.

Thanks to all the elders, staff, members, and attenders of Cuyahoga Valley Church for allowing me the privilege of growing as a man of God as we served together for almost 30 years in NE Ohio. You've followed the Lord and have given me the freedom to lead and grow and write.

Thanks to all the CVC church plants, the CVC Missions Development Team, and the NEO360 churches that have provided me with opportunities to learn, teach, and practice as a discipler.

The administrative help for this project has been amazing. Elena Golsch has made room in my calendar for me to write and has set appointments for me to maintain my current discipleship relationships in a way that permits margin in my life. She's also helped to edit the material and produced a list of references. Thanks to Jackie Petak, our gracious and capable editor, who was so very generous with her time and expertise. Thanks to Jane Rutti who faithfully, graciously, repeatedly applied her considerable skills to the layout and organization of these materials.

Finally, a very special thanks to CVC Lead Pastor Chad Allen whose vision for this project mobilized me and gave me the freedom to write. Chad's powerful contributions via his message notes occur throughout. This project could not have been completed without his initial vision, his thoughtful writing, and his wise editorial help.

If this material is helpful in any way, then all the glory goes to God who has graced us with the calling to be His Beloved Children.

Joining Jesus in His Joy,

Rick Duncan

PREFACE

In 2010, leaders at Cuyahoga Valley Church (CVC) began a process of reframing our vision. As Founding Pastor, I felt called to pass the torch of leadership to a younger lead pastor. We felt it was an opportune time to clarify our mission, values, strategy, measures, and vision. As a result, we more clearly defined what our "win" was. Winning for us is restoring brokenness—inviting people to new life in Christ, making disciples who "live new."

If making disciples is the win, then what does a disciple actually look like? When people are living new, then what does the fruit of new life look like? We defined it this way: Beloved Child, Self-feeder, Servant, Investor, Discipler, and Missionary. These are the characteristics that we want to see developed in the lives of people who are part of the Cuyahoga Valley Church family. To know if we are winning as a church, we look and listen for stories of changed lives that reflect these fruits.

Our new lead pastor, Chad Allen, asked me to write materials that would help us engage with the Lord and His Word so that our lives would reflect the Fruit of New Life. The weekly lessons have been intentionally written so that you will be encouraged to grow as a Beloved Child, Self-feeder, Servant, Investor, Discipler, and Missionary.

This discipleship material has been shaped by many different tools I have used over the years. Studies like Growing Strong in God's Family, Operation Timothy, Master Life, Navigator's 2:7, 10 Basic Steps Toward Christian Maturity, Experiencing God, and Practical Christian Living have all been very formative and useful for me over the years. If you have used any of these tools, you will, no doubt, hear echoes of truths from them as you work through this material.

Recently, I have been leading discipleship groups and have utilized the tools in this material with key men in my life. Steve Tuckerman, John Campbell, Jason Van Horn, Sam Morgano, Rich Profant, and Josh Barucky have made investments in my life over the last few years. Their contributions as a part of my discipleship groups have been invaluable.

Several leaders at CVC also contributed to the writing of this material. Various portions of content from Chad Allen's weekend messages, along with his editing, occur throughout the entire book. The sections on Prayer and the Holy Spirit were enhanced by Bill Gunsalas. Ed Jackson made contributions to the studies on Discipling and Spiritual Warfare. Dick Seawright shared his spiritual insights in the chapters on Biblical Worldview and Spiritual Gifts. Mike Hopkins wrote material that was helpful in the section on what it means to be a Missionary.

In this book, you will find 13 weeks of lessons divided into five daily readings with a variety of learning activities incorporated into the material. Head knowledge alone will not transform a life. We believe that when the mind, heart, and will are engaged in God's truth over a steady period of time, in the context of community, with a focus on application, then believers will experience the Fruit of New Life.

Although an individual believer might gain insight and growth from using the book on his own, the best way to engage with the material is in the context of a discipleship group or LifeGroup. In the appendix, you will find lesson plans for leaders to use as they guide others on their discipleship journey.

May God help you bear the Fruit of New Life!

Live New!

Rick Duncan

Week 1

ASSURANCE:
EXPERIENCING SECURITY
AS A BELOVED CHILD

M EMORY VERSE
I give them eternal life, and they will never perish, and no one will snatch them out of my hand. John 10:28

WEEK 1, DAY 1: HOW CAN I KNOW . . .?

- "How can I know for sure that I'm going to heaven?"
- "How can I be sure that I am a beloved child of the heavenly Father?"
- "How can I know for sure that my sins are forgiven?"
- "How can I know for sure that I have a relationship with Jesus?"
- "How can I know for sure that I have eternal life?"

These are common questions that many followers of Christ ask when they lack assurance.

Do you know that it's possible for you to know without a shadow of a doubt that you have eternal life? In your Bible, look up and circle or highlight 1 John 5:13.

Now, circle that word "know." Notice that the verse doesn't say "hope" or "think." God wants us to know that we *know* that we have eternal life. Assurance of our New Life in Christ and our eternal destiny is possible.

Assurance is a positive declaration intended to give confidence. For Christ-followers, our assurance is based on the promises of God.

In fact, it's the privilege and responsibility of every follower of Jesus to make our calling and election sure. *Give diligence to make your calling and election sure* (2 Peter 1:10, KJV).

Assurance of our salvation flows from a biblical truth that has been called "Perseverance of the saints" or "Eternal security of the believer." Theologian Wayne Grudem writes, "The perseverance of the saints means that all those who are truly born again will be kept by God's power and will persevere as Christians until the end of their lives, and that only those who persevere until the end have been truly born again" (*Systematic Theology*, by Wayne Grudem, p.788).

Assurance of your salvation is one of the highest blessings that you can experience in life. It's the birthright and privilege of every true believer in Christ. Once you gain assurance, you'll have more peace and joy, greater love and gratitude, and increased strength and obedience to God.

Key question:

If you were to die today, how sure are you that you would spend eternity in heaven with God?

(Place a mark on the scale to indicate your level of confidence.)

0%   25%   50%   75%   100%

When it comes to assurance of salvation, we have four options.

1. We can be saved/unsure. These are people who do have eternal life. But if asked, they would say that they do not know that they are going to heaven.
2. We can be unsaved/unsure. These are people who do not have eternal life. They don't know whether they are headed to heaven.
3. We can be unsaved/sure. These are people who do not have eternal life. But if asked, they would say that they know for sure they are going to heaven.
4. We can be saved/sure. These are people who do have eternal life and they do have assurance. They know for sure that they are going to heaven.

Consider where you are and place an X in the quadrant that you feel best describes your life.

God wants us to live in the love, joy, hope, confidence, and peace of Quadrant 4. This study is designed to help you move to Quadrant 4—to come to a solid assurance of your salvation.

IT IS COMMON FOR BELIEVERS TO HAVE DOUBTS ABOUT THEIR SALVATION.
Maybe you are wondering if you are really saved or not. Maybe you've looked at your struggles with your life-style, actions, and thought life and you've concluded, "How could I be saved if I'm struggling like this?"

Doubting your salvation is not the same thing as being unsaved. A person can have a strong, vibrant faith in Jesus Christ while still feeling some level of doubt. Don't make *doubt* and *unbelief* synonymous terms.

The presence of doubt is not the absence of faith. Brief periods of doubt do not necessarily indicate serious unbelief in a person's heart.

There are many reasons we tend to doubt our salvation.

- Spiritual immaturity may contribute to doubt. With greater maturity comes a greater understanding of God's love and His rescue of us through the work of Christ on the cross. We generally expect doubts to decrease as a person grows in spiritual maturity.
- Sensitivity to sin may cause confusion about assurance. New believers have a new sensitivity to sin. When we sin, we can question our conversion, "If I was really saved, how could I do that, think this, say that?" Believers need to remember the fact that even though they are saved, they are still sinful and, in this life, are going to continue to struggle with sin. An extra tender conscience is not a bad thing. But it can be leveraged to make us feel accused and condemned. An increased sensitivity to sin is actually a sign of salvation.
- Comparisons with other Christians may cloud our assurance. But we must understand that people mature in the faith over time and through the faithful application of spiritual disciplines. It's unrealistic to compare ourselves with believers who are far more mature.
- Our enemy, Satan, plants seeds of doubt. This is what is commonly called "spiritual warfare." It can sound like this: "You didn't really mean it . . ." "See, you haven't really changed." "You don't think your sins are forgiven just by trusting in Christ, do you? Salvation isn't free!" We must remember that if Satan can't keep us from experiencing salvation, he will seek to keep us from enjoying salvation. We dare not fall prey to his tactic of planting seeds of doubt in our minds.
- Trials or difficult circumstances sometimes cause us to have doubts about our relationship with Christ. New believers especially sometimes think that believers should be shielded by God from pain and suffering. But pain and suffering, as well as benefits and blessings, are the tools God uses to mature us in the faith.
- A lack of intimacy with God. When we don't spend regular time with God in His word and prayer, we begin to feel distant from God. That eventually leads to questioning whether we know God or love God.

Indicate how often these reasons for doubting your salvation erodes your assurance. (Put an X in the appropriate boxes.)

Spiritual immaturity	☐ Often	☐ Sometimes	☐ Rarely	☐ Never
Sensitivity to sin	☐ Often	☐ Sometimes	☐ Rarely	☐ Never
Comparisons with others	☐ Often	☐ Sometimes	☐ Rarely	☐ Never
Spiritual warfare	☐ Often	☐ Sometimes	☐ Rarely	☐ Never
A wrong perspective about trials	☐ Often	☐ Sometimes	☐ Rarely	☐ Never
A lack of intimacy with God	☐ Often	☐ Sometimes	☐ Rarely	☐ Never
Other	☐ Often	☐ Sometimes	☐ Rarely	☐ Never

Doubts about our relationship with Christ and questions about our salvation are common experiences for believers. But they are unreliable gauges of a person's relationship with Christ.

The reliability of God and His Word, rather than our subjective experiences, is what gives us true assurance. Look up and underline or highlight Philippians 1:6 in your Bible.

Based on the truth you see in Philippians 1:6, when we come to - faith in Christ, what did God begin in us?

_____

_____

_____

According to Philippians 1:6, because God is faithful, what has He promised to do for us?

_____

_____

_____

As you complete this day's study, re-word or re-write this short prayer asking God for a greater assurance of salvation for your life.

Dear Heavenly Father, thank You for providing the way for me to be saved through Your Son, Jesus Christ. I do believe that Jesus died on the cross for my sins and rose again. I want to follow Him as the Lord of my life. Help me to know that I have eternal life. Help me to make my calling and election sure. May You who began the good work in me be faithful to complete it. Help me to be eternally secure in my relationship with You.
In Jesus' name, Amen.

The presence of doubt is not the absence of faith.
Rick Duncan - Founding Pastor, Cuyahoga Valley Church

WEEK 1, DAY 2: LOOK TO GOD FOR YOUR ASSURANCE

Assurance of salvation comes when we look outside of ourselves to who <u>God is</u> rather than looking to ourselves to what <u>we are</u>. When it comes to our salvation, God Himself is our safeguard, our lifeguard, our protector.

OUR ASSURANCE RESTS ON THE NATURE OF GOD'S CHARACTER.

Think about the character of God. God is good. God cannot lie. God is faithful. He finishes what He starts. He can be trusted. Look up and underline or highlight 2 Timothy 1:12.

The great Apostle Paul wrote these words. Based on 2 Timothy 1:12, what was the basis of Paul's assurance?

_____

_____

_____

Paul rested in the character of God. He knew Whom he had believed, and trusted that God was good. He believed God would preserve him and enable him to persevere. He trusted in the goodness of God and in God's desire to save His people.

God didn't save us because of our works or our goodness. He did not save us because of what is or is not in us. He saved us because of who He is. When our assurance rests on something we have done, a promise we have made, or a prayer we have prayed, we have placed our assurance on shaky ground.

OUR ASSURANCE RESTS ON CHRIST AND HIS COMPLETED WORK.

We can build our assurance on the fact that Jesus Christ died and rose again. He accomplished all that was necessary to forgive us, to redeem us, to reconcile us to God. His work was a complete work.

In fact, when Jesus hung on the cross as He paid the debt of our sin, He cried out, *It is finished* (John 19:30). The word in the Greek New Testament is *tetelestai*. In the ancient Greek culture, it was a term written across a bill when what was owed was "paid in full." Jesus paid our sin debt in full. He said, *It is finished*.

Think about that declaration "It is finished!" What are some things Jesus meant by that statement?

_____

_____

_____

The question you face as a believer is, "Do you believe that it is finished?" Do you believe that Jesus actually accomplished His mission and that His mission included saving you? *We have nothing to add to contribute to our own salvation!* Look at the cross! Which of your sins did He not die for? Look to the cross! Jesus loved you enough to die for you. Which of your sins were not covered there? When He said, *"It is finished!"* was that not good enough for you?

We can rest in the words of Jesus, *All that the Father gives Me will come to Me, and whoever comes to me I will never cast out* (John 6:37). Jesus will never reject anyone who truly comes to Him, who rests in Him for salvation.

> **I believe hundreds of Christian people are being**
> **deceived by Satan now on this point, that they have**
> **not got the assurance of salvation just because they are**
> **not willing to take God at His word.**
> *D. L. Moody - Founder, Moody Bible Institute*

OUR ASSURANCE RESTS ON THE PROMISES OF GOD'S WORD.
If our assurance of salvation rests on God's good character and the good work of His Son, then we can also trust in God's good promises. Here are a few of God's promises in the Bible regarding our salvation:

Look up the following verses and match the sentence to the appropriate verse.

1.	God promises us eternal life.	A. John 5:24
2.	Everyone who calls upon the name of the Lord shall be saved.	B. John 3:16
3.	Whoever believes Jesus does not come into judgment.	C. Acts 16:31
4.	Belief in the Lord Jesus saves.	D. I John 2:25
5.	Whoever believes in Jesus will not perish.	E. Acts 2:21

God's promises are sure and true. If God assures us that He accepts us, who are we to argue? Who are we to doubt? If the Bible is trustworthy in telling us how we can be saved, it must also be trustworthy in how we can have confidence in that salvation. If we will not trust the Bible, who or what can we trust?

PRAYING THE PRAYER OF SALVATION OVER AND OVER?
To bolster their assurance, some people pray to receive Christ over and over and over–acknowledging sin and asking Jesus to be Savior and Lord. It can become something of a ritual if we are not careful. Yes, it can mark the moment of salvation. But like any ritual, we can wonder if we've done it right–whether we were sincere and really meant it. At that point, it becomes a kind of good work, something we do to get saved. And like every good work, it's not good enough to assure us of salvation.

It's not wrong to ask Jesus into our hearts. But what saves us is not the recitation of a prayer. It's repentance and trusting in the gospel of Christ Jesus. We are saved by grace through faith (Ephesians 2:8-9), not by doing a good enough job praying the Sinner's Prayer.

Pastor J.D. Greear provides a helpful analogy here. He encourages us to think of faith as a kind of "heart posture." Like the physical posture of sitting, it began at a specific moment. But if you want assurance that you really are sitting, do you try to remember when you first sat down, or do you make a point of noticing where you're resting right now?

Greear writes, "Many believers are troubled because they can't 'remember' the moment when they first made the decision to trust Jesus. That doesn't really matter at all. All that matters is that you're trusting Him as Lord and Savior right now. Think of it like this: I walk into a classroom and sit down in a chair. About halfway through the class you ask me if I ever made a decision to sit in the chair. I say 'yes,' and you ask me how I know that I made that decision. I don't walk you through the decision-making process that led me to sit in the chair, reviving the logic and emotions that caused me to take a seat. I simply show you that I am currently seated" (*How Can I Know I'm Saved?* by J. D. Greear, www.jdgreear.com).

Faith is the resting of your soul in Christ and His finished work. It's not totally irrelevant to remember when you first rested your weight in that posture, but it's not the most helpful question to ask. Just as you may truly be in a sitting posture without remembering when you first decided to sit down, you may have true faith even if you can't remember all the details of when you first trusted in Christ.

Our salvation does not rest in our sincerity or in anything we have done. Rather, our salvation rests entirely in the character of God, the completed work of Jesus Christ, and the promises of God. We *can* have assurance. Let's pray that every true believer experiences it to God's glory.

Question: What are some key truths about God that encourage you to believe that you are His Beloved Child?

_____

_____

_____

As you close your time today, thank Him for these truths.

Our assurance rests on God's faithfulness, character, and work—not ours.
Chad Allen - Lead Pastor, Cuyahoga Valley Church

WEEK 1, DAY 3: CONSIDERING TRUTHS ABOUT YOUR RELATIONSHIP WITH CHRIST

Many exciting things are true in your relationship with Christ. Understanding the following truths will help you build a firm foundation on which to grow in your assurance.

1. CHRIST FORGAVE ALL YOUR SIN—PAST, PRESENT, AND FUTURE.
Look up and highlight or underline Ephesians 1:7.

When Jesus died on the cross to pay for your sins, all of them were in the future from His vantage point. That means that His death paid for all your sins—even the ones you have not committed yet.

Question: How should it impact your life to know that all your sins have been forgiven?

_____
_____
_____
_____

2. YOU WILL NEVER BE JUDGED ON THE BASIS OF YOUR SIN.
Look up and highlight or underline Romans 8:1 and John 5:24.

Question: According to these verses, what 3 changes took place when you placed your faith in Jesus Christ?

_____
_____
_____

Question: According to Romans 8:1, do you have to fear condemnation from God once saved?

_____
_____
_____

3. YOU HAVE BECOME A CHILD OF THE HEAVENLY FATHER.
Look up and highlight or underline John 1:12.

You may have had a great dad growing up. Or you may have had an earthly father who failed you. Either way, God is a better Father than any earthly father ever has been or will be. He takes care of His children. He will never abandon His children. He will never kick His children out of His family.

Questions: What are some of the benefits of being a child of God? How does knowing I'm a child of God help me with assurance? In living my life?

_____

_____

_____

4. CHRIST CAME INTO YOUR LIFE AND HE WILL NEVER LEAVE YOU.
Look up and highlight or underline John 6:37 and Hebrews 13:5.

Question: According to these verses, under what circumstances might Christ leave you?

_____

_____

_____

5. YOU HAVE BEEN GIVEN ETERNAL LIFE.
Look up and highlight or underline John 6:40.

Eternal life is not something we gain after we die. It's something that we who believe in Jesus have already been given. It's not so much a quantity of life that we will be given someday, but a quality of life we have already been given in the here and now.

Questions: Based on this verse, who are the ones who have eternal life? When did eternal life begin for you?

_____

_____

_____

6. NO ONE CAN STEAL YOU AWAY FROM GOD; HE MAKES SURE YOUR SALVATION IS SURE.
Look up and highlight or underline John 10:27-29.

When you trusted in Jesus, you became one of His sheep. Jesus became your Shepherd. That means that you are safe and secure in His hands. In fact, you are in a double divine grip—in the hand of Jesus and in the hand of the Father. You are not holding onto God. God is holding on to you!

Questions: According to these verses, what will never happen to you? Can anyone take you away from God?

_____

_____

_____

7. THE HOLY SPIRIT LIVES INSIDE YOU AND GUARANTEES YOUR INHERITANCE IN HEAVEN.
Look up and highlight or underline Ephesians 1:13-14.

When these verses were written, the seal was an official mark of identification placed on a letter or legal document. The seal indicated authenticity, ownership, and security. The Holy Spirit becomes our down payment, our guarantee of heaven.

Question: How can this truth make you feel more secure?

_____

_____

_____

Which of these 7 truths gives you the most comfort and assurance? Why?

_____

_____

_____

What difference might these truths make in how you live your life day-to-day?

_____

_____

_____

As you close your time today, take some time to thank God for the truths that comfort and encourage you most.

> **To be assured of our salvation is no arrogant stoutness.**
> **It is faith. It is devotion. It is not presumption.**
> **It is God's promise.**
> St. Augustine

WEEK 1, DAY 4: EVIDENCE OF GENUINE CONVERSION

WHAT ABOUT PEOPLE WHO FALL AWAY?

Throughout the history of the church, some people profess Christ as Savior and Lord but eventually fall away from the faith. This has happened even after they have given many external signs that they were saved.

Look up the words of Jesus in Matthew 7:21-31.

The ability to do good works did not guarantee that these people were saved. Jesus said, "I never knew you." He did not say, "I knew you at one time but you strayed and fell away," but rather, "I never knew you." They never were genuine believers. At one time, they appeared to be saved. They appeared to love God. They appeared to have sorrow for sin. They appeared to be connected to Christ's church. They said that they believed the gospel. They may have even been baptized. But Jesus never knew them.

If a person falls away, they demonstrate that they never were saved in the first place. They had "the appearance of godliness" but not the ability to become truly godly (2 Timothy 3:5). Look up and highlight or underline 1 John 2:19.

"John clearly states that when people fall away from the fellowship with the church and from belief in Christ, they thereby show that their faith was not real in the first place and that they were never part of the true body of Christ" (*Systematic Theology*, by Wayne Grudem, p.794).

What about people who start out on fire for Christ, but who fall away? We all know people who started well, but drifted away.

Jesus gives us a story that gives clarity to this issue: *A sower went out to sow his seed. And as he sowed, some fell along the path and was trampled underfoot, and the birds of the air devoured it. And some fell on the rock, and as it grew up, it withered away, because it had no moisture. And some fell among thorns, and the thorns grew up with it and choked it. And some fell into good soil and grew and yielded a hundredfold* (Luke 8:5-8).

Some seed grows for awhile and eventually withers. Some seed grows for awhile and is eventually choked out. Some seed falls into good soil and eventually bears fruit. Jesus is teaching us that good fruit is the proof of the good root. He is teaching that there is a difference between saving faith and temporary faith.

If all the fruit in a person's life is in the past and there is no heart for God—no worship of Christ, no love for the Savior, no love for His people, no hunger for the truth of the Word, no hatred of sin, no love of righteousness, no desire to see others saved, no ability to grow in grace—then that person is not saved, no matter how holy he/she might have looked in the beginning. That's when Hebrews 6:4-6 and 1 John 2:19 apply.

WHAT IS EVIDENCE OF GENUINE CONVERSION TO CHRIST?

To grow in assurance of salvation, we can learn to ask ourselves 3 basic questions:

1. Do I have a present trust in Christ for salvation?

A question from the ministry Evangelism Explosion may be helpful: "If I were to die tonight and stand before God and He were to ask, 'Why should I let you into heaven?' what would I say?"

Please don't read ahead. Simply use the space provided to write your answer.

_____

_____

_____

If you wrote about your good deeds or if you are depending on your own human goodness in any way, then you are not yet resting solely on the merits of Christ. You may instead be trusting in yourself or in religion; thereby, you would be your own savior, or religion would be your savior. Both make poor saviors.

We should without hesitation or qualification be able to say that we are depending only on the work of Jesus on our behalf when He died and rose again. We must be confident that He is a sure and sufficient Savior.

2. Is there evidence of transformation produced by the Holy Spirit in my life?

When a person comes to faith in Christ, the Holy Spirit takes up residence in that person's heart. He then begins to produce His fruit. Look up and highlight or underline Galatians 5:22-23.

"Of course the question is not, 'Do I perfectly exemplify all of these characteristics in my life?' but rather, 'Are these things a general characteristic of my life? Do I sense these attitudes in my heart? Do others (especially those closest to me) see these traits exhibited in my life? Have I been growing in them over a period of years?'" (*Systematic Theology*, by Wayne Grudem, p.804).

Look at that list of traits in Galatians 5:22-23. Circle 2 or 3 where you have seen some growth. Put a star by 2 or 3 where you would like to see more growth.

3. Do I see a long-term pattern of growth in my Christian life?

The Apostle Peter tells us that the way we confirm that God has truly called us and chosen us is that we continue to grow. Look at 2 Peter 1:5-11.

Note the areas where growth is supposed to occur: faith, virtue, knowledge, self-control, steadfastness, godliness, brotherly affection, and love. How are you growing? Again, on this side of heaven, we cannot perfect any of these traits. But, over time, we ought to be seeing growth. If we practice these qualities, Peter says, we will never fall.

Consider the 3 questions:

1) Do I have a present trust in Christ for salvation?
2) Is there evidence of transformation produced by the Holy Spirit in my life?
3) Do I see a long-term pattern of growth in my Christian life?

Which question gives you the most confidence? Which question gives you the least? Why?

_____

_____

_____

Use these three questions as a basis for prayer. In your own words, ask God for the grace to truly trust in Christ for salvation. Ask Him to help you bear the fruit of the Spirit, especially the 2 or 3 where you need the most growth. Finally, ask God to help you demonstrate a long-term pattern of growth in your life.

WEEK 1, DAY 5: GAINING A "KNOW SO" ASSURANCE

Remember the verse that began this week's study? Look up 1 John 5:13 again and circle that word "know" once again . . . for double emphasis!

The preceding context for that verse can be very helpful to you as you seek to know whether or not 1 John 5:13 applies to you.

And this is the testimony, that God gave us eternal life, and this life is in His Son. Whoever has the Son has life; whoever does not have the Son of God does not have life (1 John 5:11-12).

Notice that the verse says that God *gave* us eternal life. It doesn't say "might give" or even "will give." It's "gave." Eternal life is a gift, something Christ-followers already have. We didn't earn it. We just were given it.

Now, look carefully at 1 John 5:11-12 and answer a few questions.

Where is eternal life found? And who does God give eternal life to? Who has eternal life?

_____

_____

_____

Whoever has the Son has eternal life. So, the question we must ask ourselves is this: Do I truly have Jesus? It is infinitely important to know how to have the Son. So, how do we come to "have" the Son?

The answer is not complicated or hard to find. We see the answer in verse 13. The way to HAVE the Son is to BELIEVE the Son. The word *believe* in the original Greek is *pisteuo*. It means to trust in, to place confidence in, to rely upon, to depend upon.

Jesus gives eternal life to those who believe in Him, who trust Him, who place their confidence in Him, who depend upon Him. You can have the Son of God if you trust the Son of God.

If an Advocate, a lawyer, makes an offer to defend you, you could reject him. You could say, "I can handle this case by myself." But, spiritually, none of us can handle our case by ourselves because we are sinners by nature and by choice. We simply can't defend ourselves. We can't plead our own case. So, Jesus says, "I'm coming to be your defense attorney who will not only plead your case, but also stand in your place and pay the penalty for your sin. Why do I do this? You matter to Me!" God loves to glorify Himself by saving the least likely candidates for eternal life.

Are you exclusively trusting Christ and Christ alone for your salvation? If so, then you have the Son. And you have the life!

1 John 5:11-13 applies to you. You can have a "know so" assurance.

Perhaps now we are ready to re-ask and re-answer a key question that we asked and answered earlier in the week.

Question: If you were to die today, how sure are you that you would spend eternity in heaven with God?

(Place a mark on the scale to indicate your level of confidence.)

0%   25%   50%   75%   100%

TRUE SAVING FAITH IS A FAITH THAT IS FRUITFUL.
Although it is true that we must first look outside our lives to God as the root of our salvation, we must also look at our lives for the fruit of our salvation. We should be "fruit inspectors." Does the evidence show that we have experienced new life in Christ? As someone once asked, "If you were on trial for being a Christian, would there be enough evidence to convict you?"

Therefore, if anyone is in Christ, he is a new creation. The old has passed away; behold, the new has come (2 Corinthians 5:17).

When you trusted Christ to be your Savior and Lord, you began a brand new life. God will increasingly produce many new qualities in you as you grow in Him. Has your life changed? If so, that's evidence that can help fuel your assurance. Our assurance grows when we show forth the fruit of new life. Truly saved people are truly changed people.

Which of the following changes have you experienced in your life? (Check the appropriate ones.)

- ☐ Inner peace
- ☐ New awareness of sin
- ☐ Greater victory over sin
- ☐ New love for God
- ☐ Desire to read the Bible
- ☐ Attitude changes
- ☐ Sense of forgiveness
- ☐ New concern for others
- ☐ Desire to pray more
- ☐ Increased concern for those who do not know Christ.
- ☐ Other

God's Word encourages us to be fruit inspectors. *Examine yourselves, to see whether you are in the faith. Test yourselves. Or do you not realize this about yourselves, that Jesus Christ is in you? —unless indeed you fail to meet the test*
(2 Corinthians 13:5).

Look up the following verses and match the question to the appropriate verse.

Key questions to help you grow in your assurance:

1. Has my life truly changed?
2. Am I really growing to love God more and more?
3. Do I actually seek to love God's people?
4. Do I genuinely desire to obey God's Word?
5. Am I honestly hating sin more and more?
6. Does God's Spirit whisper in my heart that I am a child of God?
7. Am I persevering in the faith?

A. 1 John 3:14
B. 1 John 2:3-4
C. 1 John 2:19
D. Matthew 22:37
E. Romans 8:16
F. 1 John 3:6
G. 2 Corinthians 5:17

Questions: Which of the above questions give you the most confidence? Which give you the most concern? Why?

_____
_____
_____
_____
_____
_____

SAVING FAITH WILL PERSEVERE TO THE END.

The true test—the final fruit—of whether or not we are saved is our perseverance. In His messages to the 7 churches in Revelation 2 and 3, Jesus shows us the importance of our being conquerors or overcomers. In the verses below, circle the word "conquers" wherever it appears.

To the one who conquers I will grant to eat of the tree of life, which is in the paradise of God (Revelation 2:7).

The one who conquers will not be hurt by the second death (Revelation 2:11).

To the one who conquers I will give some of the hidden manna (Revelation 2:17).

The one who conquers and who keeps my works until the end, to him I will give authority over the nations . . . And I will give him the morning star (Revelation 2:26-28).

The one who conquers will be clothed thus in white garments, and I will never blot his name out of the book of life. I will confess his name before my Father and before his angels (Revelation 3:5).

The one who conquers, I will make him a pillar in the temple of my God (Revelation 3:12).

The one who conquers, I will grant him to sit with me on my throne (Revelation 3: 21).

People who have saving faith will, by the power of God, persevere to the end. We will work out what He's worked in (Philippians 2:12-13). We will fight the good fight, finish the race, and keep the faith (2 Timothy 4:7). We will overcome. We will, by God's grace and for God's glory, conquer.

True saving faith is a faith that perseveres. The faith that fizzles before the finish was flawed from the first. But the converse is also true. The faith that flourishes to the finish was for real from the first.

The fruit of a believer's life certainly can't be defined as sinless living or as near-perfect behavior. We will all have ongoing struggles with sin and even, perhaps, doubt. Periods of backsliding are possible, too. But those who are being saved will lead lives that end in faith and fruitfulness, not unbelief and barrenness.

> **It is possible to profess faith in Christ but not possess faith in Christ. Those who persevere are the ones who truly possess faith in Christ.**
> *Chad Allen - Lead Pastor, Cuyahoga Valley Church*

IT'S FAITH IN GOD AND HIS WORD, NOT OUR FEELINGS THAT MATTERS MOST.
Even though feelings are important, your relationship with Christ is based on unchanging facts, not on feelings that can change daily. Some days, you may not feel saved. You may not feel eternally secure. Doubts may arise, particularly when we've succumbed to temptation. But believers are to live by faith in the reliability of God and His unchanging Word, not by feelings.

The classic example to illustrate this point is the steam engine, coal car, and a caboose. To run, the train needs the engine and the fuel car that holds the coal. It can run with or without the caboose.

The engine represents God and His Word. Let the fuel car represent our faith in God and His Word. And let the caboose represent feelings.

To help make the point, put a big "X" through the caboose. Our new life in Christ runs with or without feelings. For assurance of our salvation, we put our faith in God and His Word, not our feelings.

THANK GOD FOR YOUR SALVATION.

Now take a few moments to thank God for all He has done for you in Jesus Christ. Perhaps this prayer might help to fuel your own. Write your own prayer in the space provided.

Lord Jesus Christ, please be merciful to me, a sinner. Thank You for dying on the cross in my place for my sin. Thank You that my debt was paid in full. Thank You for rising from the dead and giving me new life. Thank You that I do not have to earn my salvation, that I have been saved by grace through faith. I believe in Your death and resurrection as the only basis for my salvation. Just as I trusted You in the past, I am trusting You today. Help me to bear fruit for Your glory. Help me to persevere, to overcome, to conquer. Grant to me assurance of my salvation. In Jesus' name, Amen.

_____

_____

_____

_____

_____

_____

Week 2

PRAYER: CONNECTING WITH GOD AS A BELOVED CHILD

MEMORY VERSE
Do not be anxious about anything, but in everything by prayer and supplication with thanksgiving let your requests be made known to god. Philippians 4:6

WEEK 2, DAY 1: AN INTRODUCTION TO PRAYER

Rudyard Kipling was a British writer who is most famous for having written *The Jungle Book*. He once wrote a little poem to help us remember six vital words that can help clarify things for us.

I have six honest serving men.
They taught me all I knew.
I call them What and Where and When
And How and Why and Who.

As we begin our week exploring the topic of prayer—a key way for us to express our God Dependence—let's use these 6 words to help us grow in our prayer lives.

WHO SHOULD PRAY?

Everyone should, of course. And anyone can. But prevailing prayer is a special privilege for those who have become Beloved Children of God through faith in Jesus. We have a Father in heaven who loves to give good gifts to His children. Read Matthew 7:11.

If you then, who are evil, know how to give good gifts to your children, how much more will your Father who is in heaven give good things to those who ask Him (Matthew 7:11).

"We can pray with perfect confidence to the Father as one who will never fail us. Human fathers may let us down, but not God. We can know with certainty that our praying will be heard and responded to in the way that is not only wisest in terms of God's own total purposes, but also is best in the long run for us as the individuals we are. Thus we see that it is a truly wonderful thing to be in God's paternal hands" (*Praying*, by J.I. Packer, p.31).

List 2-3 ways your prayer life could be different if you became truly convinced that God is your benevolent Father who wants the very best for you?

_____
_____
_____

How does it make you feel to know that God the Father not only invites us, but desires for us to talk with Him in prayer?

_____
_____
_____
_____

WHAT IS PRAYER?

Prayer is truly a gift from God. He has given us many incredible gifts. We have received new life in Christ and the forgiveness of sins. God has provided us with the power to become holy people. God has furnished us with the Bible, His written Word, and in its pages we find a model of how we are to live our new life. But one of the best gifts that God has given us is prayer, the ability to communicate with Him directly. In your Bible, read and highlight or underline Hebrews 4:16.

Prayer is entering the presence of God the Father and communicating directly with Him. Prayer is a conversation with God. We speak with Him and He speaks with us. It's important to remember that prayer is a conversation, and in conversation, people speak and they listen. When we pray we must be sure to give God time to talk, He has so much to teach us, let's be sure that we take time to listen.

Prayer is an opportunity for us to grow in our love for God, and for us to understand more fully His great love for us. We draw near to God with our thanksgiving and praise, with our confession and repentance, and with our needs and desires. He draws near to us with His comfort and promises, with His warnings and corrections, and with His mercy and grace.

In the preceding 2 paragraphs, circle the 2-3 phrases that most encourage you to become more faithful in prayer.

WHY PRAY?

Prayer changes things. God has created a world in which the actions of humans affect history. One human action that changes things is prayer—asking God to act. God chooses to weave our requests into His divine purposes. Through prayer, God may change my circumstances or God may change me despite my circumstances.

God uses the means of prayer to accomplish His ends. C.S. Lewis explains: "[God] could, if He chose, repair our bodies miraculously without food; or give us food without the aid of farmers, bakers, and butchers; or knowledge without the aid of learned men. . . Instead, He allows soils and weather and animals and the muscles, minds, and wills of men to co-operate in the execution of His will."

It is not really stranger, nor less strange, that my prayers should affect the course of events than that my other actions should do so" (*The World's Last Night and Other Essays*, by C.S. Lewis, pp.8-9).

So, why pray? Again, it's because prayer changes things. Below are 8 changes prayer makes. Match the change with the appropriate Scripture. <u>Through prayer we</u>:

1. accomplish the will of God.
2. see God work in the lives of others.
3. receive wisdom from God.
4. receive blessings from God.
5. overcome temptation.
6. overcome anxiety.
7. see more harvest workers serving.
8. glorify God.

A. James 4:2b
B. James 1:5
C. Psalm 50:15
D. I John 5:14-15
E. Philippians 4:6-7
F. Matthew 26:41
G. Ephesians 6:18
H. Luke 10:2

Prayer accomplishes even more. We develop our friendship with Jesus. We find freedom from sin. We find comfort for our grief. We gain peace. We discover healing for our pain. An old hymn says it well:

What a friend we have in Jesus,
All our sins and griefs to bear;
What a privilege to carry
Everything to God in prayer.
O what peace we often forfeit,
O what needless pain we bear,
All because we do not carry
Everything to God in prayer.

In the space below, write out a prayer asking God to help you live out the <u>WHO</u>, <u>WHAT</u>, and <u>WHY</u> of prayer.

Dear Heavenly Father,

_____
_____
_____
_____
_____
_____

What was one of the most helpful insights that you received during this lesson?

_____
_____
_____

WEEK 2, DAY 2: AN INTRODUCTION TO PRAYER (CONTINUED)

Yesterday, as we explored the topic of prayer, we considered 3 words to help us grow in our prayer lives: who, what, and why. Today, we'll consider when, where, and how.

WHEN SHOULD WE PRAY?

It's important for us to have a set time—designated time—in our schedules for prayer. We see this over and over in the life of Jesus. *He went up on the mountain by himself to pray. When evening came, he was there alone* (Matthew 14:23). *And rising very early in the morning, while it was still dark, He departed and went out to a desolate place, and there He prayed* (Mark 1:35). *But He would withdraw to desolate places and pray* (Luke 5:16). We must build routine, unhurried time in our lives for regular Bible reading and prayer, commonly called "the quiet time."

But prayer must go beyond a once-a-day quiet time. The Bible says that we should "always" pray. Look up the following three verses and in your Bible circle the words that indicate the frequency of prayer: Luke 18:1, Ephesians 6:18a, and 1 Thessalonians 5:17.

These verses obviously do not mean that we must always be "on our knees" in prayer. After all, we see Jesus doing many other things besides prayer in the gospels. We see Him healing, serving, conversing, preaching, counseling, etc.

To pray "always" means that we live in a constant spirit of prayer. We must constantly live in a state of God dependence. This means that "even when we are not speaking consciously to God, there is a deep, abiding dependence on him that is woven into the heart of faith." This also means that we pray repeatedly throughout the day. "We should pray over and over, and often. Our default mental state should be: 'O God, help' . . ." (*When I Don't Desire God*, by John Piper, p.157).

Texting has changed communication. You can have a conversation throughout the day by communicating through ongoing short texts to another person. Ongoing prayer is similar – touching base with God multiple times throughout the day.

Record in the space below what seems to be the best opportunity for your set time for regular, unhurried prayer.

_____

_____

_____

Use your imagination. What are a few tangible things you can do to remind you to "pray without ceasing"?

_____

_____

_____

WHERE DO WE PRAY?

We must pray alone and in secret. Jesus instructs us: *But when you pray, go into your room, shut the door and pray to your Father who is in secret* (Matthew 6:5). Someone once said, "Seek the face of God before you see the face of men." Make private prayer a part of the routine rhythm of your life.

We must also pray in a caring community with others. In the Bible, believers regularly gathered together for corporate prayer. *All these with one accord were devoting themselves to prayer, together . . .* (Acts 1:14a). Pray with your family and friends. Pray with your LifeGroup. Pray with others in large church-wide prayer gatherings.

Where is a secluded place that you can regularly go to for prayer?

_____

Take some time to list a few benefits that are unique to praying alone and praying with others:

ALONE:

_____   _____
_____   _____
_____   _____

WITH OTHERS:

_____   _____
_____   _____
_____   _____

HOW DO WE PRAY?

Jesus' followers once asked Him, *Lord, teach us to pray* (Luke 11:1b). Following this request, He taught His disciples a pattern for prayer. We find the same pattern for prayer in Matthew's gospel. Before He gave the pattern in Matthew 6, Jesus showed His disciples a few things *not* to do.

First, He says that your prayers should never be done for show. You aren't supposed to publicly pray to draw attention to how righteous or holy you are. *When you pray, you must not be like the hypocrites. For they love to stand and pray in the synagogues and at the street corners, that they may be seen by others* (Matthew 6:5a). If you pray simply so others notice you, you're missing the point.

Second, Jesus says that you shouldn't use "empty phrases" or "vain repetition," expecting God to hear you because of the language you use. *And when you pray, do not heap up empty phrases as the Gentiles do, for they think that they will be heard for their many words* (Matthew 6:7). God isn't impressed with big, holy-sounding words, and righteous phrases. Prayer is a conversation with God. So, talk like you're talking to a friend. Be yourself. Use the language you normally use. It's not the words you use that grab God's attention, but your heart that offers them.

Third, implied with both of these, we see that prayer must come from a heart of humility. When we look at the prayers offered through the Bible, we see how crucial humility is in prayer. In prayer we are creaturely servants who are coming before our awesome Creator and Sovereign King. At the Holocaust Museum in Washington, D.C., a damaged sign from an old synagogue is on display. It was placed in the Jewish house of worship to remind worshipers to be reverent and humble. It says, "Know before whom you stand." In prayer we come before a holy God. We dare not be arrogant when we do.

"God requires all men to pray to Him, and to give thanks, this being part of our natural worship. But to render such prayer acceptable, several things are requisite: it must be made in the name of God's Son, it must be Spirit-aided, and it must accord with the will of God. It must also be reverent, humble, fervent, persevering, and linked with faith, love, and understanding" (*The 1689 Confession: A Faith to Confess*, author unknown, p. 50).

In the space below, write out a prayer asking God to help you live out the when, where, and how of prayer.

Dear Heavenly Father,

_____
_____
_____
_____
_____
_____

What was one of the most helpful insights that you received during this lesson?

_____
_____

WEEK 2, DAY 3: THE DISCIPLE'S PRAYER (PART 1)

Maybe you are familiar with what many people call the "Lord's Prayer" or the "Our Father." It's found in Matthew 6:9-13.

Open your Bible to the prayer and circle it, highlight it, underline it, or put a box around it.

Our Father in heaven,
hallowed be your name.
Your kingdom come,
Your will be done,
on earth as it is in heaven.
Give us this day our daily bread,
and forgive us our debts,
as we also have forgiven our debtors.
And lead us not into temptation,
but deliver us from evil (Matthew 6:9-13).

The prayer might be better called the "Disciple's Prayer" or the "Model Prayer" because Jesus is giving us a pattern or outline for our prayers. We aren't meant to simply repeat the prayer mindlessly. In prayer, we are to "click on" each phrase and be launched into a meaningful, expansive conversation with God.

Today, we are going to focus on the first half of the Disciple's prayer—the half of the prayer that keeps our prayers God-focused and unselfish—that can help keep us from a "gimme" approach in prayer.

"OUR FATHER IN HEAVEN"

God is on high, He is holy. While we must respect Him, we must also remember that He is more than God in heaven who must be praised. He is also our Father. When we receive new life in Christ, we become Beloved Children of God. Open your Bible and read Galatians 4:4-6.

Abba is the Hebrew equivalent to "Daddy." Think of it. We are being invited to call God "Daddy!" It's a term of love and affection from a young child to a loving and generous Father. It's a term of confidence in the love of the Father. We know that no matter what happens, the Father's love will always be there for us, and our Father will always listen. He desires to provide for you, His child. You can always know the love and protection of your Father in heaven.

When we pray, let us come before God humbly, but confidently, knowing His love and desire for us to pray and communicate with Him.

The Model Prayer teaches us to start our praying by recognizing that even though we are undeserving, we have been adopted by God.

In the space provided below, write out a short prayer thanking God that you are His child. Praise Him for some of the benefits you now have because you are in His family. Then write a sentence or two praising God for the fact that He is in heaven ruling over all things, as your childlike spirit gives way to a spirit of devout adoration.

_____

_____

_____

_____

"HALLOWED BE YOUR NAME"

As we enter into prayer, we must remember to Whom we are speaking. God is a holy God, the Creator of the universe, perfect in His holiness and complete in His power. Some versions of the Bible use the word "holy" rather than "hallowed," i.e., *May your name be kept holy* (New Living Translation). Therefore, we come humbly before Him, acknowledging His holiness, with the realization that He is on high. He is hallowed, consecrated and set apart. He is above all.

God's power is beyond comprehension. By His word, the universe was created. He spoke and the earth and everything on it was made. He formed man from the dust of the earth and breathed life into him. He is the Author of life. He commands nature and the cosmos. In the Bible, we see time and again that in the fear and reverence of God's tremendous power, He shows up, and the people are terrified.

That's why when we come before God, we must do it reverently. God is not the "Big Guy" or "The Man upstairs." He is God in heaven, Who alone is worthy of praise. When we come before Him in prayer, let us give Him the respect and honor that He is due.

The Israelites had seen God's power firsthand, they knew what He was capable of, and they had a deep respect for His holiness, so much so that they wouldn't even say the name of God. When they built the Temple in Jerusalem they made it so that they couldn't enter the presence of God casually. The southern steps of the Temple, the main entrance in the first century AD, were built very uniquely. The first step would be tall and narrow, the next would be short and wide. Each step had to be taken intentionally and carefully. This was done purposely so that no one would casually or haphazardly enter the presence of God. It had to be done reverently and intentionally.

When we come to God in prayer, we must come with the same humble attitude, knowing before Whom we stand. We praise God like the angels who sing, *Holy, holy, holy* (Isaiah 6:3).

In the space provided below, write out a short prayer acknowledging some of the ways you see God as holy, set apart, consecrated, and above all. Ask God to make His name famous—to build His reputation, to make Himself known, to make a name for Himself—through you, through your family, and through your church. Ask God to work in you a passion for His passion—that His name be glorified in everything you do.

_____

_____

_____

_____

"YOUR KINGDOM COME"

And as we continue in prayer, it is important to remember that God is the Sovereign King. But we also acknowledge that there are individuals, families, communities, nations, businesses, and realms that have not yet submitted to His rule. We also remember that there are large parts of our own lives that are not fully under the reign of Christ. So, we pray, "Your kingdom come!"

In "The Westminster Shorter Catechism," we learn that in this petition "we pray that Satan's kingdom may be destroyed; and that the kingdom of grace may be advanced, ourselves and others be brought into it, and kept in it; and that the kingdom of glory may be hastened" (Psalm 68:1, Revelation 12:10-11; 2 Thessalonians 3:1; Romans 10:1; John 17:9, 20; Revelation 22:20).

How often do we pray and do nothing but tell God everything we're going through and everything we need Him to do for us? Where does this prayer have its focus? Fully on us. Many prayers are ultimately focused on asking God to set us up as miserable little kings and queens of our own myopic kingdoms. Prayers like this bring an attitude of entitlement, no matter how subtle or unintentional. These kinds of prayers look at God almost as a Heavenly Vending Machine. But that isn't the role God plays. When God invades our lives and we begin to Live New, our self-centered orientation must change. Prayers become God-centered, not self-centered.

Heaven is God's throne room. Sin does not exist there. There, God is glorified as He should be, and all is right. In this petition, we are seeking this same reality to come to earth. As we pray, we are asking God to bring His restoration to the world. We are asking Him to bring His Kingdom to earth. This petition moves us from pure worship into a missionary passion.

In the space provided, write out a short prayer asking God for His kingdom to come in your life and throughout the world. In what areas of life is He not truly the King of kings and Lord of lords over you? How is He not king in your family, in your neighborhood, in your church, in your region/nation/world? Be specific. Ask God to rule and reign in these particular individuals and situations.

_____

_____

_____

_____

"YOUR WILL BE DONE ON EARTH AS IT IS IN HEAVEN"

Let's face it. Often in prayer, we are seeking to bend God's will to ours. But God will have none of that! One of the main points of prayer is that we seek to line up our desires with God's will.

In "The Westminster Shorter Catechism," we learn that in this petition "we pray that God, by His grace, would make us able and willing to know, obey, and submit to His will in all things, as the angels do in heaven" (Psalm 67; Psalm 119:36; Matthew 26:39; Job 1:21; Psalm 103:20-21).

As we pray for the Kingdom to come and God's will to be done, what we are really asking is, "God empower us to do Your will, so that we can help usher in Your kingdom here on earth." Imagine how quickly the angels carry out God's will. Now, imagine what life would be like if you carried out His will just as quickly and cheerfully. What would your family, your church, and your workplace look like if everyone was focused on doing the will of God?

How often have we prayed this prayer, "Your will be done," without even realizing what we are asking? How often have we prayed this without thinking and then lived in a way that doesn't work to accomplish God's will here on earth?

In the space provided below, write out a short prayer asking God for His will to be done. Ask God to help you learn to submit cheerfully to and work passionately for God's will in your every circumstance. Ask God for His will to be done in your family, in your neighborhood, in your church, in your region/nation/world. Again, be specific as you write down a prayer about particular individuals and situations.

_____

_____

_____

_____

What was one of the most helpful insights that you received during this lesson?

As we focus our prayers on the Father's fame, His kingdom, and His will, we prepare our hearts by acknowledging God for who He is. If we don't begin prayer correctly with a God-focused orientation, we quickly get off track.

Prayer begins by acknowledging God for who He is. He is on high and He is to be glorified. Life is about Him receiving the glory. He alone is worthy. Beginning your prayer time by acknowledging God for who He is, sets the precedence for the rest of your prayer life.

As you close your time today, slowly and thoughtfully recite the Matthew 6:9-13 Model Prayer phrase-by-phrase. After each phrase, add a thought or two in your own words as you approach the Father in prayer.

***Prayer as merely communication with God can tend to be short
and shallow; but prayer as connection with God tends to be longer and richer in nature.***
Chad Allen, Lead Pastor - Cuyahoga Valley Church

WEEK 2, DAY 4: THE DISCIPLE'S PRAYER (PART 2)

Yesterday, we asked you to open your Bible to Matthew 6:9-13 to the "Disciple's Prayer" or the "Model Prayer" where Jesus gave us a pattern or outline for our prayers. As you open your time today, slowly and thoughtfully recite the Matthew 6:9-13 Model Prayer phrase-by-phrase. Just as you did yesterday, after each phrase, add a thought or two in your own words.

Our Father in heaven,
hallowed be your name.
Your kingdom come,
Your will be done,
on earth as it is in heaven.
Give us this day our daily bread,
and forgive us our debts,
as we also have forgiven our debtors.
And lead us not into temptation,
but deliver us from evil (Matthew 6:9-13).

The first half of the prayer focuses on God's name, God's kingdom, and God's will. This keeps us from being self-focused and me-oriented. In prayer, we begin by acknowledging God for who He is. We continue the focus on God by asking Him to bring His kingdom to earth and accomplish His will. Prayer is to be God-focused.

But keep in mind that Jesus encouraged us to approach God as our "Father" in the opening statement. God is our loving Father and we are His precious, beloved children. He knows that we deal with hardships. He knows that there are things we need. And prayer is the opportunity to present our requests to God.

As our Father, God is passionate about us as His beloved children. He rejoices over us (Zephaniah 3:17). Our names are engraved on the palms of His hands (Isaiah 49:16). We are the apple of His eye (Psalm 17:8). Therefore, He wants us to come to Him with our requests.

Look up Philippians 4:6 in your Bible. Circle the word that tells us how many things we are supposed to bring before God in prayer. God says, *Do not be anxious about anything, but in everything by prayer and supplication with thanksgiving let your requests be made known to God* (Philippians 4:6). We are invited to bring everything—all our requests—to God in prayer.

Jesus made some amazing promises regarding our asking. Look up and highlight or underline John 14:13-14, John 15:7, and John 16:24.

Look carefully at these verses and make a list of 2-3 qualifications that might help us define or qualify the "whatever" of our asking:

_____

_____

_____

Even though these words from Jesus are super-strong invitations for us to ask God, these are not "blank check" promises for answered prayer. This is not an invitation for us to write in whatever amount, so to speak, for whatever we want or think we want, and God will make it happen. Praying in Jesus' name means "that we should ask God for things that the Lord Jesus will also ask for on our behalf. We are to make requests to the Father that the Lord Jesus will back" (*Praying*, J.I. Packer, p.154).

Now, with that as our background, let's turn our attention to the three key requests in Matthew 6. We can come boldly and confidently to God's throne of grace to ask 1) for provision,
2) for pardon, and 3) for protection.

"GIVE US THIS DAY OUR DAILY BREAD"

It is fitting for us to make requests of God in prayer. But prayer isn't to become a selfish request for more. In prayer we ask, "Father, give us today what we need." God has promised to meet our need, not our greed (Philippians 4:19). We don't seek excess because that could turn us into greedy, selfish, materialistic, worldly consumers. Having too much can also turn us from God dependence to self-reliance (Proverbs 30:8-9). This is a prayer that cultivates a greater trust in God. Every day we look to Him to provide.

"The term 'bread' refers to all [our] physical needs. . . God cares that our physical needs are met. He is concerned with the fact that we need food to eat, clothes to wear, and a place to rest. . . Everything necessary for the preservation of this life is 'bread.' This includes food, a healthy body, a house . . . good government, and peace. . . All the physical necessities of life—the necessities, not the luxuries—[are] 'bread'" (*The Disciples' Prayer*, by John MacArthur, p.55).

God as Father loves to bless His children. *If you then, who are evil, know how to give good gifts to your children, how much more will your Father who is in heaven give good things to those who ask Him* (Matthew 7:11). Count on it. God loves to give good gifts.

Notice that the prayer is for "us," not merely for "me." This reminds us that we're instructed to address God as "Our Father," not "My Father." Our asking must be for others and not ourselves alone. We must never forget that we are to be a Caring Community. God blesses us so that we can in turn be a blessing to others. So, we boldly ask God to provide for our needs so we can meet the needs of others. We remember that often we have more than we need to help people in need. God loves to give gifts to His children who think like that!

Just as we did yesterday, in the space provided below, write out a short prayer asking God to give to you (and to others) daily bread. Today, what are your needs? What are the needs of some other people you know? Express your dependence on God. Ask God to meet needs this day.

_____

_____

_____

_____

What was one of the most helpful insights that you received during this lesson?

_____

_____

_____

_____

_____

WEEK 2, DAY 5: THE DISCIPLE'S PRAYER (PART 3)

"FORGIVE US OUR DEBTS"

Prayer is a time to confess our sins to God. In Romans, Paul says, *All have sinned and fall short of the glory of God* (Romans 3:23). We need God's forgiveness. And God wants to forgive us. So, in the Model Prayer, Jesus tells us to seek it.

It is true that, for every true follower of Jesus, our sins—past, present, and future—are *already* forgiven. Ephesians makes this clear: *In [Christ] we have redemption through His blood, the forgiveness of our trespasses, according to the riches of His grace* (Ephesians 1:7). We already have forgiveness. This means that we will never stand before God as a condemning judge. Jesus said, *Whoever hears My word and believes Him who sent me has eternal life. He does not come into judgment . . .* (John 5:24).

Because our eternal forgiveness is secure and we no longer face a condemning judge, we now have a relationship with God as our holy Father. Our actions and attitudes can grieve and offend Him. We sin against the Father, and our fellowship with Him can be disturbed. That's why we must confess. The forgiveness we seek is a child's forgiveness—the pardon that a child who has hurt his Father seeks. When we confess our sin, our fellowship with the Father is restored. Look up 1 John 1:9 and underline or highlight the verse.

Question: Is there anything you need to confess? Use the space below to list some sins you need to confess. Then, find a sharpie, and in big, bold letters, write over the list of words the word FORGIVEN!

_____

_____

_____

_____

Here in the Disciple's Prayer in Matthew 6, we see something else that is very important regarding forgiveness. The more we are focused on God and the more we desire to see His kingdom come to earth, the more forgiving we will be toward others. So, we pray, *"Forgive us . . . as we also have been forgiven."*

Do we realize what we are saying when we pray this way? "Father, forgive us to the same degree that we have forgiven others." How many times have we asked God to forgive us with unforgiveness in our hearts? How many times have we confessed something with anger, or even hatred, toward someone else? If we seek forgiveness as Beloved Children, we must also be forgiving.

"The proof that you and I are forgiven is that we forgive others. If we think that our sins are forgiven by God and we refuse to forgive somebody else, we are making a mistake; [we are proving that] we have never been forgiven. The man who knows he had been forgiven, only in and through the shed blood of Christ, is a man who must forgive others. He cannot help himself. . . Whenever I see myself before God and realize even something of what my blessed Lord has done for me, I am ready to forgive anybody anything. I cannot withhold it. . ." (*Studies in Sermon on the Mount, Volume II*, by Martin Lloyd-Jones, pp.75-76).

Forgiven people forgive people. "The point is not that a forgiving spirit causes us to merit God's forgiveness, but simply that forgiven people forgive others, and that those who persistently refuse to forgive others have no basis to claim they have been forgiven by God" (*Choosing Forgiveness*, by Nancy Leigh DeMoss, p.69).

In your Bible, look up and read Matthew 18:21-35. In the space below, write a brief summary of the main points of the story told by Jesus.

_____
_____
_____
_____

Every time we sin against God, we owe Him. But in Christ, God has forgiven us and released us from a huge mountain of debt. The debt others owe us because of the sins they have committed against us does not even remotely compare with the mountainous debt we owe God. If He has forgiven us of our huge debt of sin against Him, how can we not forgive others of the smaller debt of sin against us? Living without forgiving is like drinking poison and waiting for the other person to die.

Forgiveness is a choice. So, do not merely pray, "Lord, help me to forgive this person who has hurt me." Instead, go the distance. Pray, "Lord, I know You have forgiven me of so very much. Because I have been forgiven by You, I have the desire and the ability to forgive others. You can take care of the injustice that has been done against me. Lord, by Your grace and in obedience to You, I *choose* to forgive—to clear the record, to press the delete button, to release the offender, to let the offense go. The one who has hurt me doesn't have to pay. I *do* forgive."
(*Choosing Forgiveness*, by Nancy Leigh DeMoss, p.135).

Question: Is there anyone you need to forgive? Use the space below to list some names of people who have hurt you. Or list some of the sins that have been committed against you. Then, find a sharpie and, in big, bold letters, write over the list of words the word FORGIVEN!

_____
_____
_____
_____

Now, in the space provided below, write out a short prayer confessing your sin and asking God Your Father to forgive you. Then, thank Him for the grace He's provided you to forgive the people who have hurt you.

_____
_____
_____
_____

"LEAD US NOT INTO TEMPTATION"

We have died to sin, and found new life in Christ, and we don't ever want to go back. So we seek God's help as we live our new life in Him. We ask Him to not lead us into temptation, but rather in the paths of righteousness. We are seeking to live a life that pleases God, that glorifies God, and helps bring His kingdom to earth.

Even after gaining new life in Christ and experiencing forgiveness of our sins, in this life we will find ourselves in a battle against the world, the flesh, and the devil. These spiritual enemies work powerfully to entice us to sin. If left to ourselves, our spiritual weakness, our foolishness, our lusts, and our lack of vigilance will conspire to cause us to fall. We are human, and we live in a fallen world, and so we must daily seek God and His guidance so that we are not led astray.

Open your Bible to Matthew 26:41. Highlight or underline the verse.

Because our flesh is weak, the devil's snares are enticing, and the world's temptations are strong, we must ask God for grace to overcome. "There are situations which will be dangerous to you; watch and pray, always be on guard lest you fall into temptation" (*Studies in the Sermon on the Mount*, by Martin Lloyd-Jones, p. 76).

So, in the Disciple's Prayer, we are encouraged by Jesus to pray that God will overrule the world, subdue our flesh, and restrain the devil. We ask the Father to bless our time in the Word of God, our time in the fellowship of God's people, and our time in prayer so that we are kept from temptation and/or strengthened to resist temptation.

And if we fall, we are being taught in the Disciple's Prayer to ask to be lifted out of sin and shame. We ask to be restored so that we will grow in our sanctification until that day when we will be fully free from sin, temptation, and all evil forever.

Seek God's guidance to avoid temptation. The more you seek God, the more you will become like Christ and the more you will desire to walk the path of righteousness. And the more you walk in righteousness, the more you will be delivered from evil.

This highlights our sanctification—being saved from the power of sin. If we are really forgiven, we are anxious not to offend again. Our justification inevitably leads to a desire for our sanctification. We ask God for the grace to persevere in personal righteousness.

Now, in the space provided below, write out a short prayer asking God Your Father for deliverance—to help you overcome some particular temptations. Be specific.

_____

_____

_____

_____

What was one of the most helpful insights that you received during this lesson?

_____
_____
_____
_____
_____

Bonus exercise: Over the last 3 days, you have been encouraged to personalize each of the 6 petitions found in the Disciple's Prayer. Go back and look at each day's entries. In the space below, edit and write down all the prayers you have written in the previous days. Don't forget to follow the sequence Jesus gave us in Matthew 6:9-13. Then use the written prayer as fuel for your prayer to God your Father.

_____
_____
_____
_____
_____
_____
_____
_____
_____
_____
_____
_____
_____
_____
_____
_____
_____
_____
_____
_____
_____
_____

ADDITIONAL READING FOR WEEK 2: HINDRANCES TO PRAYER

It is possible for us to jam our line of communication with God. We call these hindrances to prayer. Below is a list of seven obstacles we can build that will impede our progress in prayer.

1. CHERISHED SIN.

If I had cherished iniquity in my heart, the Lord would not have listened (Psalm 66:18, see also Isaiah 59:1-2).

The word cherished means "looked forward to" or "aimed for." To "cherish iniquity," then, is to aim at it. This means it is futile for us to pray for God's help while aiming to commit some form of sin. It's important to note that we will always struggle with ongoing sin until we reach heaven. Therefore, it would be a misinterpretation to read this as implying that absolute sinlessness is a condition for answered prayer. But make no mistake about it: unconfessed and unforsaken sin hinders prayer. As long as we hold onto sin, we cannot expect God to heed our prayers.

2. WRONG MOTIVES.

You ask and do not receive, because you ask wrongly, to spend it on your passions (James 4:3).

Our motives must be to seek to honor God and advance His kingdom purposes. James is not saying all pleasure is wrong, only pleasure that does not have the glory of God as the goal. Selfish prayers are always those that are intended to gratify our own selfish desires. We should not expect God to respond to such prayers.

3. UNRECONCILED RELATIONSHIPS.

If you are offering your gift at the altar and there remember that your brother has something against you, leave your gift there before the altar and go. First be reconciled to your brother, and then come and offer your gift (Matthew 5:23–24).

Reconciliation with the person who has something against you must take precedence even over offering your gift, including prayer, in worship. The one who initiates the reconciliation here is the one who has wronged the other person. Sometimes, it is not possible to reconcile because the other person may be unwilling. But the willingness on our part to reconcile must be present. We cannot be wrong with man and right with God.

4. PRACTICAL UNBELIEF.

Let him ask in faith, with no doubting, for the one who doubts is like a wave of the sea that is driven and tossed by the wind. For that person must not suppose that he will receive anything from the Lord; he is a double-minded man, unstable in all his ways (James 1:6-8).

Praying without doubting means praying in the secure belief and understanding of God's character, nature, and motives. When we come to God in prayer while doubting His character, purpose, and promises, we insult Him. Our confidence must be in His ability to grant any request that is in accordance with His will and purpose for our lives. Some have not because they ask not; others have not because they believe not.

5. NEGLECTING SCRIPTURE.

If one turns away his ear from hearing the law, even his prayer is an abomination (Proverbs 28:9).

Indifference to the Word of God hinders effective praying. We must learn to pray according to God's will. The very best way for us to understand His will is to immerse ourselves into His Word. Remember that prayer is not getting God to accomplish our agenda. It's getting our hearts set on accomplishing His agenda. Reading the Bible is the way we make sure our prayers align with God's purposes and priorities.

6. AVOIDING GENEROSITY.

Whoever closes his ear to the cry of the poor will himself call out and not be answered (Proverbs 21:13).

Stingy, self-focused believers will find that their lack of generosity to the poor will be a great hindrance to their effectiveness in prayer. The one who gives generously to others will receive generously from God. The open-handed are powerful in prayer; the tightfisted are powerless in prayer. If we would get from God, we must give to others.

7. MARITAL DISCORD.

Likewise, husbands, live with your wives in an understanding way, showing honor to the woman as the weaker vessel, since they are heirs with you of the grace of life, so that your prayers may not be hindered (I Peter 3:7).

If husbands do not treat their wives in a godly way, the Lord will pay no heed to their prayers. Strained relationships in marriage hinder effective praying. R. A. Torrey has said that any man or woman whose prayers seem to bring no answer should just spread their whole married life out before God, asking Him to put His finger on anything in it that is displeasing in His sight. How tragic it would be to allow any of these things to hinder our prayers from the answers our Heavenly Father delights to give His beloved children.

Which of these hindrances to prayer have been the most difficult for you to overcome in the past?

_____

_____

_____

_____

Fortunately, all these prayer hindrances can be overcome immediately when we come to God in confession and repentance. We are assured in 1 John 1:9 that *If we confess our sins, he is faithful and just to forgive us our sins and to cleanse us from all unrighteousness.* Once we have done that, we will enjoy a clear and open channel of communication with God, and our prayers will be heard and answered according to His will.

What was one of the most helpful insights that you received during this lesson?

_____
_____
_____
_____
_____

Another helpful prayer guide:

Praise   Spend time in worship of God for Who He is.
Repent   Search your heart for all unconfessed sin.
Ask   Bring your needs and desires to God, thanking Him for all He's given you.
Yield   Seek God's direction and will in your life and the lives of those you pray for.

Week 3

SANCTIFICATION: PURSUING HOLINESS AS A BELOVED CHILD

MEMORY VERSE
But as he who called you is holy, you also be holy in all your conduct, since it is written, "You shall be holy, for I am holy." 1 Peter 1:15-16

WEEK 3, DAY 1: THE CALL TO BE HOLY

As you spend time in God's Word and with God's people, you will hear words, phrases, and concepts that you ordinarily will not hear in most conversations in our culture. One of those words is "holiness." CVC exists "to invite people to new life in Christ." One of the unmistakable marks of our new life in Christ is personal holiness.

We have been called to be holy as God is holy.

Look up and highlight or underline the following 3 verses in your Bible.

In fact, the Bible says that only those who are holy are the ones who are headed to heaven.

Draw a line matching the following reasons we should be holy with the appropriate verses mentioned above.

1. We won't make it to heaven without holiness.
2. The children of a Father who is holy must be holy, too.
3. An impure life is out of character for one who is called by God.

A. 1 Peter 1:14-16
B. 1 Thessalonians 4:7
C. Hebrews 12:14

The pursuit of holiness ought to be a primary concern for every follower of Christ.

Sometimes you might hear this pursuit described as the process of sanctification, growth in godliness, or a life of righteousness. These are different ways of saying essentially the same thing: spiritual progress must characterize the lives of God's people.

Continual spiritual growth is vital for us. It is not acceptable for believers to stay stagnant or to regress in spiritual development. Make it your aim to grow in holiness for the rest of your life. We ought to be more holy this year than last year and more holy next year than this year.

WHAT IS HOLINESS? WHAT IS SANCTIFICATION?

In your own words (without reading any further) define holiness/sanctification:

_____

_____

_____

_____

_____

Consider the following definitions and circle the words/phrases that encourage you the most and put a box around the words/phrases that challenge you the most:

"To be holy is to be morally blameless. It is to be separated from sin and, therefore, consecrated to God" (*The Pursuit of Holiness*, by Jerry Bridges, p.16).

"Sanctification is a progressive work of God in man that makes us more and more free from sin and like Christ in our actual lives" (*Systematic Theology*, by Wayne Grudem, p.746).

"Holiness means separated and set apart for God, consecrated and made over to Him. . . This means taking God's moral law as our rule and God's incarnate Son as our model" (*Rediscovering Holiness*, by J.I. Packer, p.19).

"Sanctification is that inward spiritual work which the Lord Jesus Christ works in a man. . . He not only washes him from his sins in His own blood, but He also separates him from his natural love of sin and the world, puts a new principle in his heart, and makes him practically godly in life" (*Holiness*, by J.C. Ryle, p.19).

"Sanctification is the work of God's free grace, whereby we are renewed in the whole man after the image of God, and are enabled more and more to die unto sin, and live unto righteousness" (*The Westminster Catechism*).

Now, after reading these definitions, combine words and phrases to take another stab at a definition of holiness/sanctification.

_____

_____

_____

_____

Although we don't use a traditional pulpit at CVC, we do have a table on the stage that our pastors use for holding the Bible and message notes. It's a tall table that has been "set apart" for sacred use. Most people would think that it would be highly inappropriate, offensive, and disrespectful to use that table for wild partying—to do drugs or for binge drinking. Why? It's holy. It's been set apart for sacred use.

"To be holy is to be set apart for a purpose. If you set apart a special suit, you keep it spotless and clean for special occasions. . . When a life is consecrated, it is fully devoted to God's service. You see yourself as a temple of the Holy Spirit, and there are certain things that aren't permitted in the temple" (*It's Personal*, by Brian Bloye, p.205).

In a similar way, every believer has been set apart for sacred use. We are to be holy. That means we have been called to use our minds, emotions, and bodies for righteous purposes. It also means that we have been called to avoid unrighteous thoughts, emotions, and activities.

Open your Bible and read Galatians 5:19-25 where the fruit of the Spirit stands in vivid contrast to the works of the flesh.

Which 2-3 of these "works of the flesh" do you most wish to overcome?

_____

_____

Which 2-3 examples of the fruit of the Spirit do you long to most experience?

_____

_____

People sometimes think of holy people as joyless people. But when we overcome the works of the flesh and bear the fruit of the Spirit—when we grow in holiness—we begin to experience more joy, not less!

J.I. Packer wrote, "Holiness is the substance of which happiness is the spin-off. Those who chase happiness miss it, while those who pursue holiness through the grace of Christ, happiness of spirit comes unasked" (*Rediscovering Holiness*, p.37).

Jesus Himself promised, *Blessed are those who hunger and thirst for righteousness, for they shall be satisfied* (Matthew 5:6). If we strive for happiness over holiness, we will get neither. If we strive for holiness over happiness, we gain both.

What was one of the most helpful insights that you received during this lesson?

_____

_____

_____

As you close this session, spend some time asking God to make you increasingly holy. You can use the space below to write out a short prayer to God:

_____

_____

_____

_____

_____

_____

_____

_____

WEEK 3, DAY 2: OUR SOURCE OF HOLINESS

We have been called to be holy as God is holy. The pursuit of personal holiness originates with the holiness of God Himself. Look up and highlight or underline 1 Peter 1:14-16 in your Bible.

Every believer has been adopted into God's family. As God's children, we are to become increasingly like our Father in heaven: like Father, like daughter; like Father, like son.

What are some characteristics you share with your earthly mother or father?

_____

_____

What are some characteristics that you think you should share with your heavenly Father?

_____

_____

Since our Father is holy, we, too, must be holy. If we are not becoming more and more like our Father in heaven, it is foolish for us to claim to be God's children. We dare not say that we have royal blood in our veins and that we are children of God unless we can prove our pedigree by being holy (paraphrased from the book *Holiness*, by J. C. Ryle, p.51).

THE HOLINESS OF GOD

Since holiness originates with God, then we must seek to understand the holiness of God.

Who is like you, O Lord, among the gods? Who is like you, majestic in holiness, awesome in glorious deeds, doing wonders? (Exodus 15:11).

Most of the time, when we think of God's holiness, we think of His purity. To be sure, He is infinitely pure. But the holiness of God goes beyond purity. It takes purity to a transcendent level.

"The primary meaning of holy is 'separate.' It comes from an ancient word that meant 'to cut' or 'to separate.' To translate this basic meaning into contemporary language would be to use the phrase 'a cut apart.' Perhaps even more accurate would be to use the phrase 'a cut above something.' When we find a garment or another piece of merchandise that is outstanding, that has a superior excellence, we use the phrase 'a cut above the rest.' When the Bible calls God holy, it means that God is transcendently separate." (*The Holiness of God*, by R.C. Sproul, pp.54-55).

God is above and beyond anything we can comprehend or imagine. The holiness of God applies to all of His attributes. His love is holy love. His grace is holy grace. His wrath is holy wrath. His goodness is holy goodness. His wisdom is holy wisdom.

"We cannot grasp the true meaning of the divine holiness by thinking of someone or something very pure and then raising the concept to the highest degree we are capable of. God's holiness is not simply the best we know infinitely bettered. We know nothing like the divine holiness. It stands apart, unique, unapproachable, incomprehensible, and unattainable . . . [God] is the absolute quintessence of moral excellence, infinitely perfect in righteousness, purity, rectitude, and incomprehensible holiness. And in all this, He is uncreated, self-sufficient, and beyond the power of human thought to conceive or human speech to utter" (*The Knowledge of the Holy*, by A. W. Tozer, p.104-105).

Read and underline or highlight the following verses about the holiness of God in your Bible.

>God is unique in His holiness: 1 Samuel 2:2
>God dwells in a place that is holy: Psalm 24:3
>God is called the Holy One: Psalm 71:22
>God in His holiness is incomparable: Isaiah 40:25
>God in His holiness is high and lifted up: Isaiah 57:15

What feelings are stirred up in you as you think of living your life in the presence of such a holy God?

_____

_____

_____

OUR RESPONSE TO GOD'S HOLINESS
Our response to God's holy nature brings about changes in our attitudes and actions.

Read the following passages in your Bible that deal with our response to God's holiness, and then match the verses to the correct response.

1.	2 Corinthians 6:14-7:1	A.	Worship and praise
2.	Isaiah 6:1-7	B.	Separation from anything or anyone unclean
3.	Revelation 15:4	C.	Awareness of our own impurity
4.	Psalm 99:9	D.	A reverential fear and awe of God
5.	Leviticus 11:44-45	E.	Sacrificial generosity
6.	Hebrews 12:10	F.	A devotion to be holy/consecration of one's life
7.	1 Chronicles 16:29	G.	A proper response to God's discipline

Of the 7 responses to God's holiness listed above, which 2-3 responses are most needed in your life today? Why did you choose those responses?

_____

_____

_____

DEALING WITH OUR UNHOLINESS

As we better understand the holiness of God, we will surely become increasingly broken by our own unholiness.

The prophet Isaiah once had a vision of God. The holiness of God caused him to see himself as "undone"—as someone who does not "have it all together." Read Isaiah 6:1-8 in your Bible.

We see a pattern here in Isaiah 6, a pattern that occurs throughout the Bible. First, God appears as holy. Second, because of our sin, we are terrified and broken. Third, God takes initiative to forgive and to heal. Then, God sends us on a mission for His purposes.

Yes, the holiness of God reveals our sinfulness. But we must never forget that Christ Jesus came to take away our guilt, to atone for our sin, and to empower us to live holy lives. "We must hide our unholiness in the wounds of Christ. . . We must take refuge from God in God. Above all we must believe that God sees us as perfect in His Son while He disciplines and chastens and purges us that we may be partakers of His holiness" (*The Knowledge of the Holy*, by A. W. Tozer, p.107).

Use the space below to compare and contrast God's holy nature and character and your own sinful nature and character.

God is . . .

I am . . .

_____   _____
_____   _____
_____   _____
_____   _____
_____   _____

Now, compose a brief prayer thanking God that you have been forgiven in Christ and that in Christ you have been made holy in His sight.

_____
_____
_____

What was one of the most helpful insights that you received during this lesson?

_____
_____
_____

I am sure the reason I have a deep hunger to learn
the holiness of God is precisely because I am not holy.
R. C. Sproul

WEEK 3, DAY 3: SAINTS OF GOD

As you read through the New Testament, you will find that believers are often called "saints." Use the space below to write your current understanding of a person who would be called a saint.

_____

_____

_____

In some religious traditions, the word saint is reserved for persons now in heaven who lived especially virtuous lives on earth. These people must be recognized by church officials as someone worthy of veneration in order to be classified as a saint. In some cases, people even pray to these individuals.

But in the Bible, the saints are people who are on the earth as well as in heaven. Everyone who has received Jesus Christ by faith is called a saint. Saints are not to be prayed to. Instead, saints are called to revere, worship, and pray to God alone.

UNDERSTANDING THE WORD "SAINT"

The word "saint" comes from the Greek word *hagios*, which means "consecrated to God, holy, set apart." The words "sanctified" and "holy" come from the same Greek root as the word that is commonly translated "saints." According to God's Word, saints are all the people who make up the body of Christ, the church. A saint is any follower of Jesus, any believer in Christ, every Christian. Every Christ-follower is a saint.

Underline or highlight 1 Corinthians 1:2 in your Bible. The Apostle Paul is writing: *To the church of God that is in Corinth, to those sanctified in Christ Jesus, called to be saints together with all those who in every place call upon the name of our Lord Jesus Christ* (1 Corinthians 1:2).

Have you called on the name of Jesus to save you?	☐ Yes	☐ No
Are you His follower?	☐ Yes	☐ No
Have you surrendered your life to Him?	☐ Yes	☐ No

If the answer to these questions is "yes," then beside 1 Corinthians 1:2, write these words: "I am a saint!"

Because we are saints, we can live like saints. Look up Philippians 2:12b-13. *Work out your own salvation with fear and trembling, for it is God who works in you, both to will and to work for his good pleasure* (Philippians 2:12b-13). Now, based on the truths of this Scripture, fill in the blanks: We are to work _____ what God has worked _____.

The pursuit of holiness, then, is "living out" who God has made us to be.

WHOSE YOU ARE AND WHO YOU ARE

Before their kids walk out the door and into the world, some effective parents tell them, "Remember whose you are and who you are." That knowledge empowers those sons and daughters to "live up"—to represent their families well.

If we are going to grow in holiness, we must remember whose we are (we belong to God!) and who we are (we are saints!). This will empower us to "live new"—to represent our Father in heaven well.

True followers of Jesus become saints at the moment when we put our faith in Christ as our Savior and Lord. God transfers to our account all the righteousness of Jesus. His holiness becomes ours when we trust in Him. It's a spiritual transaction called justification. He takes away our sin and gives us His holiness. He makes us "just as if we'd never sinned."

Read Romans 3:23-24, 26b. Circle the words "justified," "just," and "justifier" in your Bible.

All have sinned and fall short of the glory of God, and are justified by His grace as a gift, through the redemption that is in Christ Jesus . . . so that He might be just and the justifier of the one who has faith in Jesus (Romans 3:23-24, 26b).

Yes, we still sin, but He justifies. We must never forget that we've been made just in the sight of God by the righteousness of Christ. God applies Jesus' holiness to our spiritual bank accounts while we are still sinners.

R.C. Sproul, in his excellent book, *The Holiness of God*, asks, "How much time before the sinner begins to become pure? The answer is *none*. There is no time between our justification and the *beginning* of our sanctification. But there is a great time lapse between our justification and the *completion* of our salvation" (p. 214). This explains why we can see ourselves as saints even though we still sin.

"Luther used a simple analogy to explain it. He described the condition of a patient who was mortally ill. The doctor proclaimed that he had medicine that would surely cure the man. The instant the medicine was administered, the doctor proclaimed the patient was well. At that instant the patient was still sick, but as soon as the medicine passed his lips and entered his body the patient began to get well. So it is with our justification. As soon as we truly believe, at that very instant we start to get better; the process of becoming pure and holy is underway and its future completion is certain" (*The Holiness of God*, by R.C. Sproul, p.214).

HOW GRACE PRODUCES HOLINESS

This is amazing grace. This is what fuels our pursuit of holiness. We begin to strive for holiness out of faith, not fear; gratitude, not guilt.

If a friend came to you and, for no good reason, paid off a $100,000 mortgage, how would you behave toward that friend? Would you slash his/her tires? Would you throw eggs at his/her house? Would you steal his/her stuff? Of course not! You would want to do things to bless him/her. "Can I cut your grass? Can I go grocery shopping for you? Can I clean your carpets?"

List some other things that you might want to do for someone who paid off your mortgage:

_____
_____
_____
_____

God has done infinitely more for us than paying off a $100,000 mortgage when He paid our sin debt when Jesus died on the cross in our place! We once owed Him everything. But in Christ, we now owe Him nothing. Jesus paid it all. That fact—that amazing grace—is what must motivate our desire to live holy lives.

In the space below, list some things that you would like to do for Jesus:

_____
_____
_____
_____

Question: If you were able to do the things for Jesus that you listed above, would they make you more acceptable in His sight?

☐ Yes   ☐ No

There is nothing you can do to make God love you more and nothing you can do to make God love you less.

Read and highlight or underline the following verse in your Bible: *There is therefore now no condemnation for those who are in Christ Jesus* (Romans 8:1).

Write the following statement on a 3x5 card. Put it in a prominent place as a reminder. Read it aloud several times a day for the next 7 days. Or type it into a note on your phone with a weekly alert. (The statement originated with Robert S. McGee, from *The Search for Significance*, p.61.)

I have great worth apart from my performance because Christ gave His life for me and imparted great value to me. I am deeply loved, fully pleasing, totally forgiven, accepted, and complete in Christ. I am a saint. By God's grace and for God's glory, I can and I will pursue holiness.

What was one of the most helpful insights that you received during this lesson?

_____
_____
_____

WEEK 3, DAY 4: DEVELOPING A LIFESTYLE OF HOLINESS

Romans 12:1-2 tells us how to live lives that are holy and acceptable to the Lord. Please read the passage in your own Bible.

I appeal to you therefore, brothers, by the mercies of God, to present your bodies as a living sacrifice, holy and acceptable to God, which is your spiritual worship. Do not be conformed to this world, but be transformed by the renewal of your mind, that by testing, you may discern what is the will of God, what is good and acceptable and perfect (Romans 12:1-2).

Fill in the blank: We are not to be conformed to the world. Instead, we must be _____. We don't let the world "squeeze us into its mold." We are to be "non-conformists."

Throughout history, believers have struggled to define what non-conformity means. Some individuals have sought to be totally separated from the world, like monks or nuns who live their whole lives in a monastery. Others have tried to blend into the culture only to find that the culture shapes their lives more than Christ.

It has also been tempting for church leaders to make superficial man-made lists of dos and don'ts that they use to define what is (or isn't) holy behavior. What's confusing is that the lists tend to change over time depending on the lifestyles of the leaders and the culture that surrounds them. The simplistic way of deciding what is non-conforming is to see what culture approves and then forbid people to do it.

In the space below, create a list of man-made, superficial rules that you have seen Christians make. Complete the sentence:

Good Christians don't . . .

_____
_____
_____

HOLINESS IS DEEPER THAN EXTERNALS

The kingdom of God is not about whether or not believers go dancing, drink alcohol, or watch movies. *The kingdom of God is not a matter of eating and drinking but of righteousness and peace and joy in the Holy Spirit (Romans 14:17).*

"The call of nonconformity is a call to a deeper level of righteousness that goes beyond externals. . . When we make dancing and movies the test of spirituality, we are guilty of substituting a cheap morality for a genuine one. . . Anyone can avoid dancing or going to movies. These require no great effort of moral courage. What is difficult is to control the tongue, to act with integrity, to show forth the fruit of the Spirit" (*The Holiness of God*, by R.C. Sproul, pp.207-208).

I have been told several times that the Bible doesn't say that we can't smoke pot, to which I reply,

*"The Bible also doesn't say we can't smoke poison oak;
but I don't see people rolling that up."
Let's not play games with the obvious.*
Chad Allen, Lead Pastor - Cuyahoga Valley Church

QUESTIONABLE ACTIVITIES

Even though we must resist the urge to define holiness by a list of rules and regulations, we are faced with many lifestyle decisions that are not specifically addressed in Scripture. This is why we often can struggle to know what is right or wrong for a follower of Christ. ("Should I go there?" "Should I do this thing?" "Should I buy that?" "Should I date him/her?" etc.)

What are some activities that you have questions about? What are some things you are not sure that God would approve?

_____

_____

_____

Certain activities have been justified by some believers with the statement, "Well the Bible does not specifically condemn it." Every follower of Christ must understand that while the Bible may not directly speak to an issue, there are basic principles that can guide every decision in life.

The following 13 questions can guide us in knowing right from wrong and holy from unholy when it comes to questionable things, i.e., the "grey areas." You may be able to say yes to certain behaviors after asking and answering these questions. But you'll have to say no to others.

13 QUESTIONS TO EVALUATE QUESTIONABLE ACTIVITIES

1. Can I ask God to bless it? Psalm 67:1
2. Is there a direct command from God about it? Luke 6:46
3. Does the activity promote evil? Romans 12:9
4. Does it cause others to stumble? Romans 14:21
5. Does it harm my body? 1 Corinthians 3:16, 17
6. Do I master it or does it master me? 1 Corinthians 6:12
7. Is this activity helpful? 1 Corinthians 10:23
8. Does it glorify God? 1 Corinthians 10:31
9. Does it waste time? Ephesians 5:16
10. Do those I admire most engage in this activity? Hebrews 13:7
11. Is it "of the world" or "of God"? 1 John 2:15-17
12. Will it cause me shame in the day of judgment? 1 John 2:28
13. Based on my past experience, my present circumstances, and my future hopes and dreams, would this be a wise thing to do? Ephesians 5:15

Put a check by the top 5 questions that you believe will help you the most as you seek to live a holy life. Then, write the list in your Bible in an easy-to-find location for future reference.

OTHERS MAY; YOU CANNOT

Each believer must wrestle with these kinds of questions concerning questionable activities. Some believers find it helpful to say, "Others may; you cannot" about certain activities. Some followers of Jesus may engage in certain activities, but others may feel the Lord convicting them not to engage in them.

It's hard to not make what the Lord has said to you apply to everyone else. We must refrain from falling to the temptation of making our particular position on a questionable activity the litmus test of everyone else's holiness. If we aren't careful here, we can become legalistic, Pharisaical, judgmental, holier-than-thou types. (Remember that Jesus saved His harshest words for that crowd.)

DEFEATING SIN AND PURSUING HOLINESS

Augustine of Hippo was an influential leader in the early church. Before his conversion, Augustine felt pulled in two directions. He was pulled toward holiness by his mother, Monica, a saintly woman. He was pulled toward sin by a mistress. The conflict was long and terrible. Augustine struggled.

But when the Lord shined into Augustine's heart through the words in Romans 13:14—*Put on the Lord Jesus Christ*—everything changed.

Instantly he arose. He had made his decision. He had counted the cost. He told his friend, Alypius, and they went and told his mother Monica.

The next day, he went down the main street of his city. As he walked, he saw the woman who had been the source of so much temptation. She enticed him once again for another fling. In those days, that might have meant several weeks of sensual pleasure.

Augustine said, "No thank you." She thought, "Maybe he didn't really recognize me." So, she called out, "Augustine, it is I!" He said, "Yes, I know. But it is not I. I am not the former I."

Augustine was applying the truths found in Romans 6. Look up the passage in your own Bible. *Thanks be to God, that you who were once slaves of sin have become obedient from the heart to the standard of teaching to which you were committed, and, having been set free from sin, have become slaves of righteousness* (Romans 6:17-18).

Dr. Timothy Keller, pastor of Redeemer Presbyterian Church in New York comments, "When Jesus died, we died. Our old self was crucified. That's past tense. Therefore, you are not the same person now. Your body is now under the reign of your new spiritual master. Because of this new identity, you can break the reign of your old spiritual masters. You must learn to remind yourself of who you are. If you're not changing, it's not because you don't lack any spiritual resources. It's because you're not deploying them. They don't deploy automatically. If you're still sinning in the same old ways, you're not remembering who you really are."

What is one snare of unholiness that you need to be freed from to grow in your sanctification? Write it down and attack it through prayer, asking God to purge it from your life.

_____

_____

What was one of the most helpful insights that you received during this lesson?

_____

_____

_____

Like yesterday, close your time today by reading the following prayer aloud to God. Then pray through this prayer again in your own words.

AN EARNEST PRAYER FOR HOLINESS

Thank You, Lord, that through Christ I have died to sin. I am now alive to God and united to Christ. I have the all-powerful Holy Spirit living in me.

Lord, reveal my sin and help me to repent truly. Thank You for creating a desire for holiness in me. Thank You for giving me the strength to live a holy life. I know that You have given me everything pertaining to life and godliness.

Now, I choose to put off sin, to put it to death, to submit to God, to resist the devil, to work out my salvation with fear and trembling, and to say no to temptation. I am not the former I!

It is now my responsibility to obey You in thought, word, and deed. You have given me the ability to obey. I make no excuses. I now choose to live a holy life.

I know that my personal holiness is worth the effort and pain required for me to mortify the misdeeds of my flesh. By Your grace and for Your glory, I will fight, wrestle, labor, strive, and war against the world, the flesh, and the devil.

I passionately want my life to be aligned with the Word of God.
I shall not be squeezed into the mold of the world.

I will do only those things that are helpful to me—spiritually, mentally, and physically. I will not be mastered by anything.

I will not do something that will hurt others or cause them to stumble. I will say/do/be only those things that glorify God. I will give up any practice or habit or relationship that keeps me from holiness.

Thank You for Your grace that forgives and makes all things new. Now make me holy as You are holy.

In Jesus' name, Amen.

Prayer inspired by the Word of God and the book, *The Pursuit of Holiness*, by Jerry Bridges.

WEEK 3, DAY 5: BEARING THE FRUIT OF HOLINESS

One of the highest compliments that a man or a woman of God could ever receive is this: "She is a holy woman" or "He is a holy man." Have you ever said this or thought it about anyone? If so, who and why?

_____

_____

_____

_____

We usually think of holiness being made up of things we avoid doing that we know we shouldn't do. Or we see holiness as doing all the things we should do. Doing the dos and not doing the don'ts = holiness, or so we think.

But holiness is deeper than the externals. It's also made up of those inward graces that flow out of the heart—things that are listed in Galatians 5:22–23. Today, read a passage we read earlier in the week: Galatians 5:19-25.

Match the fruit of the Spirit with its corresponding "anti-fruit."

LOVE	HARSHNESS
JOY	IRRITABILITY
PEACE	INDIFFERENCE
PATIENCE	HEARTLESSNESS
KINDNESS	DISLOYALTY
GOODNESS	DISORDER
FAITHFULNESS	IMPULSIVENESS
GENTLENESS	MALICE
SELF-CONTROL	DISCOURAGEMENT

LOVE	HARSHNESS
JOY	IRRITABILITY
PEACE	INDIFFERENCE
PATIENCE	HEARTLESSNESS
KINDNESS	DISLOYALTY
GOODNESS	DISORDER
FAITHFULNESS	IMPULSIVENESS
GENTLENESS	MALICE
SELF-CONTROL	DISOURAGEMENT

Which fruit of the Spirit do you most need to bear?

_____

Which "anti-fruit" do you most want Jesus to defeat in your life?

_____

THE FRUIT OF HOLINESS
The fruit of the Spirit is produced by the Spirit, of course, in us and, ultimately, through us. He is called the Spirit of Christ. He is called the Spirit of God. But perhaps the name that we use most often for the Spirit is the Holy Spirit.

Therefore, it is possible to call the fruit of the Holy Spirit, the fruit of holiness. The aim of the Spirit of holiness is to produce personal holiness in us. Simply put, if we are not bearing the fruit of the Holy Spirit, we are not holy.

This is of vital importance because, as it says in Hebrews 12:14, we won't go to heaven without holiness. It is ludicrous for us to think that we shall go to a holy heaven without the fruit of holiness evidenced in our lives.

TAKING RESPONSIBILITY FOR HOLY LIVING
We began today's lesson with this: One of the highest compliments that a man or a woman of God could ever receive is this: "She is a holy woman" or "He is a holy man." Would anyone close to you ever say that about you? Would the people who know you best and live with you most—your family—say about you that you are a holy man or a holy woman?

Sadly, many of us would have to say that the people in our family would not characterize us as people who bear the fruit of holiness. Love, joy, peace, etc. are not the common characteristics of our lives, especially at home.

This is a heart-breaking sin from which we need to repent. Instead, we often blame circumstances and other people for our impatience and irritability.

We dare not excuse, minimize, or rationalize this sin. The burden of responsibility for our sin rests entirely on us rather than on those around us.

WHEN YOU ARE TIPPED OVER
Think of yourself as a pitcher or a vase. Think of the problems that come your way as pressures that tip you over. Those pressures that tip us over simply reveal what is inside our hearts. Often, what comes out is ugly. Instead of love, we bear the fruit of harshness. Instead of joy, we bear the fruit of irritability. Instead of peace, we bear the fruit of impatience. We are not holy at home.

Draw a vase that represents your life in the space below. Beside the vase, draw some of the pressure you have been facing lately. Next, draw the vase tipped over with a puddle next to it. Put some words in the puddle that illustrate what has been coming out of you lately. (Illustration taken from *The Peace and Joy Principle*, by Joe Propri, pp.7-14).

"Anti-fruit" should not be flowing out of us—especially at home. If there is any place we ought to be holy people, it should be in our homes with those closest and dearest to us.

The test of our holiness comes when a situation tempts us to cut loose with some form of ungodly tit-for-tat. Anyone can appear to be bearing the fruit of the Spirit when all is going well. But the test of holiness happens when things go wrong.

> *Love is the Christ-like reaction to people's malice.*
> *Joy is the Christ-like reaction to depressing circumstances.*
> *Peace is the Christ-like reaction to troubles, threats, and invitations to anxiety.*
> *Patience is the Christ-like reaction to all that is maddening.*
> *Kindness is the Christ-like reaction to all who are unkind.*
> *Goodness is the Christ-like reaction to bad people and bad behavior.*
> *Faithfulness/gentleness is the Christ-like reaction to lies and fury.*
> *Self-control is the Christ-like reaction to every situation that goads you to lose your cool.*
> (Taken from *Rediscovering Holiness*, by J. I. Packer, p.174).

THE SECRET TO HOLY LIVING
In John 15, we see the secret to bearing the fruit of holiness.

Read and underline or highlight John 15:1-5.

The secret to fruit bearing, according to Jesus, is abiding.

Consider what Jesus said in John 15:5 and in your own words, describe what it means to abide in Christ.

_____

_____

_____

The word "abide" is *meno* in the Greek Language, the original language of the New Testament. It literally means to remain, stay, live, dwell, or lodge. Figuratively, it describes someone who does not leave the realm or sphere in which he finds himself. It denotes an inward, enduring personal communion (*A Greek-English Lexicon of the New Testament*, by Walter Bauer, pp.503-504).

We must stay connected to the Vine. We remain in Christ, stay connected to Jesus, and make our home with Him. Without Jesus we cannot bear the fruit of holiness in our homes—or anywhere else!

When we fail to bear the fruit of holiness in our homes, it is a sure sign that we have stopped abiding in Christ. But when we, as branches, abide in Him, we can do nothing other than bear the fruit of the Holy Spirit, the fruit of holiness.

BEARING THE FRUIT OF HOLINESS
The branch that bears the most fruit is the branch with the widest, deepest, purest, and most consistent connection to the Vine.

List what you see in yourself when you abide in Christ (or not). Then ask 1 or 2 people who know you well what they see!

When I *abide* in Christ, I . . .

_____
_____
_____
_____
_____

When I *don't abide* in Christ, I . . .

_____
_____
_____
_____
_____

How might you widen and deepen the connection of your life to Christ? How might your connection to Jesus become more pure and more consistent?

_____
_____
_____
_____

Somehow, in our homes we have decided that our goal is not absolute 100% holiness. We can start to settle for 50%, 75%, or 90% holiness. We have decided that our lives are OK as long as we do not sin very much.

Perhaps you don't do the really bad things at home. You don't hit, slap, yell, cuss, get drunk, or watch R rated films with your family. But do you grumble, complain, and show your resentment?

Why do we excuse this behavior? We are not aiming at 100% holiness. We have not made it our goal to not sin at all.

What soldier goes in the battle having it as his aim to not get shot very much? He does not want to get shot at all! In a similar way, in our homes we should not want to be hit by sin at all!

May we make it our aim to abide in Christ so deeply, so consistently, so widely, and so purely, that we avoid being hit by sin at all and bear the fruit of 100% holiness at home. May the people closest to us give us one of the highest compliments we could ever receive. May the people who know us best—our families—say about us, "She is a holy woman " and "He is a holy man."

What was one of the most helpful insights that you received during this lesson?

_____

_____

_____

Like yesterday, close your time today by reading the following prayer aloud to God. Then pray through this prayer again in your own words.

A PRAYER FOR HOLINESS

O God, You are glorious and majestic in Your holiness. Your love is holy love. Your grace is holy grace.

You have called me to be holy as You are holy. But I have excused, minimized, and rationalized my sin. I have not been bearing enough of the fruit of Your Holy Spirit at home. Too often, I have been impatient, irritable, joyless, and unkind.

O Lord, be merciful to me a sinner. May the merits of Your holy Son, Jesus, make me acceptable in Your sight. May the blood of the holy Lamb of God, Jesus, wash me and make me whiter than snow. Clothe me in the robe of His holiness.

Give me the desire to not sin at all. Help me abide in Christ so deeply, so consistently, so widely, and so purely that I will bear the fruit of holiness. May the people who know me best—my family—say about me, "He/She is truly holy."

I will not play with sin. I will avoid the "just-one-more-time" syndrome. I will make it my aim not to sin at all. I will seek not to do anything that I would be afraid to do if it were the very last hour of my life.

And when I fall, I will not rationalize, minimize, or excuse my sin. Instead, I will repent again and again. I will run to Jesus who died on the cross to forgive me of all my sins—past, present, and future.

Jesus, I know You love me just like I am. But I also know You love me too much to let me stay like I am. Change me from the inside out. Make me holy from the heart.

Make it so. In Jesus' name, Amen.

Week 4

BIBLE INTAKE: GROWING AS A SELF-FEEDER (PART 1)

MEMORY VERSE
But be doers of the word, and not hearers only, deceiving yourselves.
James 1:22

WEEK 4, DAY 1: TRUSTING THE BIBLE

Polls say that even though most people in America believe that the Bible is holy, inspired, and sacred, only about one-third of Americans believe the Bible is absolutely accurate in all that it teaches. About 1 in 5 Americans believe the Bible is an ancient book of fables, legends, history, and moral precepts recorded by man.

Is it true that the Bible was written by humans who were inspired by God? Does the Bible truly have God for its author? Is the Bible absolutely true, without any mixture of error? Is the Bible the supreme standard that should guide all human conduct, all creeds, and all religious opinions? Can we trust the Bible?

Well, the Bible itself claims to be the very Word of God. In your Bible, look up and highlight or underline 2 Timothy 3:16-17.

The words "breathed out by God" means "inspired by God." The entire Bible is the revelation of God by God. *Everything we need for living new in Christ* is contained within the Word of God. When the writers of the Bible put the words of God on paper, it was God's Spirit who enabled them to write the words they wrote. Even the men God used to generate Scripture knew it was done so through divine inspiration.

Now, look up 2 Peter 1:20-21.

Our confidence in the trustworthiness of the Bible ultimately rests in our confidence in the character of God. "If God is omniscient, He must know all things. He cannot be ignorant of or in error on any matter. Further, if He is omnipotent, He is able to so affect the biblical author's writing that nothing erroneous enters into the final product" (*Christian Theology*, by Millard Erickson, p.225).

Now, look again carefully at 2 Timothy 3:16-17 and 2 Peter 1:20-21, as well as Galatians 1:12 and 1 Corinthians 2:12-13.

Based on these passages, answer the following questions:

Who is the primary author of the Bible?

_____

What part did humans play in writing the Bible?

_____

What kind of impact should the Bible have on our lives? _____

_____

_____

Sometimes people who say that they trust Jesus have a struggle trusting the Bible. But if we have a problem with the Bible, we have a problem with Jesus. Why?

JESUS BELIEVED THAT THE OLD TESTAMENT WAS TRUSTWORTHY.
Consider this: Jesus believed that the Scripture that was written before He was born was true. The part of the Bible that Jesus had when He walked on this planet was the Old Testament (OT).
The evidence points to the fact that Jesus believed the Old Testament was God's Word.

In Mark 7, Jesus affirms that what Isaiah, the OT prophet, wrote was "the commandment of God." After referring to Isaiah's prophecy, He said to the Pharisees, *You leave the commandment of God and hold to the tradition of men* (See Mark 7:1-8).

Jesus "had the highest possible regard for the OT text and recognized in its words the voice of God" (*New Testament Theology*, by Donald Guthrie, p.957).

Jesus didn't talk about OT people such as Isaiah, Noah, Abraham, Moses, David, and Elijah like they were myths. He believed they actually lived and that they did what the Bible says they did.

Jesus believed that OT teaching and prophecy would be fulfilled. Look up Matthew 5:18 and fill in the blanks. *For truly, I say to you, until heaven and earth pass away, not an _____, not a _____, will pass from the Law until all is accomplished* (Matthew 5:18). The iota is the smallest Greek letter. Jesus is saying that even the tiniest parts of the OT will be fulfilled—that all the "t's" will be crossed and all the "i's" will be dotted.

Jesus once rebuked two of His followers for being slow to believe the OT Scriptures. *O foolish ones, and slow of heart to believe all that the prophets have spoken* (Luke 24:25). He's saying, "Don't be slow of heart to believe all the Old Testament. Be quick to believe all of it!"

According to Jesus, the Old Testament can be trusted.

Jesus believed that His own words were trustworthy.

Jesus trusted the Bible that was being spoken through His very own words at the time of their speaking! He believed in His own words that would be written down later.

Jesus spoke about the eternal nature of His own words.

Heaven and earth will pass away, but My words will not pass away (Matthew 24:35). Why would He say such a thing unless His words were eternally true?

In the Old Testament, the prophets often opened statements by saying, "Thus says the Lord." Jesus didn't introduce comments that way. He would begin His teachings by saying, *Truly, truly I say to you . . .* (John 3:5). "It was enough for Jesus to speak in His own name" (*New Testament Theology*, by Donald Guthrie, p.961).

Jesus was confident that His words were God's words.

Jesus said that if we build our lives upon His words, we will stand when everyone else falls. Look up and highlight or underline Matthew 7:24-25.

He says, "If you build your lives on Me and My words, you will stand when everyone else is falling."

What are some storms that you are now facing?

_____

_____

_____

What difference does it make for you to know that building your life on Christ's words will help you stay stable as you face your storm?

_____

_____

_____

Think. If you were to say, "My words will not pass away," no one should trust you. If you were to say, "Truly truly I say to you" and act like what you are saying has the same authority as God, no one should listen to you. If you were to say, "If you obey me, you are building on a solid foundation," then the people around you should run away from you as fast as they could run. But these are the things Jesus said. Why would He say such things? He believed His words were God's words.

According to Jesus, the Gospels that recorded His words—Matthew, Mark, Luke, and John—can be trusted.

JESUS BELIEVED THAT THE REST OF THE NEW TESTAMENT WOULD BE TRUSTWORTHY.
Jesus trusted the Bible that would be written in what would be His future. Look up and highlight or underline the following three passages: John 14:26, John 16:13-14, and John 17:20.

Jesus promised that the Holy Spirit would assist His followers to remember His words: *The Helper, the Holy Spirit, whom the Father will send in My name, He will teach you all things and bring to your remembrance all that I have said to you* (John 14:26). Jesus is saying that before the New Testament (NT) was written, the Holy Spirit was working to make sure that the followers of Jesus would verbally communicate truths that could be trusted. And then the Holy Spirit would work to make sure that what they later wrote could be trusted.

This explains that what was written by the first followers of Jesus was seen by the early church as having the same authority as the OT: *When the Spirit of truth comes, He will guide you into all the truth . . . and He will declare to you the things that are to come* (John 16:13-14). The work of the Holy Spirit was to guide the followers of Jesus so that their memory of the words and the work of Jesus was completely accurate.

Later, in John 17, Jesus prays for His first followers and their impact on future followers—on people like us. And notice how He prays: *I [pray] for those who will believe in Me through their word . . ."* (John 17:20). He's praying so that what was said and written in the future could be trusted.

Jesus taught that the words and the writings from His followers that were yet to come could be trusted. The first followers of Jesus were simply passing along what they had received from Jesus.

According to Jesus, the Old Testament can be trusted. The Gospels can be trusted. And the rest of the New Testament can be trusted.

In your experience, what are some of the reasons people say that the Bible cannot be trusted?

_____
_____
_____
_____

What is one possible answer you might give to them based on what you learned today?

_____
_____
_____
_____

What was one of the most helpful insights that you received during this lesson?

_____
_____
_____
_____

WEEK 4, DAY 2: SELF-FEEDERS

Think about how some people react when you mention the words "soul food." To those people who really enjoy it, they get a longing in their eyes. Their mouths begin watering. They use wonderfully descriptive words to describe the flavor, aroma, and taste of it. They get excited about the mere mention of "soul food."

Do we get that way when we hear the mere mention of God's Word, the Bible? It is our soul food. But do we get as excited about the Bible as some people do about ribs, pulled pork, slaw, cornbread, and iced tea? Do we get a longing in our eyes? Do our mouths water? God's Word is full of flavor, aroma, and taste.

LIVING TRUTH

One of our passions at CVC is Living Truth. We believe that the Word of God is the living and active truth of God. Look up and highlight or underline Hebrews 4:12 and John 17:17.

What does it mean that God's Word is *living*?

_____

_____

What does it mean that God's Word is *active*?

_____

_____

What does it mean that God's Word is *piercing*?

_____

_____

What evidence can you share that the Bible has been alive, active, and penetrating in your life?

_____

_____

_____

_____

How does believing God's Word is *truth* help us?

_____

_____

Why do some people struggle to believe this?

_____

_____

When we open the Bible with good and teachable hearts, its living truth pierces our hearts and changes our lives. We long to see the power of the Living Truth evident in the lives of all who make CVC their church home.

THE BIBLE, OUR SOUL FOOD.
The Bible is our spiritual food, our "soul food." It nourishes us. We feed ourselves from God's Word. It is God who has prepared a table of spiritual food for us. *You prepare a table before me in the presence of my enemies* (Psalm 23:5). Are we feeding at the table our loving Father has prepared for us?

It's important that we become Self-Feeders, one of the fruits of our new life in Christ. When we grow in maturity, we aren't totally dependent on others for our spiritual nourishment.

When we become Self-Feeders, we will take in the Bible as a part of our daily lives. We won't just show up at Sunday services to get a bite-sized snack that is supposed to energize us for the week. We realize that if we take in the Bible, its living truth will have great benefit for us all day every day.

In the Old Testament, Job said about God's Word, *I have not departed from the commandment of his lips; I have treasured the words of his mouth more than my portion of food* (Job 23:12). In other words, Job is saying that he would rather eat of the Word of God than eat a juicy steak, apple pie, or ice cream.

God gives us several important ways of looking at God's Word as our necessary food.

GOD'S WORD IS LIKE BREAD.
We have been specifically designed to eat a particular kind of soul food: God's Word. That's why in both the Old and New Testaments, God emphasized that His Word is our bread (Deuteronomy 8:3, Matthew 4:4). Jesus Himself made this point. Jesus, as our pattern, took the Word of God in the Scriptures as His bread and lived on it. Look up and highlight or underline the words of Jesus in Matthew 4:4.

In the space below, write in your own words the truth that Jesus expressed in Matthew 4:4.

_____

_____

GOD'S WORD IS LIKE HONEY.
Most of us find that a glob of honey slathered thickly on buttered toast tastes amazing. It's not just that it's good for us. It also tastes sweet going down. Look up and highlight or underline Psalm 19:9b-10.

What have been some things you have found in God's Word that have been sweet to your taste?

_____

_____

_____

_____

GOD'S WORD IS LIKE MILK.

God's Word is milk to nourish the newborn ones so they may grow in the spiritual life. Look up and highlight or underline
1 Peter 2:2.

To "long for" is "to desire." It's a compelling craving. Think of how a newborn baby cries for milk when he's/she's hungry. That's what our craving for God's Word should be like. We just "have to have it!"

On a scale of 1-10 (10 being highest), rate your desire (your level of craving) for God's Word by circling a number.

1   2   3   4   5   6   7   8   9   10

What might you do to increase your craving for the Word of God?

_____

_____

_____

_____

GOD'S WORD IS LIKE MEAT.

The Apostle Paul wanted the believers at Corinth to take in the deeper truths from the Word of God. He reminded them that the Bible contains solid food, i.e., meat. He was saddened by the fact that they were still so immature that they weren't yet ready for the meat of the Word. Look up and highlight or underline
1 Corinthians 3:2 and Hebrews 5:14a.

What might be some differences between a believer who can only drink the milk of God's Word and a believer who can not only drink the milk of the Word but also eat the meat of the Word?

_____

_____

_____

_____

To be nourished by God's Word, we need to eat God's Word as bread and honey, drink God's Word as milk, and feed on God's Word as meat (solid food). We must be like Jeremiah, who found God's words and "ate them" (Jeremiah 15:16). By receiving the Word of God as our daily nourishment, we will experience an inward transformation, and we will grow in our New Life in Christ until we are "like Him" (1 John 3:2).

WE MUST ACTUALLY EAT!
There is only one thing we need to do as we sit down to feast on the Word of God. We have to partake of it. We can have the most wonderful food on our table. The table can be set with the most exquisite tablecloths and napkins. The china can be the most expensive in the world. The crystal can be glowing and the silverware can be shining. The food can look and smell tantalizing. The table can be beautiful, but if we never eat any of the food, it will not fill us up or satisfy. We must eat.

Believers who consistently bear the Fruit of New Life are people who feed on the Word of God. Without a steady diet we get weaker and weaker. If we are dissatisfied with our Christian walk, we must check the way we are feeding on the Word of God.

"Compare the way you eat. Suppose that you start the day with a glass of orange juice. It's good, and good for you. It takes you maybe five minutes to drink it, if you read the newspaper at the same time. Then you go off to work or school. You don't eat anything else until the next morning. And you have another glass of juice. And so you go on drinking one glass of juice a day until you drop. That's the way a lot of Christians try to survive as believers. They feed their faith with five minutes of food in the morning, or evening, and then don't eat again until 24 hours later. Some even skip one or two mornings and don't give their faith anything to eat for days" (*Desiring God* blog, by John Piper).

The effect of starving yourself spiritually is that . . . well, your spirit starves. That's not hard to understand. And when your soul is starving, it is weak and not able to do much. That's why you'll have a hard time trusting God, worshipping, rejoicing, and resisting sin. You'll be weak. You'll stumble and fall.

YOU ARE WHAT YOU EAT.
If we choose not to feed on God's Word, whether we recognize it or not, we will still be feeding on something. Whatever thoughts we chew on during the course of a day are what actually have become our soul food. If we are thinking anxious thoughts, prideful thoughts, self-pitying thoughts, bitter thoughts, lustful thoughts, or greedy thoughts, then our souls are actually feeding on those thoughts and not feeding on God's thoughts. Whatever thoughts our souls feed on will be what we eventually become, because our spirits will assimilate the very nature of those thoughts.

"You are what you eat." This is usually heard in reference to physical food. But it can also be applied to what we feed our souls. The health of our souls depends on our spiritual food choices. We can either nourish, or deplete ourselves spiritually. We have to eat the right things, true things. And this comes from God's Word. We don't want to suffer from spiritual anorexia or bulimia.

Sadly, too many followers of Jesus are eating junk food. It has no nutritional value. Spiritual junk food has both short-term and long-term negative effects on the soul. Certain TV shows, media, web sites, magazines, ungodly music, unedifying conversations, worldly thoughts, and perspectives fill our lives. This kind of spiritual junk food will keep our souls malnourished and open to the attacks of the enemy.

What are some things you have been taking in that could be called spiritual junk food that you need to eliminate from your spiritual diet?

_____
_____
_____
_____

SOUL FOOD SATISFIES.

Soul food is usually considered to be the most satisfying food there is. God's Word is the most amazing soul food and can satisfy us beyond measure. Think of all of the wonderful things found in the Bible that we can feast upon. There are promises, comfort, direction and instruction, salvation, love, joy, and wisdom. The list could go on and on. The menu is full.

As you close your time today, use the images—bread, honey, milk, meat—to thank God for His Word. Ask Him to give you a greater hunger for His Word. Ask Him to strengthen you as you eat His Word. Write out your prayer in the space below.

_____
_____
_____
_____
_____
_____
_____

What was one of the most helpful insights that you received during this lesson?

_____
_____
_____
_____
_____

WEEK 4, DAY 3: RELIABILITY OF THE BIBLE

The trustworthiness of the Bible is a controversial topic in today's world. It's vital that we understand that the teachings of the Bible are scientifically plausible, historically reliable, and culturally relevant.

Last week, we spent time considering the trustworthiness of the Bible as we began our studies regarding Bible intake. We want to conclude our investigation of Bible intake by bolstering our confidence in the Bible. Remember, it claims to be more than just a book.

At CVC, we believe the Bible contains Living Truth. The centerpiece of each worship service is a message based on a text from the Bible. We listen to the Bible carefully. We build our lives on its truths. We submit our wills to its demands. We believe that following the principles and precepts of the Bible is tantamount to following Christ.

But many people today think that our attitude toward the Bible is foolish and archaic. "Most would say that they know there are many great stories and sayings in the Bible, but today 'you can't take it *literally*.' What they mean is that the Bible is not entirely trustworthy because some parts—maybe many or most parts—are scientifically impossible, historically unreliable, and culturally regressive" (*The Reason for God*, by Tim Keller, pp.99-100).

So, why should we believe the Bible?

THE WITNESS OF INTERNAL CONSISTENCY

The Bible was written over a period of about 1,500 years. It was written by 40 people from many different walks of life: Peter, a fisherman; Solomon, a king; and Luke, a doctor. The Bible was written on 3 different continents: Asia, Africa, and Europe. The Bible was written in 3 languages: Hebrew, Greek, and Aramaic.

The Bible was written under many different circumstances. David wrote during a time of war. Solomon wrote in a time of peace. Mark wrote while Israel was under Roman domination.

The writers of the Bible had different reasons for writing. Isaiah wrote to warn about God's judgment. Matthew wrote to prove to the Jews that Jesus is the Messiah. Paul wrote addressing problems in different churches.

Put it all together. The Bible was written over a period of 1,500 years, by 40 different authors, on 3 continents, in 3 languages, under different circumstances, and for different reasons. But with all that diversity, there is unity: The glory of God as He reconciles a fallen creation to Himself. The internal consistency of the Bible, despite all its variety, is incredible.

Ask 40 people today to write down their views on a controversial topic. How about, "Who should be the Cleveland Browns head coach and/or quarterback?" Do you think you could get 40 Clevelanders to agree about that?

Yet when it comes to the Bible, all 40 authors, over 1,500 years, wrote on many controversial subjects, and they do not contradict one another. How did it happen? Someone guided these writers through the whole process: the Holy Spirit. *For no prophecy was ever produced by the will of man, but men spoke from God as they were carried along by the Holy Spirit* (2 Peter 1:21).

THE WITNESS OF MANUSCRIPT RELIABILITY
The reliability of the Bible is often challenged by critics. But if you see the Bible as unreliable, then you also have to disregard other ancient writings by people like Plato, Aristotle, and Homer. Why? The biblical documents are better preserved and more numerous than any other ancient writing.

Take Plato's writings. The time span between the original and the earliest copies we have? 1,200 years. How many copies? 7. Take Aristotle's writings. The time span between the original and the earliest copies we have? 1,400 years. How many copies? 49. Take Homer's writings. The time span between the original and the earliest copies we have? 500 years. How many copies? 643. Take the New Testament. The time span between the original and the earliest copies we have? About 70 years. How many copies? 5,600.

There are thousands more New Testament Greek manuscripts than any other ancient writing. And scholars tell us that the New Testament documents are about 99.5% textually pure.

If you dismiss the New Testament as reliable, then you must also dismiss the reliability of the writings of Plato, Aristotle, and Homer. We have more reason to trust the New Testament than to trust any other ancient writing.

THE WITNESS OF EYEWITNESS CREDIBILITY
Most biblical scholars agree that the NT documents were all written before the close of the first century. That means that the entire New Testament was completed in about 70 years.

So what? There were people around when the New Testament was being written who could have said, "That's not true!" But we have no ancient documents written in the first century that contest the New Testament.

"The Biblical accounts of Jesus' life were circulating within the lifetimes of hundreds who had been present at the events of His ministry . . . The New Testament documents could not say Jesus was crucified when thousands of people were still alive who knew whether He was or not. If there had not been appearances after His death, if there had not been an empty tomb, if He had not made these claims, and these public documents claimed they happened, Christianity would never have gotten off the ground. The hearers would have simply laughed at the accounts" (*The Reason for God*, by Tim Keller, pp.101-102).

THE WITNESS OF FULFILLED PROPHECY
There are dozens and dozens of prophecies made about Jesus in the Old Testament: where He would be born, how He would be rejected, how He would die. All these prophecies were made hundreds of years before Jesus ever came to earth.

Some say these prophecies were fulfilled by chance, but the odds against that happening would be huge. It would take more faith to believe in that chance happening than in the fact that Jesus is God and these prophecies are divinely inspired.

Consider just 8 prophecies about the events surrounding the death of Jesus.

1. Betrayed by a friend — Prophecy: Psalm 41:9 — Fulfilled: Matthew 10:4
2. Silent before accusers — Prophecy: Isaiah 53:7 — Fulfilled: Matthew 27:12
3. Beaten and spit upon — Prophecy: Isaiah 50:6 — Fulfilled: Matthew 26:67
4. Hands and feet pierced — Prophecy: Psalm 22:16 — Fulfilled: Luke 23:33
5. Crucified with thieves — Prophecy: Isaiah 53:12 — Fulfilled: Matthew 27:38
6. Gambled for His clothes — Prophecy: Psalm 22:18 — Fulfilled: John 19:23, 24
7. Pierced side — Prophecy: Zechariah 12:10 — Fulfilled: John 19:34
8. Buried in a rich man's tomb — Prophecy: Isaiah 53:9 — Fulfilled: Matthew 28:57-60

Peter Stoner was chairman of the science division of Westmont College. He wrote a book called *Science Speaks*. Stoner said that by using the modern science of probability in reference to eight prophecies, "We find that the chance that any [one] man might have . . . fulfilled all eight prophecies is 1 in 10^{17}." That would be 1 chance out of 100 quadrillion.

Take 100 quadrillion silver dollars and lay them on the face of Texas. They would cover the state two feet deep. Now mark one of these silver dollars with a red dot. Stir them up all over the state. Blindfold a man. Tell him he can go wherever he wants. But on one try, he has to find the one silver dollar with the red dot. He would have a 1 out of 100 quadrillion chance—the same chance that the prophets would have had of writing these eight prophecies and having them all come true in any one man. And that's just 8 fulfilled prophecies. Conclusion: There is a design, a purpose, and a guiding hand behind the Bible.

THE WITNESS OF PERSONAL TRANSFORMATION

The British pastor C.H. Spurgeon said that a Bible which is falling apart usually belongs to someone who isn't. The Spirit of God uses the Word of God to actually transform the lives of people. God has used the Bible to change the lives of murderers, drug addicts, government officials, business people, husbands, wives, and students. The Bible is not merely a book that tells us how to live. It is literally packed with life-changing power. It is the Word of God with the power to transform lives.

All Scripture is breathed out by God and profitable for teaching, for reproof, for correction, and for training in righteousness, that the man of God may be complete, equipped for every good work (2 Timothy 3:16-17, ESV).

Dennis Prager once debated Jonathan Glover, an atheistic philosopher from Oxford. Glover didn't believe the Bible. So, Prager asked Glover, "If you, Professor Glover, were stranded at the midnight hour in a desolate Los Angeles street and if, as you stepped out of your car with fear and trembling, you were suddenly to hear the weight of pounding footsteps behind you, and you saw ten burly men who had just stepped out of a dwelling coming toward you, would it or would it not make a difference to you to know that they were coming from a Bible study?"

Glover had to admit that it would make a difference. Even skeptics know that the Bible changes lives.

Why should we believe the Bible? Because of the witness of internal consistency, manuscript reliability, eyewitness credibility, fulfilled prophecy, and personal transformation.

Which of these witnesses means the most to you and why?

_____

_____

_____

_____

Who are 2-3 of your friends or family members who are skeptical about the trustworthiness of the Bible?

_____   _____

_____   _____

_____   _____

Which of these witnesses might mean the most to one of your skeptical friends or family members?

_____

_____

What was one of the most helpful insights that you received during this lesson?

_____

_____

_____

_____

Maybe you're wondering, "Can I change? Can I kick this habit?

Can I become more patient? Can I live free from fear?" You need God and His Word. The Bible is the means He's given us so everyone can live new every day.

Read it through. Pray it in. Live it out. He said, *My Word will accomplish My purpose in your life* (Isaiah 55:11). Psalm 107:20 says, *He sent out His Word and healed them* (Psalm 107:20, ESV). God can use the Bible to change your life.

WEEK 4, DAY 4: THE BENEFITS OF BIBLE INTAKE
Followers of Christ will be tempted to view the Bible as a boring book with no relevance to practical daily life. That's when taking in the Bible becomes a chore. But because the Bible is a living and active book that is full of timeless truth where we encounter our beloved Father, Bible intake, approached properly, is not a drudgery, but a delight. It's helpful to review the benefits of regular Bible intake.

SEVEN BENEFITS OF REGULAR BIBLE INTAKE

1. GREAT JOY.
Reading God's Word and applying it to your life will bring you great joy. Look up and highlight or underline Jeremiah 15:16.

How do you think internalizing God's Word can increase your joy?

_____

_____

2. PRACTICAL GUIDANCE.
Through your regular unhurried time in God's Word, you will gain guidance from God. Look up and highlight or underline Isaiah 30:21.

What is an area of your life right now where you need some guidance? How do you think the Bible can help show you the way?

_____

_____

_____

3. VICTORY OVER SIN.
Taking in God's Word will give you victory over sin. Look up and highlight or underline Psalm 119:9-11.

What are some plaguing sins in your life that you would like to overcome?

_____

_____

Seek to find and then list 2 or 3 verses that will help you fight against that temptation. _____

_____

_____

(Note: You can use the search engines on websites like www.biblegateway.com or www.esvstudybible.org (English Standard Version Study Bible) to find appropriate verses. If you are struggling with anxiety, you could type in words like "anxiety," "worry," or "peace" in the search box on the website to find great verses to help you gain victory over your besetting sins.)

4.   SPIRITUAL STABILITY, FRUITFULNESS, AND PROSPERITY.
Taking in God's Word will give lead you to flourish spiritually and give you spiritual <u>stability</u>, <u>prosperity,</u> <u>success,</u> and <u>fruitfulness</u>.
Look up and highlight or underline Psalm 1:2-3.

Of course, God's definition of success is quite different than the world's definition of success. When we find new life in Christ, we find our desires changing. We increasingly crave godly prosperity more than worldly prosperity.

Write down some synonyms for the following words:

Stability: _____
Fruitfulness: _____
Prosperity: _____

How do you think regular Bible intake will help produce these qualities in your life?

_____
_____
_____

5.   AN INCREASED ABILITY TO ENCOURAGE, HELP, AND GUIDE OTHERS.
As you get to know the Word of God more and more, your ability to be used by God to help others will be greatly enhanced. Look up and highlight or underline Psalm 119:98-100.

Match the reference to the appropriate benefit.

1.   Psalm 119:100   A. Wiser than my enemies
2.   Psalm 119:98   B. More understanding than my teachers
3.   Psalm 119: 99   C. Understand more than the aged

Which of the above 3 qualities do you need the most?

Which excites you the most? Why?

_____
_____
_____

6.   INCREASED FAITH AND TRUST IN GOD.
Life is difficult in our fallen world. Things will happen that are challenging and frustrating. If we don't gain the perspective that God's Word can bring us, then we can begin to doubt God and His love for us. Bible intake will grow our faith and our confidence in God. Look up and highlight or underline Romans 10:17.

Describe a time when your faith in God began to waver.

_____
_____
_____

How might God use His Word—the Bible—to strengthen your faith and hope in Him?

_____
_____
_____

7.   PREPARATION FOR THE DAY'S CHALLENGES AND OPPORTUNITIES.
Since God already knows what will happen in your life each day, spending time with Him gives Him the opportunity to prepare you for what will be coming your way. Look up and highlight or underline Psalm 119:105.

The Bible mentions countless other benefits in addition to the 7 benefits that are listed above.

Look up the following verses and match the reference to the appropriate benefit.

1.	Psalm 119:18	A.	An ability to know and do God's will
2.	John 14:21	B.	Growth in your love for God
3.	Psalm 40:8	C.	An ability to see and perceive God, life, and self more clearly
4.	Acts 20:32	D.	Words that will sustain weary family members and friends
5.	Isaiah 50:4	E.	Being built up (becoming spiritually "buff"!)

What was one insight from today's lesson that you really needed?

_____
_____
_____

As you end your study time today, spend some time in prayer, thanking God for His Word and its many benefits. Ask Him to give you a hunger for its life-changing truths that will enable you to live new!

What was one of the most helpful insights that you received during this lesson?

_____
_____
_____
_____
_____

WEEK 4, DAY 5: HEARING THE BIBLE

HEARING GOD'S WORD

Hearing God's Word proclaimed and explained is an important part of your new life in Christ. The leader Paul once wrote to his protégé, Timothy, *Until I come, devote yourself to the public reading of Scripture, to exhortation, to teaching* (1 Timothy 4:13). In Ephesians 4:11-12 we learn that God has given Bible teachers to the church to equip the saints (and, remember, that's you). When teachers teach and hearers hear, then the church will grow in grace.

What's something that comes to your mind when you think about "hearing the Word of God"? What does it mean? Why is it necessary? How do we do it?

_____

_____

_____

_____

Luke 4:16 tells us that Jesus made it His regular practice to attend the first century version of church services: *And as was His custom, He went to the synagogue on the Sabbath day.* Jewish synagogue services included a reading from the Scriptures and an explanation and application of the reading.

If Jesus felt that it was important for Him to be in His Father's house on the Lord's Day to hear the Word of the Lord, how much more should we make weekend services our own "can't miss" appointments? The public services of a church provide prime opportunity for us to join together to hear the Word of God. We ought to never neglect taking advantage of the opportunity to gather on weekends to hear the Word of God being taught.

"If we don't discipline ourselves to hear God's Word regularly, we may only hear it accidentally, just when we feel like it, or we may never hear it at all. For most of us, disciplining ourselves to hear God's Word means developing the practice of steadfastly attending a New Testament church where the Word of God is faithfully preached" (*Spiritual Disciplines of the Christian Life*, by Donald Whitney, p.29).

Read the following commitment. Is this a commitment that you think you could and should make?

Unless I am providentially hindered, I will seek to follow the example of Jesus by worshipping God faithfully [regularly, habitually] in order to hear God's Word being taught.

☐ **Yes**   ☐ **No**

At CVC, we have a passion for Living Truth. We value theologically-accurate, culturally-relevant, and personally-practical preaching of the Word of God. That's why on weekends at CVC, you will hear a pastor read a section of Scripture followed by explanation and application.

The preaching of the Word of God pleases God and saves hearers. *It pleased God through . . . what we preach to save those who believe* (1 Corinthians 1:21). If God values the preaching of His Word, then it must logically follow that He values the hearing of His Word.

In the Old Testament book of Nehemiah, we see an example of an expectant group of God's people hearing the Word of God.
Find Nehemiah 8:1-8 and read it.

Identify the specific verses in Nehemiah 8 that teach the following important principles about maximizing the hearing of the Word of God?

1. Attentiveness to the Word.   Verse: _____
2. Explanation of the Word.   Verse: _____
3. Reverence for the Word.   Verse: _____

What other principles about hearing the Word of God do you see in the Nehemiah 8 passage?

_____
_____

Brainstorm: Besides attending a church service, what are some other creative and accessible ways we can hear the Word of God?

_____
_____
_____
_____

Circle 3 of the following practices that might help you grow in your engagement and attentiveness to God's Word.

A. Taking notes during a message.
B. Filing your notes or keeping them in a journal.
C. Praying for the Bible teacher before the message.
D. Praying for yourself that you will have open ears, mind, and heart.
E. Tweeting the most meaningful things you hear during a message.
F. Reviewing your message notes during the week.
G. Reconciling relationships before attending a service.
H. Having a spirit of expectation that God will speak.
I. Other: _____

What was one of the most helpful insights that you received during this lesson?

_____

_____

_____

_____

_____

AS YOU CLOSE YOUR TIME TODAY, USE THE FOLLOWING PRAYER AS A GUIDE FOR YOUR OWN:

Heavenly Father, I praise You that You are a God who speaks. You are not silent. You have given us Your Word. You have given us teachers who help us understand it and apply it. Now, give me ears to hear.

Forgive me for all the times I have not listened intently to what You have been saying through Your servants. Grant to me the desire and the ability to listen with anticipation, wanting to be instructed.

May I love hearing the Word of God even when I am being exhorted, challenged, rebuked, and admonished.

May I also enjoy being comforted by the promises of the gospel. Give me discernment to reject any and all false teaching so I can hear the voice of the True Shepherd, Jesus. Give me ears to hear so that I might have a mind for truth and a heart to obey.

In Jesus' name, Amen.

Week 5

BIBLE INTAKE: GROWING AS A SELF-FEEDER (PART 2)

MEMORY VERSE

All Scripture is breathed out by God and profitable for teaching, for reproof, for correction, and for training in righteousness, that the man of God may be complete, equipped for every good work.
2 Timothy 3:16-17

WEEK 5, DAY 1: READING THE BIBLE

READING GOD'S WORD

A life-long habit that believers who Live New will be sure to develop is reading the Bible. Studies consistently show that the number one issue correlated to spiritual growth and maturity is the discipline of daily Bible reading (*The Shape of Faith to Come*, by Brad Waggoner, p.296). This is why our pastors and leaders set the example as Bible readers. This is why we emphasize Bible reading from the pulpit and in our training of new and growing believers. This is why we have a church-wide Bible reading emphasis each year. This is why all the ministries of our church emphasize Bible reading. This is why we help parents emphasize and model this in the home.

Jesus expected God's people to be Bible readers. He often referenced God's Word with an expectation that His listeners would have read it by asking, *Have you not read . . .?* (Matthew 12:3; see also Matthew 12:5, Matthew 19:4, Matthew 22:31, Mark 12:10, Mark 12:26, and Luke 6:3).

God promises blessings for those who read the Scriptures. *Blessed is the one who reads aloud the words of this prophecy, and blessed are those who hear, and who keep what is written in it, for the time is near* (Revelation 1:3). While this is a special promise for those who specifically read the book of Revelation, by extension this blessing would apply to all the other books of the Bible because they reveal their own unique truths about Jesus Christ and His gospel.

What are some practical tips for developing the habit of daily Bible reading?

1. PRAY.

Ask God to help you develop the Bible reading habit. The world, the flesh, and the devil all will battle against you to keep you out of the Bible. This is not a war you can win without divine help. Pray that God will give you the grace to develop this habit.

In the space below, please write out a prayer to God for help to build a habit of daily Bible reading.

_____

_____

_____

_____

Each time you read your Bible, ask God to give you insight into His Word and its application to your life. In Psalm 119:18 the Psalmist prays, *Open my eyes, that I may behold wondrous things out of your law.* Ask the Lord, "Why are You showing me this passage today? What is going on in my life that I need to learn this truth?"

2. PURCHASE.
We encourage you to buy a study Bible to help you understand the Bible better. The notes at the bottom of the page of a good study Bible give great insights into the context, history, and meaning of the text. Some good study Bibles include The ESV Study Bible (our highest recommendation) or The Life Application Study Bible.

When shopping for a good study Bible, you will notice that many versions of the Bible are available. Shop for a modern version that you can understand. At CVC, we mainly use the ESV—the English Standard Version. Other options include the NASB—the New American Standard Bible, the NLT—the New Living Translation, and the NIV—the New International Version.

(Note: You can politely suggest that a friend or family member buy a Bible for you for your birthday, for a Christmas present, or to help you celebrate your baptism. Make sure that they know which study Bible you are wishing for and that they know which version you prefer.)

3. PLACE (AND TIME).
Find a particular place in your home to read your Bible. It should be a place where you will be free from distractions. It should be a place that you like, that you will look forward to being in each day. Choose a particular time each day when you are alert and when you are least likely to be interrupted.

We know that this can be especially challenging for those with young children. Spouses can help each other find 10 or 15 minutes of alone time for Bible reading. Single parents may have to take advantage of rare spare moments in the day or may simply have to run straight to the Word of God before the kids awake or immediately after the kids go to sleep at night.

In the space below, describe the place and time that typically will work best for you.

_____

_____

4. PLAN.
Select a solid Bible reading plan. We strongly encourage you to join us at CVC in our church-wide Bible reading plan. Many reading plans are easily accessible online (www.bible.com).

Since you can access the Bible in so many different ways—your smart phone, your tablet, your iPod, your computer, as well as the ever-appreciated hard copy—Bible reading is extremely convenient. There are really no excuses to not read the Bible for someone who aims to experience new life in Christ.

If you make it through the readings for a day, you can make it through a week. If you can make it through a week, you can make it through a year. And if you make it through a year, at the end of this year you won't be looking at the same person in the mirror. Jesus will give you new life.

If you haven't started reading the Bible with the CVC Bible Reading Plan, please start. If you've started but gotten behind, don't beat yourself up. Just start on today's reading. Remember, reading something is better than reading nothing.

What Bible reading plan will you use in the days, weeks, and months ahead?

_____

_____

5. PERSPECTIVE.
Resist the temptation to turn your Bible reading into a spiritual chore or a religious duty. Also, refuse to turn your Bible reading into a way for you to create Bible-based, guilt-inducing "to do" lists.

Think about it. If we make the Bible primarily a book about morality—what we should or shouldn't do—then it's really not good news because we can never measure up! But if we see the Bible as a Book that, from Genesis 1 through Revelation 22, primarily points us to Jesus and His gospel, then the Bible is absolutely the best news ever.

So, see your Bible reading as a way to gaze at Jesus and the gospel. Learn to look for Jesus on each page, even in the Old Testament. In your Bible reading, you will see Jesus is the pattern for your life. He is the pardon for all your sins. He is the power Who can enable you to Live New.

AN INCENTIVE TO READ THE BIBLE
A quote from Geoffrey Thomas might encourage you to make sure that Bible reading is a regular spiritual discipline for your new life in Christ:

"Do not expect to master the Bible in a day, or a month, or a year. Rather expect to often be puzzled by its contents. It is not all equally clear. Great men of God often feel like absolute novices when they read the Word:

"Do not always expect to get an emotional charge or a feeling of quiet peace when you read the Bible . . . Let the Word break over your heart and mind again and again as the years go by, and imperceptibly there will come some great changes in your attitude, and outlook, and conduct. You will probably be the last to recognize these.

"Often you will feel very, very small, because increasingly the God of the Bible will become to you wonderfully great.

"So go on reading it until you can read no longer, and then you will not need the Bible anymore, because when your eyes close for the last time in death, and never read again the Word of God in Scripture, you will open them to the Word of God in the flesh, that same Jesus of the Bible whom you have known for so long, standing before you to take you forever to His eternal home" (*Reading the Bible*, by Geoffrey Thomas, p.22).

What was one of the most helpful insights that you received during this lesson?

_____
_____
_____
_____
_____

The Bible is not one book consisting of multiple stories, but one story consisting of many books.

WEEK 5, DAY 2: STUDYING THE BIBLE

Not only should we hear and read the Word of God, but we should also study it. In your Bible, look up and highlight or underline 2 Timothy 2:15.

The ancient King James Version of the Bible translated
2 Timothy 2:15 like this: *Study to show thyself approved unto God.*
Bible study is an important discipline for Self-feeders to develop.

STUDYING GOD'S WORD

Set aside at least 10-15 minutes for your regular, unhurried time with God. Find a comfortable, secluded place where you can be uninterrupted as you focus on the Lord. Make sure you have a good pen along with a journal and your Bible.

Use your CVC Bible reading guide to look for the appropriate Bible passage to read for the day. Open your Bible to the chapter(s) with anticipation. Expect God to speak to you about your life situation.

Before you begin to read through your daily Scripture reading, ask the Lord to illuminate His Word, to show you His will, and to reveal Jesus to you. Ask Him to lead you to some specific verse or verses for the day.

Read through the passages. As you are reading, underline, highlight, or circle anything that the Lord impresses upon you. Look for a personal word that God especially wants you to apply in your life for that day.

When you sense that the Lord is leading you to focus on a particular passage, turn to a fresh page in your journal and begin to write down what God has shown you. Since God will be speaking through His Word to you, then it makes sense to write it down. You can use the acrostic L.I.V.E. to record what God is saying to you.

LEARN:

Take your time reading the Scriptures. Allow God to speak to you. When you finish reading, be selective. Look for a verse or verses that particularly spoke to you and seek to learn the verse or verses by writing the words in your journal.

INVESTIGATE:

What do you think God is saying to you in the verse or verses?
Ask the Holy Spirit to teach you and reveal more about your new life in Christ. Write what you observe in your journal. You could use the following questions to help you get started: What is a title that you would give this passage? What does this teach you about God, about others, about yourself? What are some cross references for the passage?

VALUE:

How would you summarize the truths you learned?
Pick one thought. Write down one big idea that you will carry with you through the day.

EXPRESS:

Now, you can express yourself to God in prayer by writing out at least a portion of your prayer. *Praise* God by telling Him that you love Him and why you love Him. *Repent* of your sins of thought, sins of attitude, sins of relationships, sins of omission, sins of commission, sins of self-rule, or sins of self-reliance. *Ask* God for what's on your heart. Ask God to help you apply what you are learning. Ask Him for greater insight. Ask Him to work powerfully in, through, with, and for your family members and friends. *Yield* your life and your desires to God as you trust Him to answer your prayers according to His will. Write out a simple prayer based on God's Word.

Use the space below to create a journal entry after doing the CVC Bible reading for today.

Learn

_____
_____
_____
_____
_____
_____
_____
_____
_____

Investigate

_____
_____
_____
_____
_____
_____
_____
_____

Value

_____
_____
_____
_____
_____
_____
_____
_____

Express

_____
_____
_____
_____
_____
_____
_____
_____
_____
_____

What was one of the most helpful insights that you received during this lesson?

_____
_____
_____
_____

WEEK 5, DAY 3: MEMORIZING GOD'S WORD

From the very beginning, CVC has encouraged Bible memorization as an important tool for living new and growing spiritually. As we fill our minds with Living Truth, we will be more and more equipped to live new. The Psalmist wrote, *I have stored up Your Word in my heart that I might not sin against You* (Psalm 119:11).

Spiritual leader Dallas Willard said, "As a pastor, teacher, counselor I have repeatedly seen the transformation of inner and outer life that comes simply from memorization and meditation upon Scripture. Personally, I would never undertake to guide a program of [spiritual growth] that did not involve a continuous program of memorization of the choicest passages of Scripture for people of all ages" (*The Spirit of the Disciplines*, by Dallas Willard, p.50).

REASONS TO MEMORIZE SCRIPTURE

Match the following Scripture with the appropriate reason to memorize the Bible.

1. Brings joy.	A. Psalm 119:24
2. Helps us counsel and encourage others.	B. Romans 15:4
3. Provides comfort and hope.	C. Ephesians 6:17
4. Helps us overcome temptations.	D. Jeremiah 15:16
5. Provides guidance.	E. Proverbs 25:11

Some people view Scripture memory like it's a bad-tasting medicine. Yes, the Word of God is a medicine for our sin-sick souls. But memorizing Bible passages isn't just medicine. It's sweet-tasting food that will feed and nourish us and others. God's Word is a joy-filled feast, not a box of bitter-tasting pills.

HOW TO MEMORIZE GOD'S WORD

Every Bible memorization method has one or more of the three Rs at its heart: *Repeat, Recall, Review. Repeat* a passage over and over until you're familiar with it; practice *recalling* it until it's worn a path in your memory; then *review* it so you don't lose it.

1. REPEAT.

Write out the verse in a memory notebook or on a 3x5 card. It's helpful to include the topic and reference before and after the verse. Writing the verse out deepens the impression in your mind. If you simply copy and paste the verses from your computer, you are losing a valuable opportunity to lock in the verses by writing them out by hand.

God's Word
Psalm 119:11

I have stored up your word in my heart
that I might not sin against you.

Psalm 119:11
God's Word

Read the verse through several times. Each time you repeat it, say the topic, reference, verse, and then the reference again. Don't just say the verses in your head. Practice saying them aloud. This will engage more senses and increase your chance of long-term memory. By saying them you get a chance to use your mouth and your ears. You can even add physical gestures and walk around the room to put more of your body into the memorization process.

2. RECALL.

After learning the topic and reference, learn the first phrase of the verse. Once you have learned the topic, reference, and the first phrase and have repeated them several times, continue adding more phrases after you can quote correctly what you have already learned.

Find a friend to check you on the verse. Better yet, memorize the verse together. You don't have to both memorize the same verses, but it will help if you do. You are looking to have someone who will encourage you to consistently study and memorize God's Word. Your friend can send you an email or a text every couple of days to check up on your progress.

3. REVIEW.

Review the verse immediately after learning it and repeat it frequently in the next few days. Repetition is the best way to engrave the verses on your memory. Try to set aside time each day to work on reviewing your verses. Don't worry if you don't have large blocks of time. Even just a few minutes each day will help you commit much more Scripture to memory than most Christians do.

Find a variety of ways to review:

- You can put Bible verses on note cards around the house to help you study.
- You can keep some cards in your car to study while you are waiting at a light or in a parking lot (be aware of your surroundings and don't get hit by another car or forget to move when the light turns green).
- You can place the memory cards on your bathroom mirror or refrigerator.
- Take advantage of audio helps as well. Record the verse on your phone. Send yourself phone alerts with the verse included. Listen repeatedly to the verse using an ESV Bible app.

"No principle of Scripture memory is more important than the principle of review. Without adequate review you will eventually lose most of what you memorize. But once you really learn a verse, you can mentally review it in a fraction of the time it would take to speak it. And when you know a verse this well, you don't have to review it but once a week, once a month, or even once every six months to keep a sharp edge on it. It's not unusual, however, to reach a point where you spend 80% of your Scripture memory time in review. Don't begrudge devoting so much time to polishing your swords. Rejoice instead of having so many!" (*Spiritual Disciplines of the Christian Life*, by Donald Whitney, p.42).

Now, let's put this lesson to practice. Look up this week's CVC memory verse. Write it on a 3x5 card. Include the topic and reference before and after on the card. Now, spend some time repeating, recalling, and reviewing.

Remember, memorization is like exercise. The less you do it, the harder it gets; but the more you do it, the easier it gets!

What was one of the most helpful insights that you received during this lesson?

_____

_____

_____

_____

_____

It's convicting to realize that we may have numerous movie lines, song lyrics, and sport statistics memorized, but can only recall a few Bible verses.
Chad Allen, Lead Pastor - Cuyahoga Valley Church

WEEK 5, DAY 4: MEDITATING ON THE BIBLE

Meditating on God's Word helps to make weak Christians strong, and shallow Christians deep. Biblical meditation is an antidote to our busy-ness and superficiality.

"In contemporary society, our adversary majors in three things: noise, hurry, and crowds. If he can keep us engaged in 'muchness' and 'manyness' he will rest satisfied. . . If we hope to move beyond the superficialities of our culture, we must be willing to go down into the recreating silences, into the inner world of contemplation" (*Celebration of Disciplines: The Path to Spiritual Growth*, by Richard Foster, p.15).

Many religions—particularly eastern religions—practice meditation. But biblical meditation is radically different. Eastern meditation is an effort to *empty* the mind. Christian meditation involves *filling* the mind with truth—God's Word.

WHAT ARE THE BENEFITS OF BIBLICAL MEDITATION?

1. Meditation on God's Word is the pathway to blessedness.
    In your Bible, look up and underline or highlight Psalm 1:1-3.

Based on Psalm 1:1-3, what should we avoid if we want this blessedness?

_____
_____
_____

When is it that God's people are to meditate?

_____
_____

What are the blessings we receive from meditating on God's Word?

_____
_____
_____

2. Meditation on God's Word is the way to achieve spiritual success. Look up and highlight or underline Joshua 1:8.

When is it that God's people are to meditate?
(Hint: This might sound familiar!)

_____
_____

According to Joshua 1:8, what is a primary purpose of meditation?

_____

_____

3. Meditation on God's Word will bring us joy.
    Look up and highlight or underline Psalm 63:5-7.

WHAT IS BIBLICAL MEDITATION?

When we meditate, we muse, contemplate, and reflect on the Word of God. We see two main Hebrew words for meditation. One word is "siah" which means "to rehearse" or "to go over something in your mind" either inwardly or outwardly. Another Hebrew word used for meditation is the word "hagah" which means "to mutter." It refers to someone who murmurs "half out loud" to himself (*Theological Wordbook of the Old Testament*, edited by R. Laird Harris, pp.205, 875).

Think of a cow who "chews the cud." Cows graze on as much grass as they can during the cool hours of the morning and evening. Then during the heat of the day, they lay in the shade and "chew their cuds." The cud is undigested grass that has been regurgitated and is being chewed again.

Meditation is like that. It's "chewing" on the Word of God that you have heard, read, studied, or memorized. It's thinking about what it means for your life. We first eat the Word, then we bring it up and "chew" on it some more. When we do, we get extra nourishment and understanding. We gain insight, understanding, and perspective. Our lives start to line up with Scripture much better.

We can meditate almost anywhere—on our beds, at work, washing dishes, driving around town, walking in the park or our neighborhood.

HOW DO WE MEDITATE ON BIBLICAL PASSAGES?

We can rehearse a verse by muttering it, by emphasizing different words. Murmur a verse or a phrase over and over half out loud to yourself. The first time you repeat it, emphasize the first word. The second time, emphasize the second word. Keep going until you've emphasized the last word in the verse or passage.

This method of meditation takes a short passage of Scripture and "turns it like a diamond to examine every facet . . . [and] thinks deeply upon the light (truth) that flashes into your mind each time the verse is turned" (*Spiritual Disciplines for the Christian Life*, by Donald Whitney, p.53).

Try it. Take a few minutes and meditate on Psalm 23:6a:

Surely goodness and mercy shall follow me all the days of my life...
Surely **goodness** and mercy shall follow me all the days of my life...
Surely goodness **and** mercy shall follow me all the days of my life...
Surely goodness and **mercy** shall follow me all the days of my life...

Surely goodness and mercy **shall** follow me all the days of my life…
Surely goodness and mercy shall **follow** me all the days of my life…
Surely goodness and mercy shall follow **me** all the days of my life…
Surely goodness and mercy shall follow me **all** the days of my life…
Surely goodness and mercy shall follow me all **the** days of my life…
Surely goodness and mercy shall follow me all the **days** of my life…
Surely goodness and mercy shall follow me all the days **of** my life…
Surely goodness and mercy shall follow me all the days of **my** life…
Surely goodness and mercy shall follow me all the days of my **life…**

Spiritual leaders talk about other methods of meditation. You could picture yourself entering into a story in the Bible. "Take a single event, or a parable, or a few verses, or even a single word and allow it to take root in you. Seek to live the experience. . . Smell the sea. Hear the lap of water along the shore. See the crowd. Feel the sun on your head and the hunger in your stomach. Taste the salt in the air. Touch the hem of His garment" (*Celebration of Disciplines: The Path to Spiritual Growth*, by Richard Foster, pp.29-30).

"With your imagination anointed with holy oil, you . . . open your New Testament. At one time, you are the publican; at another time, you are the prodigal . . . at another time, you are Mary Magdalene; at another time, Peter in the porch . . . Till your whole New Testament is all over autobiographic of you" (*Lord, Teach Us to Pray*, by Alexander Whyte, p.249).

Can you think of a story in the Bible that is meaningful for you that you can use as a vehicle in which to meditate?

_____
_____
_____

What was one of the most helpful insights that you received during this lesson?

_____
_____
_____

What you tend to think about in your empty and quiet time is often that true object of your worship and ultimately who or what you serve.
Chad Allen, Lead Pastor - Cuyahoga Valley Church

WEEK 5, DAY 5: OBEYING GOD'S WORD

Why is it so hard to obey the Bible when Jesus said that His yoke is easy and His burden is light (Matthew 11:28-30)? Why does obeying the Bible sometimes seem so burdensome for us when the Bible itself says that the commandments are not burdensome (1 John 5:3)? Why do we often try very hard to obey but find ourselves failing miserably (Romans 7:15-23)?

What's the point of all our Bible intake? Why hear it, read it, study it, memorize it, and meditate on it if we find that we can't truly live it out?

The point of it all is that we come to the place where we increasingly believe the gospel. We shouldn't be trying harder, but, rather, believing more.

We simply must resist the temptation to see the Bible as a mere moral code of ethics or a book of rules to obey. To be sure, morality is in the Scriptures. After all, we are to be people who practice the Golden Rule: *Whatever you wish that others would do to you, do also to them* (Matthew 7:12).

But the Bible is not primarily a book that teaches us rules, regulations, and techniques on various topics like how to have a happy marriage or how to be a nicer person.

Instead, the Bible is a book that points us to Christ and to His gospel. And when we learn to see Jesus on every page of the Bible, we begin to increasingly believe the gospel. We are set free. That's when we find we have the desire and the ability to be obedient.

Bible intake helps us come to believe that in spite of our sins, doubts, failings, and shortcomings, we are still beloved. In the Bible, we see the deceitfulness of our sin. We see the beauty of Christ and His unfailing love for us. We see the sacrifice that Jesus made to forgive us. We see that Jesus has risen and sent His Spirit to live in us.

And because we know that we are beloved, forgiven, and empowered, we have a supernatural ability to Live New.

We can actually become holy. We can actually become conformed to the image of Christ. We actually have a new life that enables us to be obedient to Scripture.

Being obedient to the Bible—doing the will of God, becoming conformed to the image of Christ—is important. But we don't accomplish obedience through sheer willpower—by doing more and trying harder.

Instead, we become obedient when we do the hard work of believing the good news that Christ loved us enough to die for us and forgive us while we were still sinners (Romans 5:8). It's our faith in the gospel that fuels our obedience.

With that as our foundation, let's turn our attention to some simple truths about the importance of obeying the Word of God.

THE BENEFITS OF OBEDIENCE

Look up the following verses about obedience and match the appropriate summary of its teaching.

1. Psalm 40:8   A. Obedience brings about blessings.
2. Luke 6:46   B. Obedience is the way we demonstrate that Jesus is Lord.
3. Luke 11:28   C. Obedience is linked to assurance of our salvation.
4. I John 2:3   D. Obedience actually increases our sense of delight.
5. I John 5:3   E. Obedience proves that we love God.

The point that our obedience is proof that we really love Jesus cannot be emphasized enough. Jesus made this crystal clear.

Look up John 14:15, 21, and 23 and fill in the appropriate blanks.

If you _____ Me, you will _____ My commandments (John 14:15).

Whoever has My commandments and _____ them, he it is who _____ Me. And he who loves Me will be loved by My Father, and I will love him and manifest Myself to him (John 14:21).

If anyone _____ Me, he will _____ My Word, and My Father will love him, and We will come to him and make our home with him. Whoever does not love Me does not keep My words (John 14:23-24a).

Reflect and respond. Why do you think obedience is the test and proof of our love for Christ?

_____

_____

_____

_____

Because God wants us to obey His Word, every time we take in the Bible we can expect to find an application for our lives. "Open the Book expectantly. Anticipate the discovery of a practical response to the truth of God. It makes a big difference to come to the Bible with the faith that you will find an application for it as opposed to believing you won't" (*Spiritual Disciplines for the Christian Life*, by Donald Whitney, p.57).

Read the Bible while thinking that every word is expressly applicable in some way to you. When the Bible speaks out against sin, think this way: "God means *my* sins!" When a duty is commanded, say to yourself, "God wants *me* to do this thing!"

It's very helpful to ask questions about a Bible passage in order to learn how God wants us to make application of the truth to our lives. Here are some application-oriented questions.

Put on your SPECS! In the Scripture I have read today, is there a . . .

Sin to avoid?
Promise to claim?
Example to follow?
Command to obey?
Service to perform?

Take some time right now to write these questions in the front or back of your Bible or journal so you will have them at your fingertips each time you spend time in God's Word.

When you spend time in God's Word, determine at least one specific application you will live out before you go your way. "There are times when a verse of Scripture will have such evident application for your life that it will virtually jump off the page and plead with you to do what it says. More often than not, however, you must interview the verse, patiently asking questions of it until a down-to-earth response becomes clear" (*Spiritual Disciplines for the Christian Life*, by Donald Whitney, p.60).

Consider the following formulas:

Information + Application = Transformation
Information – Application = Stagnation

Which do you want to be true for you? Obey the Bible. Apply the Scriptures. *Be doers of the Word, and not hearers only, deceiving yourselves* (James 1:22).

What was one of the most helpful insights that you received during this lesson?

_____

_____

_____

_____

_____

**Either this book will keep you from sin
or sin will keep you from this book.**
*John Bunyan - 17th Century Preacher/Writer,
Author of The Pilgrim's Progress*

Week 6

SPIRITUAL WORLDVIEW: VIEWING LIFE AS A SELF-FEEDER

MEMORY VERSE

I appeal to you therefore, brothers, by the mercies of God, to present your bodies as a living sacrifice, holy and acceptable to God, which is your spiritual worship. Do not be conformed to this world, but be transformed by the renewal of your mind, that by testing you may discern what is the will of God, what is good and acceptable and perfect. Romans 12:1-2

A worldview is "a fundamental orientation of the heart, that can be expressed . . . in a set of presuppositions . . . which we hold . . . about the basic constitution of reality, and that provides the foundation on which we live and move and have our being" (*The Universe Next Door*, by James W. Sire, p.17).

It is vital that we have a worldview based on truth. Why? Our presuppositions become thoughts. Thoughts define our decisions. Decisions activate our acts. Acts become habits. Habits become character. Our character, then, directs our destiny.

Often, a person's worldview and their resulting thoughts, decisions, and behaviors are unconscious. In this week's lessons, we will seek to develop a consciously Bible-based, God-glorifying, Christ-honoring, Spirit-inspired worldview. We'll be answering the following questions:

Where did I come from?
Who am I?
Why am I here?
What is my source of authority?
What's wrong with the world; in other words, what's wrong with me?
What can make things better?
Where am I going?

How we answer these questions from the heart of what we call our worldview

A worldview is a framework of fundamental concepts of beliefs about the world. In short, a worldview comprises the lens through which we see the world.
Michael Wittmer - Heaven is a Place on Earth, p.21.

WEEK 6, DAY 1: WHERE DID I COME FROM?
In the space below, write 2 or 3 theories of the origin of life on our planet or in the universe.

_____
_____
_____

Three words carry with them the foundation of meaning, worth, purpose, and value than all other words. Once heard, translated, and understood, they change everything. They make known the beginning of the beginning. You have no choice but to either receive and believe them, or deny and reject them. There is no middle ground and what you choose to do with these words will determine the course of your life.

What are the three words?
"Bereshith bara Elohim."
בְּרֵאשִׁית בָּרֵא הַשָּׁמַיִם

You may not recognize those three Hebrew words, but you might recognize the five English words that translate them: "In the beginning God created."

Every worldview starts with basic assumptions/faith statements—ideas that can neither be proved nor disproved. Naturalists begin with the idea that the material world is all there is, all there has ever been. Christians begin where Genesis begins. Look up and highlight or underline Genesis 1:1.

These are extremely significant, vital, informative, and defining words to hear and embrace. Your entire life is impacted by them. The answers to your deepest questions, the fulfillment of your greatest longings, and the ultimate source of hope in your life all depend on whether or not you believe these words.

These words are not just the foundation of your life. They are the cornerstone to the foundation of *all* life. Believing that God made you and everything else in creation will determine your value and your values.

REASONS TO BELIEVE IN CREATION
Read the following 5 reasons to believe that God created.

- The design/order of the universe demands a Designer/Organizer.
- Something exists. Nothing cannot create something. Therefore, a necessary and eternal "something" exists.
- The effects demand a Cause—an uncaused Cause.
- Irreducible complexity. Certain biological systems—like the eye and flagella—are too complex to have evolved through the process of natural selection.
- The Rare Earth Hypothesis says that life on earth, existing in what's been called the Circumstellar Habitable Zone, requires such an improbable combination of astrophysical circumstances that Intelligent Design is a more reasonable explanation than chance.

Which of the above 5 reasons to believe in God as Creator is most compelling to you? Why? How would you explain this reason in your own words?

_____

_____

_____

Any one "proof" standing alone might seem under-whelming. But put them all together, and the reasons to believe in God as Creator are over-whelming. For many people, it's more reasonable to believe in God as Creator than to believe in random chance and evolution.

"Essentially, I realized that to stay an atheist, I would have to believe that nothing produces everything; non-life produces life; randomness produces fine-tuning; chaos produces information; unconsciousness produces consciousness; and non-reason produces reason. Those leaps of faith were simply too big for me to take, especially in light of the affirmative case for God's existence . . . In other words, in my assessment, the Christian worldview accounted for the totality of the evidence much better than the atheistic worldview" (Lee Strobel, Interview at www.patheos.com).

WHAT JESUS BELIEVED ABOUT CREATION

The cornerstone of our faith is something that happened at the hinge-point of history through Jesus. The issue is always "Who is Jesus?" Anytime that we can tie the story of creation to Jesus, we have done everybody, Christians and non-Christians alike, an incredible service. If, in the course of our conversation, we discover that our friends believe that Genesis 1 and 2 is a creation myth, we don't get belligerent and argumentative.

We simply point to Jesus. We just keep on asking, "OK. But who is Jesus to you?"

Suppose they say, "But what about the dinosaurs?" We say, "Well . . . I'm not totally sure. Obviously, they existed. And now they are extinct. I'm glad . . . because no velociraptors live in the woods behind my house. Maybe they became extinct because of the great flood. Maybe they became extinct between Genesis 1:1 and 1:2. But . . . what about Jesus? Who is Jesus to you?"

We keep on pointing them to Jesus. We say, "Here's why I believe that God created—why Genesis 1 and 2 actually happened. In the gospels—the stories about Jesus—He talks about creation. According to the gospels, He believed that Genesis wasn't a myth—that it's true, that it's history."

In Mark 10, Jesus says He believes in creation.
In Matthew 19, He talks about the fact that God made Adam and Eve.
In Matthew 24, He refers to Noah and the flood.
In Matthew 10, He talked about the judgment of Sodom and Gomorrah.

Jesus didn't treat these stories as myths. He took them as straightforward history, describing the events that actually happened just like Genesis says.

So we say to our friends, "If Jesus believed that Genesis—including creation—was actual history, then you know what? I believe it's actual history. Why? As Pastor Andy Stanley says, 'Anybody who can predict their own death and resurrection and then actually pull it off, I'm believing everything they say!'"

The cornerstone of our faith is not a particular creation theory. It's something that we believe actually happened in history. Jesus came into the world, walked on the earth, represented God, was God, and then rose from the dead. Those facts best explain the fact of the empty tomb, the changed lives of the disciples, and the growth of the church in the midst of a hostile Jewish culture. We keep on asking everyone, "What do you believe about Jesus?"

If a person can believe the miraculous regarding the resurrection at the very hinge-point of history, then why not believe the miraculous regarding the creation at the very beginning of history?

THE BIBLE ON CREATION
Match the following statements about creation to the appropriate biblical references.

1. God existed before the mountains, earth, or world.
2. We see the attributes of God through creation.
3. All things were created through Him and for Him.
4. The universe was created by the word of God
5. God is worthy of worship for He created everything.

A. Romans 1:20
B. Psalm 90:2
C. Revelation 4:11
D. Hebrews 11:3
E. Colossians 1:16

If we can eliminate God and the account of creation, we can make up our own rules. If we don't *belong* to anyone, then we're not *accountable* to anyone. If the foundation called creation erodes, then the house of the Christian faith will fall.

But faith in those powerful words— "In the Beginning God created . . ." will transform your life, and will lead you into a relationship with the Author of Life.

In the space below, write out a prayer of praise and thanksgiving to God that you have been created by Him. Ask God to give you wisdom about how this knowledge will help you live new in Christ.

_____

_____

_____

_____

What was one of the most helpful insights that you received during this lesson?

_____

_____

_____

I believe in Christianity as I believe that the Sun has risen,
not only because I see it, but because by it I see everything else.
C. S. Lewis - The Weight of Glory, p.140

WEEK 6, DAY 2: WHO AM I? WHY AM I HERE?

Yesterday's study sought to answer the question "Where did I come from?" The answer, of course, is "I came from God."

Acts 17: 24a and 28a say, *God . . . made the world and everything in it . . . In Him we live and move and have our being.* That fact is foundational for everything. It leads us to ask two important follow-up questions: "Who am I?" and "Why am I here?"

WHO AM I?

To those who seek to live without God, the answer might be:

"You are the accidental by-product of nature, a result of matter plus time plus chance. You are a highly evolved and complex animal." To those who seek to live with God, the answer is: "You have worth and value. You are highly significant. You are created in the image of God. You are an image-bearer of God in this world."

Compared to the vastness of the universe, earth is like a speck of dust floating in a giant sunbeam coming through a massive window. Yet, even though we live on this seemingly insignificant planet, we are the paramount handiwork, the crown jewel, the beloved of all of God's creation.

Read and highlight or underline Genesis 1:26-31. Circle the words "image" and "very good."

What can we learn from Genesis 1 about mankind and animals? How are we the same? How are we different? (See Genesis 1:26.)

_____

_____

_____

_____

What immediately comes to your mind when you consider that men and women have been created in the image of God?

_____

_____

"The fact that man is in the image of God means that man is like God and represents God" (*Systematic Theology,* by Wayne Grudem, p.441). This involves several main ideas that show our worth and value.

To say we are created in the image of God means that we have . . .

- an inner sense of right and wrong and are morally accountable for our actions.
- an immortal soul as well as a physical body, enabling us to relate to God.

- an ability to reason, use language, create, and experience a complexity of emotions.
- a capacity to experience interpersonal fellowship with the Lord and each other.
- a responsibility to rule over creation.

As you consider these 5 aspects of being created in God's image, write in the space below which you think is a strength for you and why you think that. Then write down which aspect you think you need to grow in the most and why you think that.

_____

_____

_____

"Every single human being, no matter how much the image of God is marred by sin, or illness, or weakness, or any other disability, still has the status of being in God's image and therefore must be treated with the dignity and respect that is due to God's image-bearer.

"This has profound implications for our conduct toward others. It means that people of every race deserve dignity and rights. It means that elderly people, those seriously ill, the mentally disabled, and children yet unborn, deserve full protection and honor as human beings.

"If we ever deny our unique status in creation as God's only image-bearers, we will soon begin to depreciate the value of human life, will tend to see humans as merely a higher form of animal, and begin to treat others as such. We will also lose much of our sense of meaning in life" (*Systematic Theology*, by Wayne Grudem, p.450).

You are a special creation of the One and only, all-powerful, all-knowing and eternal God. You have a beginning. You have a purpose. You have a Creator. You are not random. Your life is not meaningless. God *made* you. God *knows* you. God *loves* you. God has a *plan* for you. You are His.

WHY AM I HERE?
To those who seek to live without God, the answer might be: "Since you are the accidental by-product of nature, a result of matter plus time plus chance, there is really no reason for your existence." To those who seek to live with God, the answer is: "Since you are an image-bearer of God in this world, God has given you a calling, a mission, a purpose. You have the opportunity and responsibility to glorify God with your life."

The first question in the classic Westminster Shorter Catechism is, "What is the chief end of man?" The answer is, "Man's chief end is to glorify God, and to enjoy Him forever."

Read and highlight or underline 1 Corinthians 10:31.

Glorifying God is the single most important thing we can do with our lives. Every moment of every day we will make decisions that either glorify God or not. Everything in our life is an opportunity to glorify God. When we truly glorify Him, we will find our greatest sense of joy and fulfillment in life.

But exactly what does glorifying God mean? It sounds good, religious, and spiritual. But, practically speaking, precisely how do we glorify God?

Is the way to glorify God tagging on "That Thou mayest forever and ever and ever be glorified!" after everything we do? Are we, like some athletes, supposed to make the sign of the cross before we do anything relatively important? Is glorifying God a matter of constantly singing and praying praises? Are we glorifying God by driving around with Jesus bumper stickers or wearing Bible verse T shirts?

We glorify God by enjoying Him, loving Him, praising Him, and obeying Him.

We all know how to glorify. We brag about, praise, and extol stuff all the time. We praise the greatness of various things all the time. When we discover a new restaurant we love, we take others with us. When we get a new phone, notebook, or app, we show it off. When we meet a new friend, we introduce him/her to others. We follow and support our favorite sports teams. A guy who is crazy about a girl, thinks about her, sings songs about her, dreams up ways of pleasing her, and wants to tell the whole world about her. All this is what glorifying is.

God, of course, is the One who is most worthy to be glorified. As the Westminster Shorter Catechism says, "God is a Spirit, infinite, eternal, and unchangeable in His being, wisdom, power, holiness, justice, goodness, and truth." No one is more worthy to be given glory.

Just as children honor their parents when they obey them, we honor our Father in heaven when we obey Him. We don't glorify God when we obey after rolling our eyes and dragging our feet reluctantly. We glorify Him when we obey Him with joy and trust.

"Glorifying God means that we feel, think, and act in ways that reflect His greatness, that make much of God, that give evidence of the supreme greatness of all His attributes and the all-satisfying beauty of His manifold perfections" ("Message: Glorifying God . . . Period," by John Piper, July 15, 2013).

Look up and highlight or underline Romans 11:36.

Prepositions are important throughout the Bible and especially in this verse. What are implications of believing that all things are *from* God? How will this help us better glorify Him?

_____

_____

_____

What are implications of believing that all things are through God? How will this help us better glorify Him?

_____

_____

What are implications of believing that all things are to God? How will this help us better glorify Him?

_____

_____

Look up Revelation 4:11. Write it down here and circle the words that stand out/impact you.

_____

_____

_____

How does knowing a verse like Revelation 4:11 help motivate us to live a life dedicated to glorifying God?

_____

_____

_____

What was one of the most helpful insights that you received during this lesson?

_____

_____

_____

Close your time today by using the following prayer about bringing God glory as a guide for your time in prayer.

Lord heavenly Father, thank You that I have been made in Your image. I know that Your image in me has been marred by the fall and by my own sinful choices. I know that I have not glorified You as I ought. Thank You that the blood of Christ is sufficient for all the times I have lived as a broken image-bearer and fallen short of Your glory. Help me gain a greater sense of right and wrong and become more accountable for my actions. May I learn more and more what it means to worship You in spirit and in truth. Give me a greater ability to have an impact for You in this world. Help me so that whether I eat or drink or whatever I do, I shall do it all to the glory of God. Give me grace to glorify You by enjoying You, loving You, praising You, and obeying You. In Jesus' name, Amen.

I cannot at the same time accept the glory and give God the glory... Glorifying God means being occupied with and committed to His ways rather than preoccupied with and determined my own way. It is being so thrilled with Him, so devoted to Him, so committed to Him that we cannot get enough of Him!
Charles R. Swindoll - Rise & Shine: A Wake Up Call

WEEK 6, DAY 3: WHAT IS MY SOURCE OF AUTHORITY?

So far we have asked and answered 3 fundamental questions:

1. Q: Where did I come from?   A: God made me.
2. Q: Who am I?   A: I am created in the image of God and have great value.
3. Q: Why am I here?   A: My purpose is to glorify God and enjoy Him forever.

Today's question is equally fundamental: What is my source of authority? Another way to ask this is: How do I determine the difference between truth and error, between right and wrong?

In a world without God, we are left to determine right and wrong by individual choices (what feels good and right at the time), or by community-beneficial decisions that will best insure the cultural survival of the society. Truth then becomes relative. Right and wrong become arbitrary.

We commonly hear secular people say, "Every person has to define right and wrong for himself or herself." But individually or culturally determined right and wrong inevitably leads to conflict, crises, and chaos. Members of Al-Qaeda crashed jet planes into the World Trade Center. In many countries in Africa, little girls are routinely subjected to female genital mutilation in order to ensure their chastity. In American history, southern citizens in the U.S. used Bible verses out of context as a pretext to justify slavery. All these groups thought they were right.

Use the space below to share an example of a behavior that you believe to be clearly wrong yet has been justified by some group or individual.

_____

_____

Manhattan pastor Tim Keller asks people who believe that right and wrong should be individually determined, "Is there anyone in the world right now doing things you believe they should stop doing no matter what they personally believe about the correctness of their behavior?" They invariably say, "Yes, of course." Then Keller asks, "Doesn't that mean that you *do* believe there is some kind of moral reality that is 'there' that is not defined by us, that must be abided by regardless of what a person feels or thinks?" Almost always, the response to that question is silence, Keller says, either "a thoughtful or a grumpy one" (*The Reason for God*, by Tim Keller, p.47).

Clearly, we need something (or Someone) outside ourselves to determine right from wrong and truth from error. That something (or Someone) who has the authority to determine right from wrong and truth from error is God.

Follow the logic:

- God exists.
- God, in His essence, is truth or else He would not be God.
- God desires to communicate His truth to His creatures.

- God sent His Son, Jesus, to be the living truth who dwelt among us.
- Jesus was authenticated as the truth through His death and resurrection.
- Jesus trusted the written truth of God, the Bible. (See Week 2, Day 1 study.)
- Therefore, we can trust the Bible to be the true self-revelation of God.

Although there are other lines of reasoning to support the claim that the Bible is true, one of the most powerful is found in Jesus. If Jesus lived, died, and rose again, then Jesus Himself becomes an argument in support of the truth of the Bible.

What does Jesus say about God's Word? He says, *Scripture cannot be broken* (John 10:35), testifying to the authority of the Bible. In Matthew 5:17, Jesus said, *Do not think that I have come to abolish the Law or the Prophets; I have not come to abolish them but to fulfill them,* meaning that Jesus believed and trusted in the Old Testament "Law" and "Prophets." The evidence is overwhelming that Jesus believed God spoke through the Bible. He overtly upheld belief in several Old Testament stories. He saw the Bible as holy and authoritative.

The cornerstone of Christian belief is the life, death, and resurrection of Christ. Paul the Apostle wrote that if the resurrection did not happen, our faith *is futile and you are still in your sins* (1 Corinthians 15:17). In this sense, making a case for Christ's resurrection also makes a case for the truth claims of Jesus and, in turn, the reliability and truth of the Bible.

Therefore, our trust in the Scripture is based on the very character of God. The God who knew us and loved us long before we came to know Him is the God we can trust to give us a completely trustworthy revelation of Himself. The one true God, the God who reveals Himself in the Bible, is a God who defines His own existence, sets His own terms, and rules over His own creation.

In the verses below, circle the words true, pure, perfect, and sure.

And now, O Lord God, You are God, and Your words are true . . . (2 Samuel 7:28).

Every word of God proves true; He is a shield to those who take refuge in Him (Proverbs 30:5).

The words of the Lord are pure words, like silver refined in a furnace on the ground, purified seven times (Psalm 12:6).

This God—His way is perfect; the word of the Lord proves true; He is a shield for all those who take refuge in Him (Psalm 18:30).

The law of the Lord is perfect, reviving the soul; the testimony of the Lord is sure, making wise the simple (Psalm 19:7).

The sum of Your word is truth, and every one of Your righteous rules endures forever (Psalm 119:160).

Sanctify them in the truth; Your word is truth (John 17:17).

Based on these verses, what are some of the benefits we experience when we build our lives on God's truth?

_____

_____

_____

The great spiritual leader Billy Graham once struggled to believe that the Bible was trustworthy and authoritative. His friend and colleague in ministry, Chuck Templeton, had become skeptical about the truthfulness of the Bible. Templeton had a passion for intellectualism and challenged Graham, "Billy, you're fifty years out of date. People no longer accept the Bible as being inspired the way you do. Your faith is too simple. Your language is out of date. You're going to have to learn the new jargon if you're going to be successful in your ministry."

Early in his ministry in 1949, Graham sat alone in his room one evening, reading every verse of Scripture he could that had to do with "thus saith the Lord." He said he had no doubts concerning the deity of Jesus Christ or the validity of the Gospel, but wondered if the Bible was completely true.

In his 1997 biography, *Just As I Am*, Graham wrote, "I pondered the attitude of Christ toward the Scriptures. He loved those sacred writings and quoted from them constantly. Never once did He intimate that they could be wrong. In fact, He verified some of the stories in the Old Testament that were the hardest to believe, such as those concerning Noah and Jonah. With the Psalmist, He delighted in the law of the Lord, the Scriptures. . . My heart became heavily burdened. Could I trust the Bible? I had to have an answer. If I *could not* trust the Bible, I could not go on."

Graham left his room and took a walk. He remembers dropping to his knees there in the woods. He opened the Bible at random on a tree stump. He prayed, "O God! There are many things in this book I do not understand. There are many problems with it for which I have no solution. There are many seeming contradictions. There are some areas in it that do not seem to correlate with modern science. I can't answer some of the philosophical and psychological questions Chuck and others are raising."

Graham was trying to be on the level with God, but something remained unspoken. At last the Holy Spirit freed him to say it. "Father, I am going to accept this as Thy Word—by *faith*! I am going to allow faith to go beyond my intellectual questions and doubts, and I will believe this to be Your inspired Word."

When Graham got up from his knees, his eyes stung with tears. He said, "I sensed the presence and power of God as I had not sensed it in months. Not all my questions were answered, but a major bridge had been crossed. In my heart and mind, I knew a spiritual battle in my soul had been fought and won."

Which parts of Graham's story are most meaningful to you? Why?

_____

_____

_____

As you close your time today, read through Billy Graham's prayer and use it as a guide for your own.

Note: Please refer back to Week 4, Day 1 and Week 5, Day 5 for more helpful information concerning the trust-worthiness of the Bible as our source of authority. We discovered that according to Jesus, the Old Testament can be trusted; the Gospels can be trusted; and the rest of the New Testament can be trusted. We asked, "Why should we believe the Bible?" Our answer, "Because of the witness of internal consistency, manuscript reliability, eyewitness credibility, fulfilled prophecy, and personal transformation."

What was one of the most helpful insights that you received during this lesson?

_____

_____

_____

We have known the method of our salvation by no other means than those by whom the gospel came to us; which gospel they truly preached; but afterward, by the will of God, they delivered to us in the Scriptures, to be for the future the foundation and pillar of our faith,
Irenaeus - (130-202, Adv. H. 3:1)

WEEK 6, DAY 4:

WHAT'S WRONG WITH THE WORLD? WHAT CAN MAKE THINGS BETTER?
No one thinks that the world is perfect. We can all agree that things are broken. Badly.

War
Famine
The AIDS pandemic
Sex trafficking
Poverty
Oppression

Injustice
Crime
Broken relationships
Clean water shortages
Lack of education

What are some other broken areas in the world that bring sadness to your heart?

_____

_____

Everyone knows that the world is a mess. But many people disagree on what's wrong and what will make it better.

WHAT'S WRONG WITH THE WORLD?
Some people think that what's mainly wrong is a lack of education. Others think that what's primarily wrong is our world's poor distribution of wealth. Some think that our biggest problems are racism and nationalism. Others think that our most serious problems are rooted in self-righteous, fundamentalist religion.

Obviously, what we think is wrong with the world will impact what we think the solution will be.

What does a biblical worldview teach?

God didn't originally make the world to have disease, hunger, and death in it. Disease, genetic disorders, famine, natural disasters, aging, and death itself are as much the result of sin as are oppression, war, crime, and violence. What happened?
Genesis 3 happened.

Read Genesis 3:1-7.

The people rebel against God. They sin. They lose their place. Paradise is lost. Things are not very good. They are not good. In fact, things are very bad.

Sometimes, people blame Adam and Eve for our problems. Or they say, "It's not fair that we should suffer for their sins." But drawing those conclusions overestimates our own goodness and underestimates our own depravity. If we had been in the garden, we would have made the same sinful choices. Just like Adam and Eve, we choose to rebel and sin.

Look up and highlight or underline Romans 3:10 and 23.

When we decide that we are in control, instead of God, a cataclysmic collapse takes place. Because we have disobeyed God, we are separated from Him and hide from Him. We no longer love one another. We hurt and blame one another and live in shame. We no longer care for the world. And the whole world pays the price (Genesis 3:1-19).

The world is broken because of our sin, our failure to love and obey God. Each person on the planet contributes to the problem. We were designed to love and to give God glory, but we all tend to seek our own good above the good of others.

Because of the Fall, paradise was lost. We rebelled and the whole of creation was plunged into chaos. Even the beauty that we now see in the world is broken, marred, wild—a shadow of what once was.

We know things have to change. We hunger for a better world. So we try and fix it. We try to be good and do good. We try to care about justice, the environment, and the poor.

Most of the rest of the Old Testament after Genesis 3 is the story of people trying to regain what they lost. People are looking for a rescue. People are looking to fill up the hole in their lives. They try politics. They try pleasure. They try nationalism. They try education. They try religion. People think, "If we can only do enough good things—enough religious things—then maybe we can get right with God and we can fix our world."

What are some things you have seen that people do to try to fix the world? How effective are they?

_____

_____

_____

When we look in the mirror, we realize that we are part of the problem. In fact, if we are honest, we realize that we are our own worst problem. Nothing we try on our own works to fix anything—not for long anyway. Paradise is lost and stays lost. We can't fix the problem (Romans 3:20).

So, God does something for people that they cannot do for themselves.

WHAT CAN MAKE THINGS BETTER?

The Bible tells the story about the God who does for us what we cannot do for ourselves. God loved the world too much to leave it broken, so He entered into the darkness and pain of this world.

The Gospels—Matthew, Mark, Luke, and John—tell the story of Jesus dying on the cross to pay the penalty for our sins and provide forgiveness for us. These books tell the story of His resurrection—how He defeated death and the grave for all who will believe. It tells the story of His ascension into heaven. It tells the story of His sending the Holy Spirit to live in His people so they can carry out His mission.

Read John 3:16.

God sent His Son, Jesus, to show us how to live. Jesus lived a perfect life as the One who shows us how to live new. Jesus entered into the evil of this world and suffered with us. And then He died on a cross. He died in our place—paying for our sins, forgiving our personal failures to love God and love one another.

Read Romans 5:8.

As a result of His work on the cross for us, a miracle happens. We can be reconciled to God and to each other. Change happens when we turn from our sin, trust in Jesus, and seek to follow Him (Acts 3:19-20, John 1:12). Our selfishness dies with Jesus, and through the resurrection of Jesus, we are restored. All this can only happen through Jesus (John 14:6).

We can have a new life and be the people we were originally created to be because Jesus sends His Holy Spirit to live in us and empower us to live new.

Read 2 Corinthians 5:17.

Spend some time thinking through the implications of new life in Christ. Write down a few thoughts about how new life in Christ would transform various domains of society. How would new life in Christ change education? Government? Business? The arts? Entertainment?

_____

_____

_____

Today's lesson was a review of the gospel. Spend some time today thanking God for the gospel and how it has changed you. Ask Him for grace to impact your domain in society and bring new life there. Also, pray for at least one person you know whose worldview is not biblical and, therefore, is not experiencing new life in Christ.

What was one of the most helpful insights that you received during this lesson?

_____

_____

_____

Because a God who is ultimately most focused on his
own glory will be about the business of restoring us,
who are all broken images of him. His glory demands it.
So we should be thankful for a self-sufficient God
whose self-regard is glorious.
Matt Chandler - The Explicit Gospel, p.32

WEEK 6, DAY 5: WHERE AM I GOING?

So far we have asked and answered 6 fundamental questions:

1) Q: Where did I come from?   A: God made me.
2) Q: Who am I?   A: I am created in the image of God.
3) Q: Why am I here?   A: My purpose is to glorify God.
4) Q: What's my source of authority? A: God and His Word, the Bible.
5) Q: What's wrong with the world?   A: We have fallen into sin and rebellion.
6) Q: What will make things better?   A: The gospel brings new life in Christ.

Today's question is: Where am I going? What happens after I die?

"Are we there yet?" is a question that parents hear when a family is on a trip. It implies a destination. The trip is a journey with an end in view. The family is going someplace. They're traveling from point A to point B. They are not just traveling in circles.

Various worldviews have different answers to the ultimate question. Are we headed for nothingness or personal extinction? Are we going to one day undergo a transformation to a higher state? Will we be reincarnated? Will we lose our individuality and become one with the universe? Will we depart to a kind of shadowy existence on "the other side"?

We live our lives out in this world hoping to find satisfaction. But in our honest moments, most of us would admit that we experience a level of emptiness that nothing in the world has ever truly filled. And that's a sign that we were made for another world.

Your view of the afterlife determines how you live this life.
Chad Allen - Lead Pastor, Cuyahoga Valley Church

"If I find in myself a desire which no experience in this world can satisfy, the most probable explanation is that I was made for another world . . . I must take care, on the one hand, never to despise, or to be unthankful for, these earthly blessings, and on the other, never to mistake them for the something else of which they are only a kind of copy, or echo, or mirage. I must keep alive in myself the desire for my true country, which I shall not find till after death; I must never let it get snowed under or turned aside; I must make it the main object of life to press on to that country and to help others to do the same" (*Mere Christianity*, by C. S. Lewis, pp.136-137).

The Bible tells us about that other country. One day, Jesus is coming again to make all things right—perfectly and forever. God has a long-range plan with an end in view. Ephesians 1:10 says that God is seeking "to unite all things in Christ"—to restore all things so they are, once again, "very good" (Genesis 1:31).

The final book of the Bible—The Revelation—draws a picture of that hopeful future. There will be a new heaven and earth in place of this heaven and earth, with a new Jerusalem where God and His people will dwell together in loving community. It will be a place where the hard things that have oppressed humanity will be absent. The Tree of Life will be present again as it was in Eden. Death and darkness will be no more. In short, all that accursed this world will be removed.

Spend a few minutes scanning Genesis 1 and 2 and Revelation 21 and 22. In the space below, list some of the similarities you find in these chapters.

Genesis 1 and 2

_____
_____
_____
_____
_____

Revelation 21 and 22

_____
_____
_____
_____
_____

It is not a coincidence that the first two chapters of the Bible (Genesis 1–2) begin with the creation of the heavens and the earth and the last two chapters (Revelation 21–22) begin with the re-creation of the heavens and the earth. Paradise lost as a result of the Fall will one day be paradise regained. Creation will be restored . . . forever.

At the end of the biblical story, Jesus says, *Behold, I am making all things new* (Revelation 21:5). Jesus is going to purge the creation from all the results of the fall. What has been corrupted will be declared "very good" again. The good news is that Jesus is Lord over the chaos of fallen creation. He has conquered sin and death.

God takes His fallen original creation and restores it. Our eternal home is not an alternative world, but a restored and healed world. He doesn't abandon the creation. Yes, we messed up everything including the creation. But in Christ, creation is restored. This means that we can live with hope! Because we know Christ as the old song says, "There's a land that is fairer than day, and by faith we can see it afar; for the Father waits over the way to prepare us a dwelling place there!"

Heaven is our home in the future and our hope in the present.
Chad Allen - Lead Pastor, Cuyahoga Valley Church

Read and highlight or underline John 14:1-3.

Jesus has come to rescue His people and to rescue our place—the heavens and the earth. Jesus is the central character in the story of creation. One day, when Christ returns, the heavens and the earth will be restored.

You haven't tasted an awesome orange yet! The best orange you've ever tasted has been wounded by the fall. You haven't seen a perfect sunset yet. You haven't taken a walk on a real beach yet. The most beautiful rose that you have ever seen or smelled has been tainted, marred, and desecrated by the fall. But the rose will be pristine once again. No matter how great your friendships might be, you haven't had a truly fulfilling relationship. Not yet. But one day you will!

Describe a great experience you've had on earth that you anticipate being better than ever in the new heavens and the new earth.

_____

_____

Think about the restoration of all things. If you don't believe that God will one day restore all things for those who believe, you should want it to be true!

There's something in us that longs for restoration. Relationships will be healed. Guilt will be gone. Sin will surrender to the Savior. Conflict with parents, spouses, and kids will be over.

Read Revelation 21:2-4.

Which description of the new Jerusalem in these verses moves you the most? Why?

_____

_____

Most of us think that there is a heaven. According to a Barna survey in 2003, 76% of Americans believe that heaven exists. But our ideas about what heaven is are foggy. And our hope is weak. Pastors don't talk about it as much as they used to.

So, many Americans get their ideas about heaven from Hollywood. And that can be confusing and dangerous. No wonder we have all kinds of misinformation about heaven. "It's a silly myth." "We'll fly around with wings and float around on the clouds." "Won't it be boring in heaven—to have to be good all the time? Man, I like to party!"

Listen, heaven *is* a party! We've been duped by the enemy to think that God is boring. God is amazing. And wherever He is, boredom will be impossible.

We think that we are fun-loving and that God is a humorless killjoy. But we've got it backward. As author Randy Alcorn says, "It's not God who's boring; it's us! He invented laughter and adventure. In heaven, we'll never exhaust God's sense of humor and His love for excitement. The real question is not 'Won't we get bored with

God?' but 'How will God not get bored with us?' Heaven is where the One who is infinite in creativity lives. How could the home of someone like that be anything less than exciting? When an omnipotent Person creates the ultimate place, it will give maximum pleasure" (*Heaven*, by Randy Alcorn, p.395).

For those who believe, heaven is our home—our reward. It gives us relief from our trials. It's an everlasting Easter and a never-ending Christmas. It's the end of death. It's an ongoing, ever-growing experience of God. In heaven is our greatest good—God Himself.

Do you have a hunger for heaven?

Your hope for heaven is your fuel for today.
Rick Duncan - Founding Pastor, Cuyahoga Valley Church

We need to get our heads around this. We need to get our hearts fixed on this. New Life can only be lived with an ETERNAL perspective in mind. Life here is good. Life there is better. Max out in both.

At the very end of C.S. Lewis' *Chronicles of Narnia*, a little girl, Lucy, speaks with Aslan, the lion who metaphorically represents Christ. Lewis uses that conversation to give us some insight into the glory that is to be ours one day:

"And as He spoke He no longer looked to them like a lion; but the things that began to happen after that were so great and beautiful that I cannot write them. And for us this is the end of all the stories, and we can most truly say that they all lived happily ever after. But for them it was only the beginning of the real story. All their life in this world and all their adventures in Narnia had only been the cover and the title page: now at last they were beginning Chapter One of the Great Story, which no one on earth has read: which goes on forever: in which every chapter is better than the one before" (*The Last Battle*, by C. S. Lewis, chapter 16, last paragraphs).

In the space below, let your imagination run wild as you write down a prayer of praise to God for the future that He has in store for you.

_____

_____

_____

_____

_____

_____

What was one of the most helpful insights that you received during this lesson?

_____

_____

_____

How, then, will the story of human history end? At the end of the final book of the Bible, we see the very opposite of what other religions predict. We do not see the illusion of the world melt away nor do we see spiritual souls escaping the physical world into heaven. Rather, we see heaven descending into our world to unite with it and purify it of all its brokenness and imperfection . . . this as a new Garden of Eden, in which there is again absolute harmony of humanity with nature and the end of injury, disease, and death, along with the end of all racial animosity and war. There will be no more poor, slaves, criminals, or broken-hearted mourners . . . Creation itself will be liberated from its bondage to decay...The whole world will be healed as it is drawn into the fullness of God's glory.

Tim Keller - The Reason for God, pp.222-223

Week 7

THE CHURCH:
THRIVING AS A SERVANT

M EMORY VERSE
And they devoted themselves to the apostles' teaching and the fellowship, to the breaking of bread and the prayers. Acts 2:42

WEEK 7, DAY 1: THE BENEFITS OF BELONGING

The Bible clearly teaches that every follower of Jesus must care for other followers of Jesus in the context of a community of faith. We need each other.

Every believer is to participate. We are not only to be served, but we also are called to serve others. Our Father desires for us to care for our brothers and sisters through the full range of the "one another" commands that are encouraged in the New Testament.

God has provided an environment where we can enjoy these kinds of benefits. It's the local church—a Caring Community of believers. In fact, it's exceedingly difficult, perhaps even impossible, to truly practice the "one anothers" of the New Testament without a connection to a local church.

These expressions of love, and they are numerous, are to be practiced by every believer. For example, we are told to:

Care for and be cared for. *Care for one another* (1 Corinthians 12:25).

Encourage and be encouraged. *Encourage one another* (1 Thessalonians 5:11).

Show kindness and be shown kindness. *Be kind to one another* (Ephesians 4:32).

Be hospitable and be shown hospitality. *Show hospitality to one another* (I Peter 4:9).

Serve and be served. *Serve one another* (Galatians 5:13, 1 Peter 4:10).

Forgive and be forgiven. *Forgive one another* (Ephesians 4:32).

Instruct and be instructed. *Instruct one another* (Romans 15:14).

Admonish and be admonished. *Admonish one another* (Colossians 3:16).

Build up and be built up. *Build up one another* (1 Thessalonians 5:11).

Love and be loved. *Love one another* (John 13:34-35; 1 John 3:23, 4:7, 4:11).

As you look at this list of "one anothers," which 2 or 3 of these are benefits that you feel you need to experience most right now through the church body? Why?

_____

_____

_____

_____

_____

Which 2-3 are benefits that you feel you can most contribute to the church body right now? Why?

_____

_____

_____

_____

_____

DISCONNECTED CHRIST-FOLLOWERS?

You'll sometimes hear people say that they have a vital and growing relationship with Jesus without a connection to a particular church or community of faith. They say things like these:

"I'd rather worship on my own."
"I'm connected to Christ and don't feel the need to connect with a local church."
"I don't want to be a part of organized religion."
"I can't stomach all the hypocrites at church."
"I don't connect with God by singing."
"I don't learn about God from a lecture."
"I'd rather connect with other believers outside of a church, with a community of faith that's global, non-arguing, non-tribal and without walls."

What are some of the common criticisms you have heard about the local church?

_____

_____

_____

_____

We understand the concerns. Certainly, no church is perfect. But people who say they have an intimate relationship with Jesus but don't want to have a vital relationship to a local church may be misunderstanding the vital connection between Christ and His church.

CHRIST'S LOVE FOR THE CHURCH

In your Bible, look up and highlight or underline Ephesians 5:25.

Christ loved the church and gave Himself up for her (Ephesians 5:25b).

Jesus sacrificed His life and shed His blood to save His church. Surely, it hurts Him to see His followers neglect, criticize, and wound that for which He died. If we want to be like Jesus, we, too, must love the church—the community that He loved and gave His life for.

It's true that Ephesians 5:25 is referring to what theologians call the "universal church"—the community of all true believers who have ever lived or will live throughout the whole earth. But this is no reason for any follower of Christ to disengage from the church.

The best way we can demonstrate our affection for the invisible, universal church is by connecting with a visible, local church.

WHY LOVING THE CHURCH IS ALSO LOVING CHRIST.

Let's think through two biblical metaphors for the church. These will show the fallacy of believing that you can be committed to Christ without being committed to His church.

Look up and highlight or underline Ephesians 1:22-23. Now, fill in the blank in the sentence below.

The church is called the _____ of Christ (Ephesians 1:22, 23).

Jesus is the head and the church is His body. Suppose a husband wants to compliment his wife. So, he says something like, "Honey, I want you to know that I really love your eyes, your hair, your smile, and your face. I love everything about your head. But I really want nothing to do with your body." That conversation would not end well! Why? The head and the body go together! It's impossible to love the one and not the other! In a similar way, we wound Jesus if we say we love Him without a corresponding love for His body, the church.

Look up and highlight or underline Ephesians 5:25, Revelation 19:7, and Revelation 21:2. Now, fill in the blank in the sentence below.

The church is called the _____ of Christ (Ephesians 5:22-25; Revelation 19:7; 21:2).

Jesus is the Bridegroom and the church is His bride. Suppose someone invited a man over to his home for dinner, "Please come. We'd love to have you to our home on Friday evening." The man says, "Thanks so much. My wife and I would love to come." The host replies, "Oh. I'm sorry. Perhaps you misunderstood. I'm only inviting you over, not your wife. I really don't care for your wife.

I don't want anything to do with her." You can imagine that the man would be highly offended and would not accept the dinner invitation. Why? The bride and the groom go together! It's offensive to seek to relate to one without connecting with the other! In a similar way, we wound Jesus if we say we love Him without a corresponding love for His bride, the church.

To grow in our New Life in Christ, we must be rooted in a Caring Community. Look up and highlight or underline Hebrews 10:24-25.

The classic illustration is simple. Logs burning together in a bonfire keep each other burning. But take a single log out of the bonfire, set it by itself, and watch the fire go out.

And that is exactly what can happen to us if we neglect to meet together and become isolated from other Christ-followers. We will lose our fire for the things of God if we seek to live out the Christian life on our own. None of us can make it alone. We weren't meant to. We need to belong to a Caring Community of believers to help keep us ignited— "on fire" for God.

What was one of the most helpful insights that you received during this lesson?

_____

_____

_____

You can't say you truly love the Groom if you hate His bride.
Rick Duncan, Founding Pasto | Cuyahoga Valley Church

WEEK 7, DAY 2: THE CHURCH—DEFINED AND PICTURED

In the New Testament, the word "church" translates the Greek word *"ekklesia."* It's a compound word in the Greek (*ek* is a prefix which means "out of" and *kaleo* is a verb which means "to call"). The word "church" means "a gathering of people who have been called out" for God's purpose.

A church is *not* defined by the building they meet in. A church is *not* a disconnected group of people who merely gather together once a week to sing encouraging songs and hear an inspiring lecture.

Consider the following theological definitions of the church:

"The church [is] the whole body of those who have been savingly reconciled to God and have received new life" (*Christian Theology*, by Millard Erickson, p. 1034).

"The church is the body of people called by God's grace through faith in Christ to glorify Him together by serving Him in His world" (*A Theology for the Church*, by Daniel L. Akin, p. 768).

A church is "a community of God's people that defines itself and organizes its life around its real purpose of being an agent of God's mission to the world" (*The Forgotten Ways*, by Alan Hirsch, p.82).

We can say, then, that a local church is a Caring Community of mutually accountable Christ-followers who come together to be sent on mission for the purpose of 1) worship, 2) witness, 3) nurture, and 4) restoration.

FIVE WORD PICTURES TO DESCRIBE AND DEFINE THE CHURCH

1. THE CHURCH IS A FAMILY.
Look up and highlight or underline 2 Corinthians 6:18.

A family illustrates the essence of commitment—people linked together—inseparable and loyal. Certainly, family members today do disconnect themselves, but that is not the picture of family in Scripture.

Being in a family means that as children, we have a safe place to grow. It's an environment of warmth, nurture, and encouragement. We fail and fall and flounder together. We live and laugh and love together.

Fill in the blank: The fact that the church is like a family and the fact that I am a part of the family should increase my:

_____

_____

2. THE CHURCH IS A BRIDE.
Look up and highlight or underline Ephesians 5:31-32 where Paul says that the relationship between husband and wife refers to Christ and His church.

A marriage illustrates intimacy and faithfulness. In life, of course, we often see the dissolution of marriage. But this is not the picture of marriage in the Bible. Friendship, togetherness, and loyalty are experienced in marriages where couples cleave and weave their lives together unbreakably.

Jesus is to the church like a husband is to his wife. He loves the church so much that He sacrifices His life for the church (Ephesians 5:25). He nurtures and cherishes the church (Ephesians 5:28-29). He sanctifies and purifies the church (Ephesians 5:26-27). The church responds to Christ by submitting to His leadership (Ephesians 5:22-24).

Fill in the blank: The fact that the church is the bride of Christ and that I am part of the bride of Christ should increase my:

_____

_____

3. THE CHURCH IS A <u>BODY</u>.
Look up and highlight or underline Colossians 1:18.

As the head of the church, Jesus is the source of life (Colossians 2:9-10). His life thoroughly permeates the entire body (Ephesians 1:22-23). Plus, Jesus as the head of the church is the One who leads the church and the church responds to His direction and guidance.

Like your physical body, the Body of Christ has members of the Body, i.e., different parts. Every member plays an important part.

A body needs hands and feet, elbows and knees. This means that you have an important part to play. The Body of Christ needs your ministry (1 Corinthians 12:12-26). If any part is missing, the Body is deformed. If any part is not functioning, the Body is disabled. If any part is malfunctioning, the Body is dysfunctional.

Fill in the blank: The fact that the church is the Body of Christ and that I am part of the Body of Christ should increase my:

_____

_____

4. THE CHURCH IS A <u>BUILDING</u>.
Look up and highlight or underline Ephesians 2:19b-22.

By considering the verses above, match the "building materials" with the spiritual realities.

1. The cornerstone
2. The foundation
3. The occupant
4. The bricks/stones

A. The apostles and prophets
B. Christ Jesus
C. Citizens, saints, members
D. The Spirit of God

The church, then, is a spiritual building where God dwells because He seeks to be present with His people. The church is a spiritual building that provides safety, warmth, and beauty. The church is a spiritual building where sacrifices and praises are offered. The church is a spiritual building that grows as other "living stones" are added and bond together (1 Peter 2:4-10).

Fill in the blank: The fact that the church is a building that is being built by Christ and that I am a living stone in His temple should increase my:

_____

_____

5. THE CHURCH IS A FLOCK.

In Acts 20, Paul uses another metaphor describing the church as he encourages church leaders in the city of Ephesus. Read and highlight or underline Acts 20:28. Notice the image Paul uses to describe the church.

Pay careful attention to yourselves and to all the flock, in which the Holy Spirit has made you overseers, to care for the church of God, which he obtained with his own blood (Acts 20:28).

In the Bible, believers are called sheep (John 10:15). Jesus, of course, is the Good Shepherd of the sheep (John 10:14). Local church pastors are also called shepherds (1 Peter 5:2). Therefore, one key biblical image is that the church is a flock.

Through our witness, we seek to bring other sheep into the fold (John 10: 16a). Being in the flock of God speaks to our unity in Christ (John 10:16b). As a flock, even though we must beware of enemies (Acts 20:29), we need not fear because we have a Shepherd who is actively watching out for us (Luke 12:32). As our Shepherd, the Lord meets our needs, leads our paths, gives us rest, guards our lives, and takes us home (Psalm 23).

Fill in the blank: The fact that the church is a flock that is being shepherded by Christ and that I am one of His lambs should increase my:

_____

_____

Which image of the church—family, bride, body, building, flock—encourages you the most? Why?

_____

_____

_____

_____

Which image of the church—family, bride, body, building, flock—challenges you the most? Why?

_____

_____

_____

_____

What was one of the most helpful insights that you received during this lesson?

_____

_____

_____

_____

WEEK 7, DAY 3: THE PURPOSES OF THE CHURCH

Today, let's move our attention from what the church is to what the church does. What are the tasks and the responsibilities of the church? Another way to ask the question is, "What are the purposes of the church?"

FOUR MAJOR PURPOSES OF THE CHURCH

1. A PURPOSE OF THE CHURCH: <u>WORSHIP</u>

Donald Whitney defines worship well: "The word *worship* comes from the Saxon word *weorthscype*, which later became *worthship*. To worship God is to ascribe the proper worth to God, to magnify His worthiness of praise, or better, to approach and address God as He is worthy. As the Holy and Almighty God, the Creator and Sustainer of the Universe, the Sovereign Judge to whom we must give an account, He is worthy of all the worth and honor we can give Him and then infinitely more. . .

"If you could see God at this moment, you would so utterly understand how worthy He is of worship that you would instinctively fall on your face and worship Him" (*Spiritual Disciplines for the Christian Life*, by Donald Whitney, p.87).

In your Bible, look up and highlight or underline John 4:23b-24.

How would you describe a person who worships God in spirit but no truth?

_____

_____

_____

How would you describe a person who worships God in truth but no spirit?

_____

_____

_____

How would you describe a person who worships God in spirit AND truth?

_____

_____

_____

We must aim for our worship to be heartfelt. It cannot become dutiful drudgery because duty-driven worship actually dishonors God. Pastor John Piper explains, "If I take my wife out for the evening on our anniversary and she asks me, 'Why do you do this?' the answer that honors her most is, 'Because nothing makes me happier tonight than to be with you.' 'It's my duty' is a dishonor to her. 'It's my joy' is an honor." We must seek to always have awakened our childlike awe and wonder at the very thought of God. The scenic beauty, the poetic music, and the glorious majesty of God should never dry up 'like a forgotten peach at the back of the refrigerator'" (*Desiring God*, by John Piper, pp.84, 89).

Worship is more than just the music time. We can rejoice in God and honor God in many ways through corporate worship:

- praying publicly and privately during services,
- attentively listening to the teaching of God's Word,
- hearing testimonies,
- meditating during special songs,
- celebrating with those who lead us by using art in God-honoring ways,
- listening to Scripture being read, as well as
- singing praise to God.

The Archbishop of Canterbury, William Temple, once famously described worship: "Worship is the submission of all our nature to God. It is the quickening of conscience by His holiness; the nourishment of mind with His truth; the purifying of imagination by His beauty; the opening of the heart to His love; the surrender of will to His purpose—and all of this gathered up in adoration, the most selfless emotion of which our nature is capable and therefore the chief remedy for that self-centeredness which is our original sin and the source of all actual sin" (*Readings in John's Gospel*, by William Temple).

Using Temple's definition of worship, what aspect of worship do you most need right now in your life? Circle one or two.

A quickened conscience.
A nourished mind.
A purified imagination.
An opened heart.
A surrendered will.

How can real worship remedy our self-centeredness?

_____

_____

_____

_____

Make the decision now that you will make a habit of gathering weekly for worship. Luke 4:16 tells us that Jesus made it His regular practice to attend weekend services: *As was His custom, He entered the synagogue on the Sabbath.* If Jesus, God the Son, felt it necessary to practice the discipline of being in His Father's house on the Lord's Day, how much more should we make weekend services our own "can't miss" appointments?

Are you willing to make the following commitment?
I will make it my custom—my regular practice, my habit—to join with God's people for worship each weekend.

☐ Yes   ☐ No.

2. A PURPOSE OF THE CHURCH: <u>WITNESS</u>

People outside the church sometimes criticize evangelistic Christ followers by saying things like, "Religion is a private matter," or "Don't try to cram your faith down my throat," or "Who are you to say your truth is THE truth?" They see believers as "very conservative, entrenched in their thinking, anti-gay, anti-choice, angry, violent, illogical, empire builders [who] want to convert everyone (*Unchristian*, by David Kinnaman, p. 26).

We instinctively know we live in a culture that is hostile to our faith. So, we are very hesitant to witness for Christ in our spheres of influence. In the space below, suggest a few reasons why followers of Jesus might be hesitant to talk about the faith.

_____

_____

_____

_____

In spite of the obstacles, we must share our faith. Why? All people without Christ are lost. People may be moral, attractive, cultural, and educated. But without Christ, they are lost. To be lost means not to know the way home. Hell, not heaven, is the future destiny of those who do not know Jesus (2 Thessalonians 1:9-10).

One of our basic problems is that we don't really believe that people without Jesus are lost, or else we would do more to help them find Him—to discover the way home to a New Life in Christ.

Look up John 14:6 in your Bible. Circle the phrase "the Way."

Notice that He is not <u>a</u> way, but "<u>the</u> Way." We'll never be effective in sharing our faith unless we believe that nobody can ever be saved apart from Christ, and that He is the <u>only</u> hope. We must be witnesses to this truth.

Being a witness is not the only business, but it is a primary business of churches.

That means that there is not a person or place on the earth who is not our concern. There can be no spiritual, racial, or national limits to our mission. Our mission is as big as the world. As a church, and as individuals in the church, we are responsible to pray and to work so that everyone in the world can hear the gospel.

At CVC, we call this several things:

Missional Living.
Being Missionaries cleverly disguised . . .
Inviting people to New Life in Christ.

Fill in the blank. I am a Missionary cleverly disguised as a

_____.

We have all been called to reach new people for Christ. Someone once said that the church is the only society on earth that exists for the benefit of non-members.

Jesus gave us what has been called "The Great Commission" in various forms at least 5 different times—in all 4 gospels, plus Acts.

Look up in your Bible and highlight or underline Matthew 28:19-20, Mark 16:15, Luke 24:46-48, John 21:15-19, Acts 1:8.

Make a list of 3 or 4 of the action verbs that you see in these 5 passages of Scripture. What do these verbs tell you about our responsibility to a non-Christian world as individuals who are part of a church?

_____

_____

Being a witness doesn't mean being weird, rude, judgmental, obnoxious, pushy, or holier-than-thou. Instead, we earn the right to be heard by being gracious—bearing the fruit of New Life, being loving/joyful/peaceful, becoming increasingly holy in all we say and do.

Walk in wisdom toward outsiders, making the best use of the time. Let your speech always be gracious, seasoned with salt, so that you may know how you ought to answer each person (Colossians 4:5-6).

We build relationships and listen with non-judgment to outsiders as they share their stories. We learn to share our own stories with succinct clarity. Finally, we lovingly share the gospel of Christ—the story of creation, fall, rescue, and restoration. This is the way we invite outsiders to Live New.

On a scale of 1-10 (1 being highly distressed and 10 being extremely at ease), how comfortable are you being a witness for Christ? _____

Why did you choose that number?

_____

_____

_____

Now envision yourself helping a family member or a close friend come to faith in Christ and approaching you in heaven to say "Thank you." If that were to happen, what kind of feelings do you think you might have on that day?

_____

_____

_____

What was one of the most helpful insights that you received during this lesson?

_____

_____

_____

_____

_____

PRAYER: Close this time praying that Christ will increase your desire and ability to worship and witness. Pray specifically that the power of Christ will help you overcome whatever is preventing you from worshipping and witness to the capacity God desires for you.

WEEK 7, DAY 4: THE PURPOSES OF THE CHURCH (CONTINUED)
Yesterday, we explored 2 of the 4 purposes of the church: We worship and witness. *Today, we will explore 2 additional purposes of the church.* As a church, we nurture and restore.

3. A PURPOSE OF THE CHURCH: <u>NURTURE</u>
God has established the church to foster spiritual growth and maturity. We are to edify and build up one another. In your Bible, look up and highlight or underline Colossians 1:28.

Based on Colossians 1:28, who in the church is supposed to grow toward maturity?

A. Pastors
B. Staff
C. Leaders
D. Members
E. Attenders
F. All of the above

Everyone is to grow to maturity in Christ. And that means you! You can become mature in Christ. It's simply not acceptable when believers stay stagnant or regress in their spiritual development. Spiritual progress ought to characterize the lives of God's people.

The church uses a variety of words to describe this process of spiritual growth. Words and phrases like edification, a changed life, transformation, growth in godliness, the pursuit of holiness, spiritual maturity, discipleship, and spiritual formation all express the concept of nurture.

When a person initially receives New Life in Christ, Jesus says that we have been "born again" (John 3:3,7). Spiritually, we are babies. Life in the nursery can be fun—for a while! But the goal of all parents is to help their children grow out of the diaper-and-baby-food phase and into mature adulthood. That's God's goal, too, for each of us spiritually. He wants bottle-fed spiritual babies to grow into maturity (Hebrews 5:12-14).

Match the following descriptions of spiritual maturity with the appropriate verses.

1. Romans 8:29
2. Ephesians 4:11-12
3. Matthew 28:19-20

A. Being taught to observe all Jesus' commands
B. Being conformed to the image of Christ
C. Being equipped by spiritual leaders of the church

At CVC, we encourage constant spiritual growth in discipleship—in what we call the Fruit of New Life (FONL). So, each believer is taught to regularly ask himself, "How am I maturing as a Beloved Child, as a Self-Feeder, as a Servant, as a Discipler, as an Investor, and as a Missionary?"

Our worship, groups, and service environments are all designed with the goal of helping every CVCer to be nurtured toward becoming more and more mature in bearing the Fruit of New Life. Our leaders seek to be careful and strategic in placing growth opportunities on the church calendar. Our services, ministries, gatherings, groups, seminars, retreats, concerts, and missions are all designed to help you maximize your growth as a disciple.

What is a ministry of the church that has helped you grow spiritually?

_____

_____

What is a ministry of the church that you can be involved with that will help you grow deeper spiritually and what will you do to find out more about that opportunity?

_____

_____

_____

Before we leave this point, let's consider that the church not only exists to help you be nurtured, but it also exists for you to nurture others. Look up and highlight or underline 2 Timothy 2:2.

In this verse, Paul is telling Timothy to pass along his teaching to others who will in turn teach others. We see 4 generations of disciples here: 1) Paul, 2) Timothy, 3) Faithful men, and 4) Others.

We don't have to be completely mature before we can pass on what we've learned. We just need to be a step ahead of someone else.

Write down the name of a person in your life who is a step (or 2 or 3!) behind you spiritually that you can help grow:

_____

Brainstorm: How do you think you might help this person grow?

_____

_____

_____

_____

Action step: What will you do this week to initiate your thoughts above? Some ideas may include writing a note, making a call, setting a time to get together, inviting them to church, etc.

4. A PURPOSE OF THE CHURCH: <u>RESTORE</u>

The church has a responsibility to perform acts of love and compassion for those *inside* the church and for those *outside* the church. Jesus cared about the needy and the suffering. He fed the hungry, healed the sick, and restored the broken. When He launched His public ministry in Luke 4, Jesus quoted from Isaiah 61. Turn there in your Bible and highlight or underline verse 1.

The Spirit of the Lord God is upon Me, because the LORD has anointed Me to bring good news to the poor; He has sent Me to bind up the brokenhearted, to proclaim liberty to the captives, and the opening of the prison to those who are bound (Isaiah 61:1).

If we are going to follow the example of Jesus, we must show great compassion for the hurting and the needy. "Indeed, Jesus suggests in Matthew 25:31-46 that the one sign by which true believers can be distinguished from those who make empty professions is acts of love which are done in Jesus' name and emulate His example. Concern for the fatherless, the widow, and the sojourner is appropriate for those who worship a God who Himself displays such concern" (*Christian Theology*, by Millard Erickson, p.1058).

Fill in the blanks by looking up the following verses:

James 1:27
Religion that is pure and undefiled before God, the Father, is this: to visit _____ and _____ in their affliction, and to keep oneself unstained from the world.

James 2:14-16
What good is it, my brothers, if someone says he has faith but does not have works? Can that faith save him? If a brother or sister is poorly _____ and lacking in daily _____, and one of you says to them, "Go in peace, be warmed and filled," without giving them the things needed for the body, what _____ is that?

1 John 3:16-18
By this we know love, that he laid down his life for us, and we ought to lay down our lives for the brothers. But if anyone has the world's _____ and sees his brother in _____, yet closes his heart against him, how does God's love abide in him? Little children, let us not love in _____ or _____ but in _____ and in _____.

What is something in our culture that is broken that you want to see restored? Global hunger? Sex trafficking? Systemic poverty? Illiteracy? The redefinition of marriage? Orphaned children? Lack of clean water? The abortion of the unborn? Natural disasters? Spousal abuse? Homelessness? Unemployment or underemployment?

Some people have called these social concerns "global Goliaths."

In the space below, express what "global Goliath" brings a tear to your eye or makes you pound the table because you are thinking, "That's simply got to change!" Why has this issue become a burden for you?

_____

_____

_____

_____

The church as a Caring Community is to mobilize believers to be salt and light (Matthew 5:13-16) in their spheres of influence. Individual believers are to be agents of restoration, bringing justice where there is oppression.

"People who are obsessed with Jesus aren't consumed with their personal safety and comfort above all else. Obsessed people care more about God's kingdom coming to this earth than their own lives being shielded from pain or distress. People who are obsessed with Jesus live lives that connect them with the poor in some way or another. Obsessed people believe that Jesus talked about money and the poor so often because it was really important to Him. When Christians sacrifice and give wildly to the poor, that is truly a light that glimmers. The Bible teaches that the church is to be that light, that sign of hope, in an increasingly dark and hopeless world" (*Crazy Love*, by Francis Chan, pp.133, 135, 140.)

End your time today by writing out a short prayer in which you ask God to help you and your church to fulfill the purposes of the church: Worship, witness, nurture, and restore.

_____

_____

_____

_____

What was one of the most helpful insights that you received during this lesson?

_____

_____

_____

FOUR PURPOSES OF THE CHURCH
WORSHIP – WITNESS – NURTURE - RESTORE

WEEK 7, DAY 5: LIFEGROUPS

As we did on Week 5, Day 1, consider just a few of the "one anothers" of the New Testament.

Care for one another (1 Corinthians 12:25). *Encourage one another* (1 Thessalonians 5:11). *Serve one another* (Galatians 5:13). *Forgive one another* (Ephesians 4:32). *Instruct one another* (Romans 15:14). *Admonish one another* (Colossians 3:16). *Build up one another* (1 Thessalonians 5:11).

It's almost impossible to accomplish these "one anothers" in a larger worship environment. The best place for these kinds of relationships to be built is in the context of a small gathering. At CVC, we call these LifeGroups. One Christian leader, in emphasizing the value of small groups in relation to large meetings, said, "We impress people from a distance. But we impact them up close."

FELLOWSHIP

Look up and highlight or underline Acts 2:42. It's a verse that describes the Caring Community that the people in the early church experienced.

Look carefully at the verse and make a list of the four things that the earliest Christians devoted themselves to.

1. _____
2. _____
3. _____
4. _____

Fellowship translates from the Greek word *koinonia* which means "close relationship, common sharing, joint participation" (*A Greek English Lexicon of the New Testament*, by Walter Bauer, pp.438-439).

As you consider Acts 2:42, what might "devoting yourself to" fellowship look like? Why would this be important?

_____
_____
_____
_____

We passionately believe that every person at CVC should live in authentic community that is rooted in Christ, grounded in God's Word and established in love. We believe that growth happens best when we are in fellowship in a community—not in isolation—so that when we face life's problems, we have a group of people around us praying for us, encouraging us, checking in on us, visiting us, and challenging us toward spiritual growth and maturity.

LIFEGROUP DYNAMICS AND STRUCTURE

LifeGroups are a vehicle by which our adults, students, and children actively journey toward greater spiritual growth and authentic Christ-centered relationships. At CVC, a LifeGroup is a small group, usually 8-12 people, that gathers regularly and intentionally to grow toward maturity, to pursue the Fruit of New Life. In LifeGroups, our goal is that each person experiences what Acts 2:42 refers to as fellowship.

LifeGroups are an environment in which people relationally experience our church's 6 Passions, sometimes known as "Values": Living Truth, God Dependence, Caring Community, Linked Generations, Equipped Leadership, and Missional Living (see the CVC Vision Guide).

These 6 passions define the way we relate to one another and carry out our mission. They capture our uniqueness, define how we serve together, and help define the personality of CVC.

If a LifeGroup is successfully living out our passions, then the people will experience. . .

1) growth
2) discipleship
3) community
4) life-on-life learning
5) care
6) support
7) hospitality
8) encouragement
9) healthy, loving accountability
10) organic relationships
11) authentic friendships
12) a safe and disarming environment
13) service
14) Bible intake and prayer
15) the power and presence of God

Look at the list of benefits in the previous paragraph. Which of these would be most meaningful for you? Why?

_____
_____
_____
_____

GOSPEL-BASED LIFEGROUPS

Sometimes people resist the idea of connecting in a LifeGroup because their past experience has been with groups that are performance-based (do more, try harder) and guilt-inducing ("I'll never measure up"). We should want to run from small groups like that!

But thankfully, not all groups are created equal! Some groups are life-giving. We should want to run toward a Caring Community of believers who remind each other that Jesus loves us. We can remind one another that even while we were still sinners, Christ died to forgive us and that He rose again so we can share in His life (Romans 5:8-10).

A LifeGroup is a place where we can be reminded over and over by a spiritual friend, "You are a Beloved Child. I know you've messed up. But you still have great worth apart from your performance. Christ gave His life for you. He loves you deeply. You are the apple of His eye. He rejoices over you. He's forgiven you. You matter to Him. You are accepted and complete in Christ." See, it's this message that enables us to Live New.

Describe a time in your life when you either received a message like that from a friend or when you needed to receive a message like that from a friend.

_____

_____

_____

_____

A VISION FOR LIFE-GIVING LIFEGROUPS

The world, because it's fallen, is a place where we experience wounds. We are all damaged people. But God has invited us to live in Caring Community with each other where our brokenness can be restored. Author and Christian counselor Larry Crabb writes, "I envision the church as people who are connected in small healing communities, connected by what they give to each other."
(*Connecting*, by Larry Crabb, p. xiv).

Crabb continues, "When two people connect something is poured out of one and into the other that has the power to heal the soul of its deepest wounds and restore it to health . . . Something good is in the heart of each of God's children that is more powerful than everything bad . . . (*Connecting*, by Larry Crabb, p. xi).

We must believe that something amazing can happen when the Holy Spirit is released in us and through us as we gather in our LifeGroups. Christians "have been given resources that if released could powerfully heal broken hearts, overcome the damage done by abusive backgrounds, encourage the depressed to courageously move forward, stimulate the lonely to reach out, revitalize discouraged teens and children with new holy energy, and introduce hope into the lives of the countless people who feel rejected, alone, and useless . . ." (*Connecting*, by Larry Crabb, p.xiii).

Who wouldn't want to give and receive this kind of Christian fellowship?

Will you make a definite commitment to a lifestyle of devoting yourself to a LifeGroup for your personal, spiritual development?

☐ Yes   ☐ No

Admittedly, not all groups are life-giving like Crabb is describing. But groups can become increasingly better if we will learn to listen to one another from the heart, ask each other quality questions, and speak words of life and hope to one another.

In the space provided below, please write out a prayer that expresses your heart's desire when it comes to connecting in a Caring Community.

_____
_____
_____
_____
_____
_____

What was one of the most helpful insights that you received during this lesson?

_____
_____
_____
_____
_____

LifeGroups help the monologue of Sunday morning become a dialogue.
LifeGroups make friends out of strangers.
Chad Allen, Lead Pastor - Cuyahoga Valley Church

Week 8

THE HOLY SPIRIT:
Being Empowered
as a Servant

MEMORY VERSE
And I will ask the Father, and he will give you another Helper, to be with you forever, even the Spirit of truth, whom the world cannot receive, because it neither sees him nor knows him. You know him, for he dwells with you and will be in you. John 14:16-17

WEEK 8, DAY 1: WHO IS THE HOLY SPIRIT?

One of the most important and fascinating studies in the Bible is the Person and work of the Holy Spirit. But, sadly, truths about the Spirit of God are ignored in too many churches today.

For this reason, Francis Chan released a book in 2009 entitled, *Forgotten God: Reversing Our Tragic Neglect of the Holy Spirit*. He writes, "From my perspective, the Holy Spirit is tragically neglected and, for all practical purposes, forgotten. While no evangelical would deny His existence, I'm willing to bet there are millions of churchgoers across America who cannot confidently say they have experienced His presence or action in their lives over the past year. And many of them do not believe they can"
(*Forgotten God*, by Francis Chan, p.15).

Forgetting the Holy Spirit is truly tragic. When we ignore, neglect, or misunderstand the ministry of the Holy Spirit, we miss out on the adventure of seeing the fullness of God's presence and power manifested in our lives.

God has given us His Spirit so we can experience His reality in ever-increasingly powerful and joyous ways.

Let's start our study by considering some foundational truths about the Holy Spirit.

THE HOLY SPIRIT IS GOD.

The Bible teaches that there is one God, eternally existing in three Persons: God the Father, God the Son, and God the Spirit. One God. Three Persons. This, of course, is hard to fathom. But it's a truth taught in Scripture. The benediction at the end of 2 Corinthians illustrates the Tri-unity of God. *The grace of the Lord Jesus Christ and the love of God and the fellowship of the Holy Spirit be with you all* (2 Corinthians 13:14). Note: Other Trinitarian passages can be found in Matthew 28:19, 1 Corinthians 12:4-6, Ephesians 4:4-6, and 1 Peter 1:2.

The Holy Spirit is co-equal and co-eternal with the Father and Son. He is God just as the first and second Persons of the Trinity are God. In Acts 5:3-4, Peter asks Ananias, *Why has Satan filled your heart to lie to the Holy Spirit . . . You have not lied to man but to God.* The clear implication is that to lie to the Holy Spirit is to lie to God.

What is a practical application of the truth that the Holy Spirit is God? Complete the sentence: Because the Holy Spirit is God, I can . . .

_____

_____

THE HOLY SPIRIT IS A PERSON.

After understanding that the Holy Spirit is God, it should go without saying that He is a Person. But it's been a temptation for some people to consider the Holy Spirit to be an impersonal influence, energy, or power. They think that the Spirit's influence is a "may-the-force-be-with-you" kind of thing. Sometimes, people have even referred to the Spirit as an "it."

The Holy Spirit, however, is a Person. He does what only persons can do. Among other things, He teaches (John 14:26), witnesses (John 15:26), prays (Romans 8:26-27), gives (1 Corinthians 12:11), speaks (Acts 8:29), approves (Acts 15:28), and can be grieved (Ephesians 4:30). As a Person, He displays wisdom, volition, strength, and love.

"The Scriptures then teach that the Holy Spirit is a Person, having all the Divine attributes and able to do all the Divine works. The mystery is acknowledged, and it is very profound. To finally explain it is impossible; but this impossibility of explanation is to be accounted for by human limitation and by the fact that the finite can never grasp the Infinite" (*The Spirit of God*, by G. Campbell Morgan, p.30).

What is a practical application of the truth that the Holy Spirit is a Person? Complete the sentence: Because the Holy Spirit is a Person, I can . . .

_____

_____

THE HOLY SPIRIT IS HOLY.

That is stating the obvious, right? But let's not too quickly pass over this simple, yet profound fact.

Because the Spirit is holy, "one of His primary activities is to cleanse us from sin and to 'sanctify us' to make us more holy in actual conduct of life" (*Systematic Theology*, by Wayne Grudem, p. 638). When we initially become followers of Christ, the Spirit cleanses us and then makes significant changes in our lives so that we decisively break some of our old patterns of sinful behavior (1 Corinthians 6:11). Then, we begin a lifelong process of becoming more and more holy through the inner workings of the Spirit in our lives (2 Corinthians 3:18).

What is a practical application of the truth that the Holy Spirit is holy? Complete the sentence: Because the Holy Spirit is holy, I can . . .

_____

_____

THE NAMES OF THE HOLY SPIRIT

The Holy Spirit has various names in the Bible. Look up the following Scriptures and match the appropriate verses with the 10 names of the Spirit listed below. (Note: This is not an exhaustive list.)

1. The Spirit of God	A. Romans 8:9a
2. The Spirit of your Father	B. Romans 8:9b
3. The Spirit of the Lord	C. Hebrews 10:29
4. The Spirit of Christ	D. Matthew 10:20
5. The Spirit of grace	E. Acts 5:9
6. The Spirit of truth	F. Romans 8:15
7. The Spirit of adoption	G. John 14:17
8. The Spirit of holiness	H. Romans 8:2
9. The Spirit of life	I. John 14:16
10. The Helper	J. Romans 1:4

When you come across these various terms for the Holy Spirit in your Bible (and there are more!), be reminded that the Holy Spirit is just as infinite a Resource for you as are the Father and the Son. His multiple names demonstrate His multi-faceted ministry for us and in us.

Which of these names of the Holy Spirit is most intriguing for you? Why?

_____

_____

_____

_____

_____

What was one of the most helpful insights that you received during this lesson?

_____

_____

_____

WEEK 8, DAY 2: SEVEN SYMBOLS OF THE HOLY SPIRIT

Throughout the Bible, we see several different symbols of the Holy Spirit. Each one gives us an insight into His nature.

As we learn about these symbols, we should keep in mind that God uses symbols, metaphors, and images in Scripture to express realities that are more profound than words can express. Because of His omniscience, omnipotence, and omnipresence, the Spirit is infinitely greater than the symbols express.

WIND

When Jesus talked about the initial work of the Spirit in our salvation, He likened the Spirit's work to wind. Open your Bible and highlight or underline John 3:8.

The wind blows where it wishes, and you hear its sound, but you do not know where it comes from or where it goes. So it is with everyone who is born of the Spirit (John 3:8).

We can't see wind, but we can see its effects. It's the same with the Holy Spirit. Although we can't see Him, we can see the changes He makes in our lives. His work in us to transform us must be evident.

After Jesus' death, resurrection, and ascension, in Acts 2:1-2, we learn about the Spirit's empowering believers who were waiting with expectation: *When the day of Pentecost arrived, they were all together in one place. And suddenly there came from heaven a sound like a mighty rushing wind, and it filled the entire house where they were sitting* (Acts 2:1-2). The Holy Spirit is sovereign, dynamic, irresistible, and unstoppable. Like wind, He is powerful, active, and cannot be controlled.

In the space below, jot down some of the changes the Spirit has made in you—the visible evidence that the wind of the Holy Spirit has blown across the landscape of your life.

_____

_____

_____

_____

> ***If it's true that the Spirit of God dwells in us and that our bodies are the Holy Spirit's temple, then shouldn't there be a huge difference between the person who has the Spirit of God living inside of him or her and the person who does not?***
> *Francis Chan - Pastor, Author of Forgotten God*

RAIN

Rain brings refreshing where there once was dryness and barrenness. That's good news for us because we live in a dry and barren land. In Joel 2:23, 28a, we read: *Be glad, O children of Zion, and rejoice in the LORD your God, for He has given the early rain for your vindication; He has poured down for you abundant rain, the early and the latter rain, as before . . . And it shall come to pass afterward, that I will pour out my Spirit on all flesh"* (Joel 2:23, 28a). The Lord is saying that He will send rain to fields [to people] that are totally barren. This gives us hope.

In your Bible, highlight or underline Isaiah 44:3.

If we find ourselves needing to be rejuvenated, it doesn't necessarily mean that we've sinned. Sometimes a lawn or a field endures a hot day or a dry spell. That's when it needs to be revitalized with a steady rain. In the same way, the Holy Spirit, coming as a nourishing rain, brings refreshing and restoration to our lives.

In the space below, describe a time in your life when you needed to be refreshed by God's Spirit.

_____

_____

_____

_____

RIVERS

We see similarities with the symbol of rivers and the symbol of rain. But the differences seem to warrant separate consideration. The rain comes *upon* us, while the rivers flow *from* us. Find John 7:38-39 in your Bible and underline or highlight the verses.

The Holy Spirit is like a river of living water flowing out of the hearts of His followers. Rivers flow to places where life-giving water is needed. The Holy Spirit is not only life-giving and refreshment for you, but also is an overflowing channel through you so that His fullness, life, and love can flow to others.

The Lord wants thirsty people to know Him. And this means that we must let the rivers of living water flow through us and gush out of our lives. In the space below, write down some thoughts about what might block the life-giving flow of the Spirit from our lives.

_____

_____

_____

_____

FIRE

Just as fire purifies, warms, and illuminates, so does the Holy Spirit. Look up and highlight or underline Matthew 3:11, the words John the Baptist used to describe Jesus.

The Spirit works to refine us, as gold or silver is refined in a fire (Malachi 3:2, 1 Peter 1:7). As a silversmith uses fire to purge the dross from the precious metal, so the Spirit removes our sin by cleansing and refining us.

143

Fire not only purifies, it also energizes and illuminates. When the Holy Spirit began His ministry of indwelling the early church, He chose to appear as "tongues of fire" resting on each of the believers: *And divided tongues as of fire appeared to them and rested on each one of them. And they were all filled with the Holy Spirit* (Acts 2:3-4a). It is, therefore, biblical to speak of someone influenced by the Holy Spirit as being "on fire" for God.

In the space below, write down a few words to describe the life of someone who is on fire for God. How is this evidence that the Holy Spirit is at work in that person's life?

_____

_____

_____

ANOINTING OIL

In the Old Testament, oil was used to anoint priests, prophets, and kings. In the New Testament, we see that Jesus was anointed "with the Holy Spirit and with power" (Acts 10: 38). Jesus is our Ultimate and Supreme Prophet, Priest, and King. He quoted Isaiah 61:1, recognizing that He was anointed by the Spirit of the Lord to fulfill His mission to minister to the broken and the oppressed.

Anointing oil represents the empowering presence of God for ministry. Anointing is for all God's people. Look up and highlight or underline 1 John 2:20.

The anointing of the Holy Spirit consecrates us for effective service. The symbol of oil for the Holy Spirit speaks to us about the work He does to set us apart as His missionaries. When we are anointed by the Spirit, like Jesus, we will be increasingly fruitful on our mission to restore broken people.

In the space below, write down a prayer asking God's Spirit to anoint you for more effective service.

_____

_____

_____

_____

SEAL/GUARANTEE

The Holy Spirit is the "guarantee" or "seal" in the hearts of the followers of Christ. Look up and highlight or underline Ephesians 1:13b-14.

The gift of the Spirit to believers is like a down payment or a first installment on the completion of our salvation that Jesus promised and secured for us at the cross: *And it is God who establishes us with you in Christ, and has anointed us, and who has also put His seal on us and given us his Spirit in our hearts as a guarantee* (2 Corinthians 1:21-22). The Greek word translated "guarantee" in these passages means "a pledge." It's money or property given in advance as security for the rest. Because the Spirit has sealed us, we are assured of our salvation.

And this reassurance is necessary as we live in this fallen world. "Often our faith and the knowledge we have of our believing in Christ is severely shaken; the activities of indwelling sin stir up a thick cloud of doubt, and Satan avails himself of this to tell us our profession is an empty one. But in His tender grace, God has given us the Holy Spirit, and from time to time He 'seals' or *confirms* our faith by His quickening and comforting operations (*The Holy Spirit,* by A.W. Pink, chapter 24).

What can sometimes cause you to doubt your salvation? How has the Presence of the Holy Spirit reassured you that Christ will complete the work that He began in your life and, ultimately, take you to heaven?

_____

_____

_____

_____

DOVE

In Matthew 3:16, we see the Holy Spirit coming as a dove to rest on Jesus at His baptism. This pictures the Spirit's approval, beauty, gentleness, and peace. In a similar way, the Holy Spirit seeks to rest on every follower of Jesus. In order for that to happen, we must have a Christ-like disposition of humility.

"The Holy Spirit as the Dove, could only come upon and remain upon the Lord Jesus because He was the Lamb. Had the Lord Jesus had any other disposition than that of the Lamb—humility, submissiveness, and self-surrender—the Dove could never have rested on Him. Being herself so gentle, she would have been frightened away had not Jesus been meek and lowly in heart. Here then we have pictured for us the condition upon which the same Holy Spirit can come upon us and abide upon us. The Dove can only abide upon us as we are willing to be as the Lamb" (*The Calvary Road,* by Roy Hession, pp.58-59).

It's important for us to remember at this point that the Holy Spirit will never leave us or forsake us. After all, we are sealed! But the influence and anointing of the Spirit can be diminished when we have a haughty heart and a stiff-necked spirit. It's in this sense that the Dove may not rest on us.

Over the course of the next week, take one symbol of the Holy Spirit each day and invite Him to display that characteristic more and more deeply in your life.

- Ask Him to blow His mighty wind to empower your life.
- Ask Him to pour His refreshing rain onto your life.
- Ask Him to open up His rivers of living water to flow through you.
- Ask Him to refine you with His fire and to set your soul on fire.
- Ask Him to anoint you with oil so you can serve the broken with greater fruitfulness.

- Ask Him to give you a greater sense of your sealing, your assurance of heaven.
- Ask Him to rest on your life as a dove with His beauty, gentleness, and peace.

What was one of the most helpful insights that you received during this lesson?

_____

_____

_____

WEEK 8, DAY 3: WHAT IS THE WORK OF THE HOLY SPIRIT?

Based on what we have already learned about the Holy Spirit, His work can be defined as Divine, personal, sanctifying, and spiritual. In this study, we will explore specific aspects of the Spirit's work that will reflect these general characteristics.

The Holy Spirit is at work in the dynamic, eternal, loving relationship within the Trinity. He was at work in creation. The Holy Spirit was active in the Old Testament and in the life of Jesus. He inspired the authors of Scripture so that what they wrote was truly God's Word.

When we think about the work of the Holy Spirit, we must not think of Him working separately from the Father and the Son. "The work of the Son is the work of the Father, and the work of the Spirit is the work of the Son. The work of one is the work of all, and each works in and through the others. [However] the divine Persons co-operate in different offices" (*Work of the Holy Spirit,* by W. T. Conner, p.187).

In this study, we will limit our focus to how the Holy Spirit works in the lives of believers.

THE HOLY SPIRIT CONVICTS US.

Our conversion means that we have turned to God. But before we turn to God, we must turn from our sin. And before we can turn from our sin, we must be convicted of sin. That is the work of the Holy Spirit. Look up and highlight or underline John 16:8.

Without this work of the Holy Spirit, we would never experience conversion from sin to Christ.

In the space below, describe when and how the Holy Spirit brought an initial conviction of sin into your life.

_____

_____

_____

_____

THE HOLY SPIRIT REGENERATES US.

Regeneration is a word that describes being born again. It's a supernatural work of the Holy Spirit. Before the Spirit regenerated us, we were dead in our trespasses and sins (Ephesians 2:1). Because of our spiritual death, we had no ability to repent and trust Christ. That's why we need the Spirit to give us New Life in Christ. Look up and highlight or underline John 3:5–6.

If you ask enough people when they became Christians or when they were born again, you will hear, "Well, I've just always been a Christian." That shows a lack of understanding. For example, if you were to ask a married person, "When did you get married?" and they said, "Well, I've always been married," you would think they're missing the point. There was a day and a time when the "I do's" were made. In a similar way, there is a specific point in time when New Life occurs for the believer. There is a point in time when those who are spiritually dead are granted spiritual life by the Holy Spirit.

Often, true believers can't remember an exact, specific point in time when this occurred. But they can look back to a season of time when this happened. For example, sometimes, the sun appears quickly in the sky—like a sunrise over the Atlantic Ocean. Other times, the sun seems to appear gradually—like in a valley between the mountains. But in both cases, you know that the sun has risen.

In a similar way, New Life seems to appear at a point in time for some. While for others, it appears over time. In both cases, the evidence of the New Life is prominent.

In the space below, describe when and how the Holy Spirit brought about a new birth for you.

_____

_____

_____

_____

THE HOLY SPIRIT BAPTIZES US.

The word "baptize" means to dip, immerse, or plunge. Water baptism is an external symbol that identifies a believer with a particular local church family. Spirit baptism is an internal work that makes a believer part of the larger body of Christ—part of the church universal.

For in one Spirit we were all baptized into one body—Jews or Greeks, slaves or free—and all were made to drink of one Spirit (1 Corinthians 12:13).

This baptism in the Spirit occurs at our conversion to Christ. It refers "to the activity of the Holy Spirit at the beginning of the Christian life when He gives us new spiritual life (in regeneration) and cleanses us and gives a clear break with the power and love of sin (the initial stage of sanctification)" (*Systematic Theology*, by Wayne Grudem, p.768).

Therefore, people who say that you need to experience the baptism of the Holy Spirit after you become a believer are misinterpreting the Scriptures. You simply cannot be a believer without being baptized with the Holy Spirit. You have been immersed by the Holy Spirit into all the privileges of being a part of the body of Christ as a child of God.

THE HOLY SPIRIT INDWELLS US.

Sometimes, people coming to faith are encouraged to "ask Jesus to come into your heart." Certainly, there is a sense in which that is a legitimate prayer. But in another sense, it's not possible.

Remember that ever since the Incarnation, Jesus has had a body. And, right now, He is in heaven at the right hand of God the Father. So, the Person who actually comes into our hearts at the point of conversion is the Spirit of Christ—the Holy Spirit. Look up and highlight or underline John 14:16–17.

This is an especially encouraging truth. When Jesus walked the earth, He was the Master as a teacher and leader. "But His influence was that of an external word and example. The Spirit, however, is able to affect one more intensely because, dwelling within, He can get to the very center of one's thinking and emotions" (*Christian Theology*, by Millard Erickson, p.874). "Jesus merely walked beside the disciples; the Spirit would actually enter their human bodies . . . Have you marveled at it? Would you be willing to take thirty seconds right now just to dwell on the fact that God is in you?" (*Forgotten God*, by Francis Chan, p.110).

Because of the Spirit's indwelling nature, we are never alone. When Jesus says, "Behold, I am with you always, to the end of the age" (Matthew 28:20b), and "I will never leave you nor forsake you" (Hebrews 13:5b), He is speaking of the permanent indwelling presence of the Spirit of Christ with us.

What are some practical implications for your daily life that arise from knowing the Holy Spirit dwells in you?

_____
_____
_____
_____

THE HOLY SPIRIT EMPOWERS US.

It isn't just hard to live the Christian life. It's impossible. We have been called to a life that cannot be lived in our own natural human ability and strength. We have been called to a lifestyle that is, frankly, supernatural or super-human.

The good news is that God has given us His Resource—the Holy Spirit—to live beyond the norm. With the Spirit, what was impossible becomes possible. Look up and highlight or underline Acts 1:8.

Because the Spirit lives in us, we have a Power within us to become who we could not become without Him. Trying harder to do more—self-effort—is doomed to fail. The New Life in Christ is lived out "not by might, nor by power, but by my Spirit, says the Lord of hosts" (Zechariah 4:6). Human might and personal power won't work over the long haul. We need something more; actually, Someone more. We need the enablement and empowering of the Holy Spirit.

It's exciting to know that you can live in a way that the only possible explanation for your life is the work of the Holy Spirit in you and through you. You can live with a Power that can't be faked. The touch of the supernatural should be the atmosphere of your life. "You are a temple of the Holy Spirit. You are not just a person living your life by human power." (*Forgotten God*, by Francis Chan, p.111). People ought to ask, "How do you live like that? Why did that happen to you?" And we ought to be able to say, "The only explanation I have is that the Holy Spirit is working in me and for me."

In the space below, write out a prayer that God would so fill you with His Spirit that people would recognize that something is supernaturally different about you, and that the only explanation is that God's Spirit is alive and well and working powerfully in you.

_____
_____
_____
_____

THE HOLY SPIRIT TEACHES US.

The Holy Spirit has a teaching role. He illuminates the Word of God when we hear, read, or study the Bible. Turn in your Bible and highlight or underline Jesus' words in John 14:26.

When you sit down to read your Bible, it is the Spirit of God who sheds light on passages and gives you "aha" moments. People who read the Bible regularly will invariably have moments where a word, phrase, sentence, verse, or passage will "jump off the page" and meet a particular need or answer a specific question. What happened? It's the teaching ministry of the Holy Spirit operating in the person's life.

When you hear a message, a teaching, a podcast, a lesson from a pastor or Bible teacher, it is the Spirit of God who applies the truths to your life. Quite often, people will say to a Bible teacher, "You've been reading my mail," or "You must have talked to someone in my family or at work," or "You've been a fly on the wall at my house, because it felt like you were speaking right to me." What happened? The Holy Spirit has taken the Word of God and, through a Bible teacher, taught it and applied it to a particular person.

In the space below, describe a time when the Holy Spirit has shown up in an especially powerful or unique way to teach you to apply God's truth to your life.

_____

_____

_____

_____

THE HOLY SPIRIT PRAYS FOR US.

When we do not know how to pray, the Holy Spirit wisely intercedes for us when we step out and approach the Father. Look up and highlight or underline Romans 8:26.

When you do not know how to pray or what to pray, it is still supremely beneficial to approach God in prayer. When you don't know how to pray or what to pray, pray anyway. In a powerful way, the Holy Spirit takes over for us and translates our unintelligible groans into intelligible prayers that touch the Father's heart.

THE HOLY SPIRIT GUIDES US.

We can experience day-to-day direction through our relationship with the Holy Spirit. We must resist our natural tendency to decide based solely on our own limited human wisdom and common sense. We must seek the guidance of the Spirit.

Match the following verses about the Spirit's guidance to the appropriate description.

1. The Spirit's guidance is evidence we are children of God.
2. The Spirit's guidance will keep us free from sin.
3. The Spirit's guidance points us to obey God's Word

A. Galatians 5:16
B. Ezekiel 36:27
C. Romans 8:14

In the space below, write down a few ideas about how you can recognize the Spirit's guidance. How do you discern between your own thoughts and His leading?

_____
_____
_____
_____

Which of the truths about the work of the Spirit is the most meaningful for you at this point in your life? Why?

_____
_____
_____
_____

What was one of the most helpful insights that you received during this lesson?

_____
_____
_____

The Holy Spirit convicts us, regenerates us, baptizes us, indwells us, empowers us, teaches us, prays for us, guides us.

WEEK 8, DAY 4: SINS AGAINST THE HOLY SPIRIT

On day five of this week's study, we will explore various blessings that our positive responses to the Holy Spirit bring about. But the Scripture also includes sober warnings that our negative responses bring about.

So, today we will examine four sins against the Holy Spirit. The first two are sins that only unbelievers can commit against the Spirit. The last two are sins that believers can commit against the Spirit.

Sins that unbelievers can commit against the Holy Spirit

1. Do not blaspheme against the Holy Spirit.

This is sometimes referred to as "the unpardonable sin."

> And I tell you, everyone who acknowledges me before men, the Son of Man also will acknowledge before the angels of God, but the one who denies me before men will be denied before the angels of God. And everyone who speaks a word against the Son of Man will be forgiven, but the one who blasphemes against the Holy Spirit will not be forgiven (Luke 12: 8-10). (See also Matthew 12:31-32 and Mark 3:29.)

Sincere followers of Jesus sometimes read these verses and others like them, and have asked themselves and their spiritual leaders, "Could I possibly be unforgiven? I can remember a time in my life when I said horrible things about God. Am I doomed?"

Blasphemy against the Holy Spirit is connected to rejecting the Person and work of Christ. It is attributing to the devil the work that the Spirit was doing through Jesus. Theologian Wayne Grudem looks at these verses in the context of the surrounding Scripture and writes, "Jesus is speaking about a sin that is not simply unbelief or rejection of Christ, but one that includes, (1) a clear knowledge of who Christ is and the power of the Holy Spirit working through Him, (2) a willful rejection about the facts about Christ that His opponents knew to be true, and (3) slanderously attributing the work of the Holy Spirit in Christ to be the power of Satan" (*Systematic Theology*, by Wayne Grudem, p.508).

In these cases, the person's hardened heart puts him beyond the reach of God's ordinary means of bringing forgiveness through Christ and His cross since he has rejected the very idea that the Spirit of God is working in and through Christ.

If a person has a desire to respond to the Person and work of Christ and His Spirit, then that is a sign that he or she has not committed the unpardonable sin. It is not possible for a person who has received Jesus Christ as personal Lord and Savior to commit the sin of blasphemy against the Holy Spirit.

2. Do not resist the Holy Spirit.

In the Bible, a follower of Jesus named Stephen was on trial before the Jewish religious leaders for his faith in Christ. He pointed out that their ancestors refused to take seriously the Spirit-inspired messages from the prophets that God had sent to them. Stephen challenged the religious leaders of his day by saying that they were resisting the Spirit by refusing to hear and heed the gospel message of the followers of Jesus.

You stiff-necked people, uncircumcised in heart and ears, you always resist the Holy Spirit. As your fathers did, so do you (Acts 7:51).

This is a sobering verse that ought to remind us to ask God for grace so that we can maintain soft, receptive hearts to the Spirit of God and to the Word of God.

Remember that it is the work of the Holy Spirit to regenerate a person so that they can respond to the Gospel of Christ. Our New Life in Christ is evidence that we are not resisting the Holy Spirit.

So, two sins that *unbelievers* commit against the Spirit are blaspheming and resisting Him. Next, we will turn our attention to two sins that *believers* can commit against the Spirit.

Sins that believers can commit against the Holy Spirit

The Holy Spirit may withdraw His blessing if He is not pleased by the situation He sees. "In the Old Testament, the Holy Spirit came mightily upon Samson several times (Judges 13:25; 14:6, 19; 15:14), but ultimately left him when he persisted in sin (Judges 16:20)" (*Systematic Theology*, by Wayne Grudem, p.647). We must be very careful not to offend the Spirit who loves us.

1.   Do not quench the Holy Spirit.

The word "quench" means "to put out" or "to put a damper on." Look up and highlight or underline 1 Thessalonians 5:19.

It might be helpful to remember that one of the symbols of the Holy Spirit is Fire. To quench the Holy Spirit is to put out the fire that He is seeking to kindle in your life. Fire goes out when the fuel supply diminishes. This is why we must stir up our souls by spending time in the Word of God, in prayer, in fellowship, and on mission. These habits keep the Spirit's fire stoked in our lives.

The Holy Spirit seeks to guide us. He inspires us with positive encouragement and direction. Quenching the Holy Spirit is failing to do what the Holy Spirit is encouraging you to do. It is the sin of omission. Willful sin quenches the Spirit.

We can quench the Spirit when we question, belittle, or block a fresh movement or method in worship, ministry, or mission.

Have you in any sense quenched the Spirit in your life? How so? Use the space below to describe how you have quenched the Holy Spirit.

_____

_____

_____

_____

2.   Do not grieve the Holy Spirit.

Remember that the Holy Spirit is a Person. And that means that He can be hurt or made sorrowful. Look up and highlight or underline Ephesians 4:30.

Grieving the Holy Spirit is only possible because of His love for us. "We may hurt or anger one who has no affection for us, but we can grieve only a person who loves us" (*The Holy Spirit,* by Billy Graham, p.186). We can hurt and wound the heart of the Holy Spirit. We can bring pain to Him by what we do.

In this case, it might be helpful for us to remember that a symbol of the Holy Spirit is a Dove. Remember that a dove rests on those who are humble. Whenever we engage in behavior that is hurtful to ourselves and others—in behavior that is clearly prohibited in the Scriptures—we grieve the Spirit. Although He will never leave or forsake us, His presence in our lives to bless us, like a dove, can fly away. We grieve the Spirit of God when we commit sins of comission—doing what He has taught us not to do.

Describe a time in your life when you grieved the Spirit of God and what you did to restore that relationship.

_____

_____

_____

_____

Billy Graham has written that the following words regarding the Holy Spirit have been a help to him: "Resist not His incoming; grieve not His indwelling; quench not His outgoing. Open to Him as the Incomer; please Him as the Indweller; obey Him as the Outgoer in His testimony of the things concerning Christ" (*The Holy Spirit,* by Billy Graham, p.192).

When we quench or grieve the Spirit, it is important for us to run again and again to the cross and to remind ourselves about the truths of the Gospel. We confess our sins. We remember that Jesus has died to forgive us.

In brokenness and in humility, we can quickly pray, "Please cleanse me, O Holy Spirit, for quenching and grieving You. Come and be the Fire within me so I can shine brightly for Christ. Come to me as a Dove to rest on me that I might feel Your approval and know Your blessing. May those times when I quench You and grieve You become less and less as I learn to obey You more and more. In Jesus' name, Amen."

Take some time right now and use this prayer above as a basis for your own. And then use the following words from a song written by Russell Fragar to seek more of the Spirit's influence in your life:

Holy Spirit rain down; rain down.
O Comforter and Friend, how we need Your touch again.
Holy Spirit rain down; rain down.
Let Your power fall; let Your voice be heard;
Come and change our lives as we stand on Your Word.
Holy Spirit rain down.

What was one of the most helpful insights that you received during this lesson?

_____

_____

_____

Without the Spirit of God we can do nothing.
We are as ships without wind or chariots without steeds.
Like branches without sap, we are withered.
Like coals without fire, we are useless. As an offering
without the sacrificial flame, we are unaccepted.
Charles Spurgeon - 19th Century Pastor

WEEK 8, DAY 5: LIFE IN THE SPIRIT

Think of a high-level performer that you admire and would like to emulate. It could be a business leader, an athlete, a vocalist, a musician, a painter, a spiritual leader, a business leader, or some figure in history. Do you have someone in mind? Write the name down in the space provided.

What if someone came to you and said, "We have developed a new surgical technique. We can put you on an operating table. We can cut you open and put inside you the abilities of (insert name here). You will still look like you. Your personality will still be intact. You will still be you. But you will now have the ability, the skill, and the talent of this high performer."

What would you do? If you really wanted to emulate that high-level performer, you might say, "Let's get on with the operation!"

So, the surgery is performed. You get up off the operating table. You look in the mirror. It's you! But when you begin to perform the task, you're now performing it at a whole new level. You can play the violin flawlessly. You can hit a 99 mph fastball. You can dance with the stars. You can . . . Well, you get the idea.

When people see you perform, they say, "Hey. It looks like you. But it sounds like/acts like/plays like (insert name here)."

In a similar way, this is what happens when the Holy Spirit comes to live inside us. God performs an operation on us. He cuts us open, as it were, and places inside us His very Spirit. We now have a new operating system. So, when we live out our lives, people should say, "It still looks like you. But you are acting a lot like Jesus Christ."

That is the way it is supposed to work. However, we know that something happens to detract us from displaying the characteristics of Christ.

Going back to our analogy, suppose all the talents, abilities, and skill of that other person indwells you. But one day you say, "I don't really feel like yielding control to the indwelling presence. I am going to call the shots today. I am going to display my own talents today." Immediately, your performance level would drop dramatically. You would no longer be living up. You would be living down.

In the same way, when we usurp the Spirit's control, we immediately stop displaying the characteristics of Christ. And people will say, "You not only look like the old you, but you are living like the old you, too."

So, our aim is to increasingly yield more and more control of our lives to the indwelling Spirit.

How do we do that? Scripture gives us 4 habits to develop regarding yielding control of our lives to the Spirit.

BE SPIRIT-MINDED.

What occupies your thought life? Where does your mind drift when you are day-dreaming?

Many followers of Christ miss out on the fullness of the Spirit because we do not bring our thoughts captive to Christ and His Spirit. Money, sex, and power often dominate our thoughts. We set our minds on ways to achieve pleasure and affluence. We are far too worldly-minded.

We have been called to be Spirit-minded. Look up and highlight or underline Romans 8:5.

How do we set our minds on the things of the Spirit? First, we must ask, "What are the things of the Spirit?" We can only give a partial listing here. Match the appropriate verse with the correct things of the Spirit.

1. Glorifying Jesus
2. The Word of God
3. The fruit of the Spirit
4. Witnessing
5. Prayer

A. 2 Timothy 3:16-17
B. John 16:14
C. Acts 1:8
D. Galatians 5:22-23
E. Ephesians 6:18

What are some other "things of the Spirit" that you can identify?

_____

_____

Don't allow your mind to be absent, vacant, empty, wandering. Neither should you allow your mind to be corrupted by the pollution in the world. Instead, our minds need to be occupied with things pertaining to the Holy Spirit.

BE SPIRIT-ENLIVENED.
There is no resurrection without a crucifixion. In order for you to have more and more life in the Spirit, some things in your life will have to die. Look up and highlight or underline Romans 8:13.

We see a negative and a positive here in Romans 8:13. To experience the fullness of life in the Spirit, we must put to death the sinful deeds of the body. The great spiritual leader John Owens said, "The choicest believers, who are assuredly freed from the condemning power of sin, ought yet to make it their business all their days to mortify the indwelling power of sin . . . Do you mortify? Do you make it your daily work? Be always at it whilst you live; cease not a day from this work; be killing sin or it will be killing you" (*Overcoming Sin and Temptation*, by John Owen, p.9).

Some have called this "radical amputation." Jesus said, *If you find that your eye is causing you to sin, pluck it out. If your right hand is causing you to sin, cut it off...* (See Matthew 5:29-30).

We must be creative in the ways we kill sin. A person with an alcohol problem stops going to bars and liquor stores. A person with a pornography problem either stops using the computer altogether or places the computer in a public place so that others can see what is being viewed. A person who struggles with pride willfully chooses to take the back seat, the lesser role, the longer line.

If, by the Spirit's power, we put to death the sinful deeds of the body, we will find ourselves experiencing increasing vibrancy of life through the Spirit. The killing of sin allows for the life of the Spirit.

What sins must you kill so the life of the Spirit will flow more freely in you?

_____

_____

_____

_____

BE SPIRIT-FILLED.

Being filled with the Spirit is not a one-time act. There is one indwelling of the Spirit, but many, many fillings! We must cultivate an ongoing relationship with the Holy Spirit. We must actively pursue the filling of the Holy Spirit. Why? We leak! Like a balloon with a hole in it, we lose the fullness of the Spirit when we sin.

Look up and highlight or underline Ephesians 5:18-21.

How does a person get drunk with wine? By drinking a lot of it! How, then, would a person be filled with the Spirit? By drinking in a lot of the Spirit's influence!

We must develop the practice of what some have called "spiritual breathing." As soon as you realize that you have sinned and that you are "leaking," exhale by confessing your sin to God. Then inhale by asking God to fill you with His Holy Spirit. Now, you might not feel different, but by faith, believe that God has answered your prayer. Step out in faith, obey the Lord, and watch God's Spirit bear His fruit (love, joy, peace . . .) in your life once again. Spiritual breathing is something you will have to do many, many times.

As you look carefully at the verses in the above paragraph from Ephesians 5, circle the participles—words that end in "-ing": addressing, singing, making melody, giving thanks, submitting.

Greek scholars discuss the way these participles function in these verses. They may be describing behaviors that are the *result* of being filled with the Spirit. They may be describing behaviors that *cause* the filling of the Spirit. The participles may be functioning in both ways, as both means and results.

Let's work with the idea that these participles may be causal. In other words, one way to increase your filling with the Spirit is to practice giving thanks always. With that in mind, evaluate your life on a scale of 1-10, 1 being low and 10 being high:

_____ I am regularly speaking to others using biblical and spiritual content.

_____ I have developed the skill of singing and making melody in my heart to the Lord.

_____ Throughout the day, I often find myself giving thanks to God.

_____ I gladly humble myself in submission to others and, when appropriate, follow their leadership and advice.

Which of these areas provide you with the greatest growth opportunity? In the space below, write down a few thoughts about some changes you can make in your life in order to grow in this area.

_____

_____

_____

_____

BE SPIRIT-LED.

Since the Holy Spirit is a Person who lives in you and knows you and your potential and giftedness intimately, it makes sense that He would lead you to be in just the right place at the right time over and over again and again. The Holy Spirit maintains a constant, loving interest in the details and outcomes of your life. He has an amazing plan for you.

Following His leadership, however, requires a special Holy Spirit sensitivity on your part. Look up and highlight or underline Galatians 5:16 and 25.

Ask God for a special sensitivity to the Holy Spirit. Ask God to teach you to hear His still, small voice. The Holy Spirit will give you inner promptings as He seeks to guide you through the decisions and details of daily living.

The Holy Spirit will never ask you to do anything that violates His Word. Promptings from the Holy Spirit must line up with the Bible. If a prompting doesn't reflect biblical principles, then maybe you're just dealing with indigestion! Be aware that the promptings of the Spirit might be challenging to religious traditionalists. If that happens, you're in good company . . . with Jesus!

Being sensitive to the Spirit's leading can be challenging. Francis Chan writes, "I struggle to always and actually keep in step with the Spirit moment by moment. To submit and give up everything is truly radical and terrifying. However, when I think deeply about it, walking in my own wisdom, contrary to the Spirit's leading, is even more frightful. Though I struggle, I know that ultimately I want nothing more than to live in total surrender and abandonment to the Spirit every moment I have left on this earth" (*Forgotten God*, by Francis Chan, p.126).

The Spirit may lead you to spontaneously wash the dinner dishes or vacuum the family room carpet. The Spirit may lead you to ask a co-worker, "How can I pray for you?" The Spirit may lead you to secretly pay for the meal for the needy-looking family sitting next to you in a restaurant. The Spirit may lead you to advance Christ's kingdom by moving to a different neighborhood, city, state, or country.

Being Spirit-led—staying in step with the Spirit—is one of the key habits that will make your relationship with God an exciting, dynamic, interesting, amazing, grace-filled adventure.

What if you fail to stay in step with the Spirit? That's when you must remember the gospel. If you misunderstand the Holy Spirit's prompting or disobey it, then confess your failure to God. He is faithful to forgive (1 John 1:9). Your failure is not final. Remember that you are a disciple—someone who is learning to follow Jesus more faithfully. The Lord knows you're still being trained. That's why He sent the Holy Spirit to be your Teacher.

159

Share a story about a time when you sensed the Spirit was prompting you. How difficult was it for you to stay in step with the Spirit?

_____

_____

_____

_____

For the next week or so, keep a list of the times you sense the Spirit prompting you. This will help you learn to be sensitive to the Spirit. It will also strengthen your resolve to be obedient to God's guidance.

Let's close our week's study in prayer. Spend a few minutes inviting the Holy Spirit to be prominent in your life. Simply pray the words of an old song. Pray them through one time as written. Then, pray them through using your own words.

> *Spirit of the living God,*
> *Fall afresh on me.*
> *Break me, melt me,*
> *Mold me, fill me.*
> *Spirit of the living God,*
> *Fall afresh on me.*

What was one of the most helpful insights that you received during this lesson?

_____

_____

_____

We are either under the influence of the flesh, the world, a substance, or the Spirit of God. Being under the influence of the Holy Spirit produces spiritual and God-pleasing fruit. All other influences lead to rotten and worthless fruit.
Chad Allen, Lead Pastor - Cuyahoga Valley Church

Week 9

SPIRITUAL GIFTS:
TAKING SHAPE
AS A SERVANT

MEMORY VERSE

Now there are varieties of gifts, but the same Spirit; and there are varieties of service, but the same Lord; and there are varieties of activities, but it is the same God who empowers them all in everyone. To each is given the manifestation of the Spirit for the common good. 1 Corinthians 12:4-7

WEEK 9, DAY 1: AN INTRODUCTION TO SPIRITUAL GIFTS

At CVC, our strategy for inviting people to New Life in Christ is:

- Worship
- Groups
- Serve

We believe that if we will all engage in these 3 activities and environments as regular rhythms in our lives then we will experience more and more New Life in Christ. We will learn more and more to Live New. Worship—Groups—Serve. It's the way we believe we will bear more and more of the Fruit of New Life.

This week's new series study on spiritual gifts is fuel for the third piece—the Serve part—of our strategy.

As we work through our study in Week 3, be asking yourself some questions:

- Do I really believe that I am gifted?
- What are the spiritual gifts?
- What is my spiritual gift?
- Why has God given it to me?
- What happens when I use it?
- What happens if I don't?
- How can using my gift help me and help others?

You are fearfully and wonderfully made.

Look up and highlight or underline Psalm 139:13-16.

Think about how these verses apply to you. The person you are was "formed," "knitted," and "woven" by God in your mother's womb. You came into this world shaped by God.
Match the amazing truths about you with the appropriate verse.

1. I am fearfully and wonderfully made.
2. I am the apple of God's eye.
3. The Lord rejoices over me and exults over me.
4. My name is engraved on the palms of His hands.
5. I am God's workmanship, created for good works.

A. Isaiah 49:16
B. Zephaniah 3:17
C. Ephesians 2:10
D. Psalm 139:13-16
E. Psalm 17:8

Now, read these truths about you out loud. On a scale of 1-10 (10 being high), how much do you feel these truths to be true about you?

_____

How might you live differently if you fully believed that as God's beloved child you were fearfully and wonderfully made?

_____
_____
_____

And when His Holy Spirit entered your life, He brought with Him some special gifts for you.

YOU ARE GIFTED.
You are gifted. Some people might disagree with that statement. That's because we sometimes think of being gifted as being extraordinarily talented. We put excellent learners in gifted classes. We think of Mozart or Bono as gifted musicians. We say that Daniel-Day Lewis is a gifted actor. All of that is true. But, so is the statement, "You are gifted." Look up and highlight or underline 1 Peter 4:10.

Now, based on 1 Peter 4:10, answer the following questions.

Who has received a gift?

_____

What are we to do with the gift?

_____

"Each" means every believer—every Christian. So, you can't say,

"I don't have anything worthwhile to offer." If you truly know Jesus as your Lord and Savior—if you are truly a Christ-follower, then you are uniquely gifted to serve Him.   Everyone who has a real relationship with Jesus has at least one spiritual gift. Probably more than one.

The word for "gift" is closely related to the word for "grace." They are in the same word family in the Greek language. You may not think so, but you have charisma. The word for grace is "charis" and the word for gift is "charisma." Both have to do with something undeserved that is freely given by God to us. Your spiritual gift is undeserved and unearned.

That means you can't say, "Look at me. Look at what I can do. I'm somebody special." No, your gift is an unearned, undeserved grace gift. And you can't say, "Look at me. Look at what I cannot do. I'm no one special." No, you have an unearned, undeserved gift. It's a vital part of what makes you who you are. You have in you a gift or gifts that God has given you.

SPIRITUAL GIFTS DEFINED

God wants all believers to be familiar with some vital truths about true spirituality. Look up and highlight or underline 1 Corinthians 12:1.

The spiritual leader, Paul, who wrote these words is saying, "I do not want you to be unaware, ignorant, or unintelligent about these spiritual things. Paul used this phrase when he wanted to say something to correct some bad thinking about a topic. No one wants to be an uninformed, ignorant, unintelligent follower of Christ, right? That's why we must understand the truths about spiritual gifts.

Dr. Howard Hendricks was a professor for over 50 years at Dallas Theological Seminary who said, "Trying to minister without first understanding how God has gifted you is like spinning your wheels on an icy road—a lot of noise and smoke but little progress." Let's not be "uninformed" about our gifts.

A spiritual gift is a supernatural ability activated and empowered by the Holy Spirit that enables a believer to build up the body of Christ in a unique way.

Let's break down this definition:

What do you think it means that a spiritual gift is a <u>supernatural</u> ability?

_____

_____

_____

What do you think it means that the Holy Spirit activates spiritual gifts?

_____
_____
_____

What do you think it means that the Holy Spirit empowers spiritual gifts?

_____
_____
_____

What do you think it means that spiritual gifts are for believers?

_____
_____
_____

What do you think it means that spiritual gifts are to build up the body of Christ?

_____
_____
_____

What do you think it means that believers use their spiritual gifts in a unique way?

_____
_____
_____

Spiritual gifts are special abilities given by the Holy Spirit to every believer according to God's grace to be used to serve others and, therefore, build up the body of Christ. Every believer has at least one gift (1 Peter 4:10). No one has them all (1 Corinthians 7:7). It is important not to neglect your gift (1 Timothy 4:14).

Have you ever taken a spiritual gifts assessment or have any idea what your spiritual gifts might be?

Do you know what your spiritual gifts are?

Each of us has what Pastor Rick Warren has called our SHAPE (explained in more detail in Week 9, Lesson 3.). It's as much a part of us as our fingerprints. It's who we are, how we operate, and it won't go away. Most of us are not aware of it, even though it is what is in operation when we succeed in life. It is God's gift to each of us.

It is a mix of abilities, preferences, passions, and motivations that produces successful, productive outcomes for the glory of God.

Understanding and embracing your giftedness is the key to who you are and what God is calling you to do. God has a purpose for you. You have a reason for being. Your mission is to discover and develop what is already at work in you for the glory of God.

Close this day's time by praising God that you are fearfully and wonderfully made and that He has gifted you to serve Him. Ask Him for wisdom to discover, develop, and use your spiritual gifts.

What was one of the most helpful insights that you received during this lesson?

_____

_____

_____

WEEK 9, DAY 2: WHAT ARE THE SPIRITUAL GIFTS?

It's likely that God has not necessarily provided us with an exhaustive list of gifts in the Scriptures. We see a smattering of gifts listed in several passages, but that doesn't mean they are the *only* ones God has made available. But we can confidently interact with the ones He has made known.

As we explore the lists of spiritual gifts today, remember the following "don'ts":

- Don't confuse spiritual gifts with natural talents. For example, singing is a talent, not a spiritual gift. But singing might be the context for the exercise of the spiritual gift of encouragement.
- Don't confuse spiritual gifts with the fruit of the Spirit (Galatians 5:22-23). Every Christian is to bear all the fruit of the Spirit like love, joy, and peace. The fruit of the Spirit is the context out of which the gifts of the Spirit are to operate.
- Don't confuse spiritual gifts with positions within the church. A church has leaders called Pastors with a big "P" but also needs many people functioning as pastors (shepherds) with a little "p." Many people with the gift of pastoring might not be on the Pastoral staff of the church. Instead, they might exercise their gift of shepherding by being LifeGroup leaders.
- Don't confuse spiritual gifts with spiritual disciplines like prayer, Bible intake, fasting, serving, fellowshipping, or worshiping. Every Christian is to practice all the spiritual disciplines. But not every Christ-follower has all the spiritual gifts.

Look up and list the spiritual gifts mentioned in the following passages:

Romans 12:6-8 (7 gifts mentioned)

_____

_____

1 Corinthians 12:8-10 (9 gifts mentioned)

_____

_____

1 Corinthians 12:28 (8 gifts mentioned)

_____

_____

Ephesians 4:11 (5 gifts mentioned)

_____

_____

Note that some gifts appear several times in more than one passage. After you list the gifts, circle the ones that you feel might be yours.

Having gifts that differ according to the grace given to us, let us use them: if prophecy, in proportion to our faith; if service, in our serving; the one who teaches, in his teaching; the one who exhorts, in his exhortation; the one who contributes, in generosity; the one who leads, with zeal; the one who does acts of mercy, with cheerfulness (Romans 12:6-8).

Thoughts or questions:

_____
_____
_____

For to one is given through the Spirit the utterance of wisdom, and to another the utterance of knowledge according to the same Spirit, to another faith by the same Spirit, to another gifts of healing by the one Spirit, to another the working of miracles, to another prophecy, to another the ability to distinguish between spirits, to another various kinds of tongues, to another the interpretation of tongues (1 Corinthians 12:8-10).

Thoughts or questions:

_____
_____
_____

And God has appointed in the church first apostles, second prophets, third teachers, then miracles, then gifts of healing, helping, administrating, and various kinds of tongues (1 Corinthians 12:28-30).

Thoughts or questions:

_____
_____
_____

And He gave the apostles, the prophets, the evangelists, the shepherds and teachers, to equip the saints for the work of ministry, for building up the body of Christ (Ephesians 4:11-12).

Thoughts or questions:

_____

_____

_____

We're going to experience a little "Definition Feast." Here's a very brief overview of the gifts mentioned in 1 Corinthians 12, Romans 12, and Ephesians 4.

Wisdom is the supernatural ability to put knowledge to work. It's an incredible application of applying spiritual insight to specific situations. It's effectively applying God's Word.

Knowledge is the supernatural ability to perceive and systematize the great facts that God has given in His Word.

Faith is the supernatural ability to believe God to supply great needs. It is seeing what needs to be done and trusting God to do it even though it looks impossible.

Healing is a supernatural ability to help people experience restoration over physical illnesses or mental and emotional bondage. Prayers for people's healing are answered frequently.

Miracles is the miraculous manifestation of God's power beyond natural laws. This could include healing, supernatural intervention, miraculous provision for needs, etc.

Prophecy is not so much accurate predictions of the future. It is boldly and clearly telling something that God has spontaneously brought to mind or impressed on the heart. Usually, it includes an unplanned and urgent revelation from God proclaiming truth so that it becomes very clear, vital, piercing, and compelling.

Discernment is the supernatural ability to recognize truth from falsehood, to detect what is genuine from what is counterfeit, to distinguish what is of God from what is demonically influenced.

Tongues is the supernatural speaking of a language unknown by the speaker. It could be a human language or an angelic language. The Greek word is "_glossa_" which means tongue or language. (More details and guidelines for the use of this gift can be found in 1 Corinthians 14.)

Interpretation is the supernatural ability to hear someone speaking in tongues and to translate it so the meaning can be known by others. (More details and guidelines for the use of this gift can be found in 1 Corinthians 14.)

Apostle is the supernatural ability to be a pioneer and messenger of Christ who courageously goes out to start new ministries, missions, organizations, or churches. (Note: This is a little "a" gifting to be distinguished from the capital "A" office, someone who (1) had seen Jesus after His resurrection, an eyewitness, and (2) was commissioned by Christ Himself. There are no more capital "A" Apostles.)

Teacher is the supernatural ability to engage in the explanation and application of God's Word, to communicate and clarify the details and truths of God's Word for others to learn and apply.

Helps is the supernatural ability to bring immediate support and assistance to another in order to relieve a pressing burden. This person is energized by coming alongside to assist and support others.

Administration is the supernatural ability to organize, manage, and give direction toward the accomplishment of specific goals.

Serving is the supernatural ability to joyfully perform any task in such a way that it strengthens and encourages others. This person desires to help accomplish tasks in practical ways.

Encouraging is the supernatural ability to come alongside others, to draw close to them, and to lift them up in time of need with counsel, encouragement, and exhortation.

Contributing/Giving is the supernatural ability to joyfully and generously share one's material resources without selfish motives.

Leadership is the supernatural ability to guide, direct, or lead others.

Mercy is the supernatural ability to show practical and compassionate love to relieve the physical suffering of the hurting, the lowly, the sick, the poor, and the aged.

Evangelist is the supernatural ability to present the gospel with exceptional clarity and effectiveness to the unsaved so they respond with saving faith.

Pastor/teacher is the supernatural capacity to provide spiritual leadership, nurturing, and care for God's people. This person is usually enabled to preach and teach the Word of God with great effectiveness. This person delights to take responsibility for the spiritual welfare of a body of believers.

For application:
Suppose you are out to dinner with a group of friends. The server trips and spills your meal all over the floor right in front of your table. How might the various gifts be used?

Helps gets up and starts to clean up the mess on the floor.
Service notices the server's shoelace is untied and starts to tie it.
Mercy grabs a chair for the server to sit down for a few minutes to collect himself.
Encouragement starts to cheer up the server.
Giving offers to pay for the lost meal.
Administration organizes everyone to resolve the problem quickly and without confusion.

Teaching points out the reason why the accident happened.

Wisdom offers suggestions to avoid the accident in the future.

Discernment senses a sinister influence in the situation.

Faith helps everyone see that it will never happen again.

Leadership tells the manager about the hazard that they need to fix on the floor.

Pastor/Teacher consoles the surrounding people and uses the incident as an object lesson to help warn others about how easy it is to fall when our plates are full.

As you read through these definitions, certain ones may have stood out to you. You might be thinking, "I wonder if that's me?" Take some time to scan the list of gifts. Which 3-4 of these gifts do you think might be yours? Write them in the space below.

_____

_____

_____

_____

We think it is prudent at this point to make a statement about the public expression of the supernatural sign gifts (miracles, tongues, interpretation, and healing). While we do not believe, as some Christians do, that these gifts have ceased for today's church, we are not a body where the expression of these gifts is emphasized.

Since in our services we are attempting to communicate clearly to those who are without Christ, we are sensitive to the fact that the public expression of the supernatural sign gifts often makes lost people feel uncomfortable and may lead them to focus on our methods of worship, rather than the Savior Himself. 1 Corinthians 14:23 makes the point: *If the whole church assembles together and all speak in tongues, and ungifted men or unbelievers enter, will they not say that you are mad?*

Our position on the sign gifts is "seek not, forbid not" (1 Corinthians 12:31 and 14:39). We will not permit controversy concerning the gifts of the Spirit to bring division to CVC. (For a fuller understanding on the position of CVC, please read chapter 13 of Billy Graham's book, *The Holy Spirit*.)

WHAT GIFTS MIGHT YOU HAVE?

On our church's website—http://www.cvconline.org/spiritual-gifts-inventory/—you will find a "Spiritual Gifts Inventory." It is a 96-statement exercise with each statement giving you four choices. Select the "truest" choice for you for each statement. Follow the instructions for scoring the exercise.

Before you work your way through the inventory, keep the following questions in mind, based on the Scriptures indicated:

- Does my selection reflect a sane and sober estimate of my capabilities? Can I really do this thing (Romans 12:3)?

- Does my selection reflect my passion? Do I love doing what is indicated? This is crucial (Ecclesiastes 3:13; 9:10).
- Does my selection reflect things I do with the excellence God deserves? Remember Who it is you are serving (Colossians 3:23-24).

Now, proceed to work your way through the inventory. Your answers will be recorded if you use the website, so you can click where it is indicated to learn your results.

What gifts are indicated as a result of the inventory?

List the top 3 below.

_____

_____

_____

Were there any surprises? Did the gifts from the inventory match the gifts you had circled or had listed earlier after you read the definitions?

_____

_____

_____

As you close your time today, underline the commands in the following 2 verses.

Having gifts that differ according to the grace given us, let us use them (Romans 12:6).

As each has received a gift, use it to serve one another, as good stewards of God's varied grace (1 Peter 4:10).

Our human bodies are fascinating organic machines. We have different body parts that are unique in function, but are designed to work together in harmony. The same is true in the body of Christ. All our different gifts need to be appreciated and valued. The diversity that God has given us strengthens us! We all approach life and the situations of life differently.

Are you willing to invest these gifts at CVC?

☐ Yes ☐ No ☐ Maybe ☐ I don't know.

CVC's website contains a page offering various opportunities to serve. If after reviewing the various opportunities you find you have questions, feel free to send your inquiry via e-mail to connect@cvconline.org.

We don't always see a one-to-one correlation between a particular serving opportunity and a particular spiritual gift. For example, we wouldn't say that a LifeGroup leader absolutely must have the gift of teaching to be a LifeGroup leader. Several of the gifts might equip a LifeGroup leader to lead a group well. So, don't confuse specific spiritual gifts with particular positions within the church. Someone with the gift of shepherding might not be the Pastor of the church. Instead, they might exercise their gift of shepherding by being a LifeGroup leader.

However, our spiritual gifts do give us a general sense of direction to exercise our gifts in specific ministries.

Match the spiritual gifts on the left side of the page with the ministry on the right side of the page. Note: More than one gift may be useful in a particular ministry.

1.	Shepherding	A. Greeter
2.	Encouragement	B. LifeGroup Leader
3.	Teaching	C. Special Needs Ministry
4.	Hospitality	D. Stewardship Team
5.	Helps	E. Care Ministry
6.	Service	F. LifeGroup Leader Coach
7.	Mercy	G. Ministry or Event Organizer
8.	Administration	H. Sound Technician

- Someone with the gift(s) of shepherding, encouragement, and/or teaching might be an excellent LifeGroup leader in children, youth, or adult ministries.
- A greeter might have the gift of hospitality.
- A sound technician could have the gift of helps or service.
- A special needs leader may perhaps have the gift of mercy.
- A person on a team to organize a ministry or event can have the gift of administration.

Diversity is beautiful. We are unique in our function so we can serve the Lord in unity for the common good of the Body of Christ.

Based on what you have learned today about your spiritual gifts, compose a prayer to God that expresses your desire to develop and use your gifts.

_____
_____
_____
_____
_____

What was one of the most helpful insights that you received during this lesson?

_____
_____
_____

WEEK 9, DAY 3: DISCOVERING YOUR SHAPE

So far you have learned that you are gifted and have a function to fulfill in the Body of Christ. Discovering that function is crucial to what God is calling you to be and do. Using the analogy of the human body, it's important to know if you are an ear, an arm, a leg or some other part of the body.

**God made you _on_ purpose
for His purpose.**

A SANE ESTIMATE

Jesus Christ is the Head of His body, the church (Colossians 1:18). This means we take our cues from Christ who gives us our gifts to be used as He decides (1 Corinthians 12:18). That means that we are to discover and use the gifts God has given us. This requires a wise, sound, common-sense approach to where and how we will invest our lives in service through the church. Look up and highlight or underline Romans 12:3.

J.B. Phillips' translation says, _Try to have a sane estimate of your capabilities._ In Romans 12:1-2 Paul has just written about consecrating ourselves to God. He now adds a word about sober judgment. A person may want to be a doctor in service to God, but if he/she gets failing marks in biology and chemistry, he/she should rethink medicine as a calling. Someone might love music, but that doesn't make him/her a musician. (One man said, "I can carry a tune; I just can't unload it!")

In this lesson, we will explore other tools to help you gain a sane estimate of your capabilities.

Don't be disappointed if what you have discovered so far hasn't helped you locate your particular place of ministry in the Body of Christ. Just remember that God gave you the gifts and He has a place for you in His Body. Most of what we've looked at up to this point has to do with working with people and ideas. You may be gifted with working with things—making things, fixing things, or making things work. Or, you may be great at organizing and managing groups.

Remember, Paul tells us that the "Body does not consist of one member but of many." What you are gifted to do is from God and He has a place for you.

YOUR SHAPE

Key questions every spiritually gifted believer should ask is: "What body part am I? How has God shaped me?" Our S.H.A.P.E. is determined by:

S   Spiritual Gifts (God's gifting in your life)
H   Heart (what you are passionate about)
A   Abilities (what you are good at)
P   Personality (how God has made you)
E   Experiences (what you have learned in life)

Your ministry will be most effective, fulfilling, and fun when you are using your . . .

> Spiritual gift in the area of your
>> Heart's desire, and using your
>>> Abilities in a way that best expresses your
>>>> Personality and
>>>>> Experiences.

Today, we will explore your spiritual gifts and heart. Tomorrow, we will survey your abilities, personality, and experiences.

S – SPIRITUAL GIFTS

Identifying your spiritual gifts require more than simply locating the gift lists in your Bible, reading the definitions, and taking an inventory. To identify your gift or gifts, you should . . .

- Explore the possibilities. We did this in our study on Day 2. You might want to do a quick review of the results of your study and inventory.
- Experiment with as many as you can. This will take time. Simply volunteer. Try serving for 3-6 months on a "try-before-you-buy" basis. You might need to help out in a variety of ministries over a period of several months and even a few years before you become fairly certain about the spiritual gifts God has given you.

What ministries in the church do you think you might want to try?

_____

_____

_____

- Examine your feelings. God will energize you as you exercise your spiritual gift. If you are well-rested and spiritually healthy, but find yourself dreading a ministry opportunity, then that might be a strong indicator that you are serving outside your giftedness. If you are unusually depleted or drained after serving, then you probably need to experiment with another option. God wants us to be rejuvenated and invigorated when we use the gifts He's given us. When we exert ourselves in a ministry that matches our giftedness, it will be a "good tired."
- Evaluate your effectiveness. Serving according to your giftedness will bear fruit. You might not see as much fruit as you would like to see. But you will see some. If a person thinks he has the gift of teaching and the class grows from 12 to 2 in a matter of a few weeks, then maybe he should explore another option. People actually feel encouraged after spending time with a person with the gift of mercy. People really experience guidance and care from someone with the gift of pastoring. People truly follow someone with the gift of leadership.
- Expect confirmation from the body of Christ. If you are serving in your area of giftedness, then people in the church will encourage you, thank you, and help you. If positive feelings, effectiveness, and confirmation are lacking, then experiment with another gift and ministry.

Have you experimented with serving in the past? If so, use the space below to describe your feelings, effectiveness, and confirmation from others.

_____

_____

_____

Remember that the identification of your spiritual gift is a process, not an event. It's easier to discover your gift through ministry than to discover your ministry through your gift.

H – HEART
The Bible uses the term "heart" to represent the center of your motivation, desires, and inclinations.

Your heart determines . . .

- Why you say the things you do. *For out of the abundance of the heart the mouth speaks* (Matthew 12:34).
- Why you act the way you do. *Keep your heart with all vigilance, for from it flow the springs of life* (Proverbs 4:23).

Think of people who obviously have a heart for what they are doing. Bono has a heart for fighting against poverty, hunger, and injustice. Billy and Franklin Graham have a heart to reach the lost for Christ. Mother Teresa had a heart for the needy. Pastor Lee of South Korea, about whom the movie "Drop Box" was made, had a heart for abandoned babies.

Spiritual gifts direct us in *what* to do. Heart directs us *where* to do it.

TO TAKE A SPIRITUAL EKG:
Look at your past accomplishments. For example, think about your accomplishments during your grade school years, your teen years, during your college or early career years. List some of your accomplishments below.

_____

_____

_____

Dare to dream.   Ask yourself a series of questions: "If I could not fail, what would I do to make a difference?"

Complete the sentences:

At the end of my life, I'd love to be able to look back and know that I had done something about

_____

What I would most like to do for others is

_____

Listen for your own heartbeat. What conversation would keep you talking late into the night? If someone were to mention your name to a group of your friends, what would they say you were really interested in or passionate about?

_____
_____
_____

What gives you a sense of accomplishment and joy? Arthur Miller, an expert in helping people find their calling in life, encourages people to think through the things they have done in life that brought them a strong sense of delight and satisfaction. This indicates things we are good at and love to do. It highlights our strengths. It's our "motivational thrust." The sense of joy we gain in a task well done is God's pay-off for doing what He's called us to do.

Make a list of 7 accomplishments that brought you joy, a sense of real satisfaction. Put a name to that sense of accomplishment—like "I overcame great odds," or "I led the charge," or "I met a real need in someone's life."

_____
_____
_____
_____
_____
_____
_____

The people I would like to help most are:

- ☐ Infants
- ☐ Youth
- ☐ Teen moms
- ☐ Singles
- ☐ Divorced
- ☐ Young marrieds
- ☐ Parents
- ☐ Homeless
- ☐ Elderly
- ☐ Prisoners
- ☐ Hospitalized
- ☐ Business men and women
- ☐ Grieving

- ☐ Children
- ☐ College students
- ☐ Single parents
- ☐ Widowed
- ☐ Career women
- ☐ Refugees
- ☐ Empty nesters
- ☐ Unemployed
- ☐ Disabled
- ☐ Poor
- ☐ Underemployed
- ☐ Orphans
- ☐ Others: _____

The issues or causes I feel strongly about are:

☐ Environment	☐ Child care
☐ Marriage	☐ Discipleship
☐ AIDS	☐ Politics
☐ Violence	☐ Injustice
☐ Racism	☐ Education
☐ Addictions	☐ International
☐ Economic	☐ Reaching the lost
☐ Technology	☐ Health care
☐ Poverty	☐ Family
☐ Abortion	☐ Hunger
☐ Literacy	☐ The Church
☐ Slavery	☐ Special Needs
☐ Adoption	☐ Others: _____

What was one of the most helpful insights that you received during this lesson?

_____

_____

WEEK 9, DAY 4: DISCOVERING YOUR SHAPE (CONTINUED)
Let's review. Your personal ministry will be most effective, fulfilling, and fun when you are using your . . .

> Spiritual gift in the area of your
>> Heart's desire, and using your
>>> Abilities in a way that best expresses your
>>>> Personality and
>>>>> Experiences.

Yesterday, we explored your spiritual gifts and heart. Today, we will survey your abilities, personality, and experiences.

A – ABILITIES
God, in His creative wisdom, has showered His grace on all people. Each person has been granted various natural talents, abilities, and skills as an opportunity to glorify his/her Creator. Both Christians and unbelievers share in this common grace.

Our natural talents, abilities, and skills can be developed through education and experience. These can be leveraged in combination with our spiritual gifts so that we accomplish *far more abundantly than all that we ask or think* (Ephesians 3:20).

Check the abilities below that you think you may have. Note others that may not be listed:

- ☐ Entertaining ability: to perform, act, dance, speak, do magic
- ☐ Recruiting ability: to enlist and motivate people to get involved
- ☐ Interviewing ability: to discover what others are really like
- ☐ Researching ability: to read, gather information, collect data
- ☐ Artistic ability: to conceptualize, picture, draw, paint, photograph, or make renderings
- ☐ Graphics ability: to lay out, design, create visual displays or banners
- ☐ Evaluating ability: to analyze data and draw conclusions
- ☐ Planning ability: to strategize, design, and organize programs and events
- ☐ Managing ability: to supervise people to accomplish a task or event and coordinate the details involved
- ☐ Counseling ability: to listen, encourage, and guide with sensitivity
- ☐ Teaching ability: to explain, train, demonstrate, tutor
- ☐ Writing ability: to write articles, letters, books
- ☐ Editing ability: to proofread or rewrite
- ☐ Promoting ability: to advertise or promote events and activities
- ☐ Repairing ability: to fix, restore, maintain
- ☐ Feeding ability: to create meals for large or small groups
- ☐ Recall ability: to remember or recall names and faces
- ☐ Mechanical operating ability: to operate equipment, tools, or machines
- ☐ Resourceful ability: to search out and find inexpensive materials or sources needed
- ☐ Counting ability: to work with numbers, data, or money

- ☐ Classifying ability: to systematize and file books, data, records, and materials so they can be retrieved easily
- ☐ Public Relations ability: to handle complaints and unhappy customers with care and courtesy
- ☐ Welcoming ability: to convey warmth, and develop rapport, making others feel comfortable
- ☐ Composing ability: to write music or lyrics
- ☐ Landscaping ability: to do gardening and work with plants
- ☐ Decorating ability: to beautify a setting for a special event
- ☐ Other abilities: _____

_____

How can you see yourself investing this ability in the life of the church?

_____

_____

P – PERSONALITY

Your personal style is God-given. There is no right or wrong personal style. Personal style answers the "how" question.

Two elements of your personal style are how you are *energized* and how you are *organized*.

How are you energized? Are you task-oriented—energized by doing things? Or are you people-oriented— energized by interacting with people? If you are task-oriented, then the primary content of your ministry should be accomplishing tasks that serve people. The primary focus of your ministry should be on getting the job done. If you are people-oriented, then the primary content of your ministry should be direct people interaction. The primary focus of your ministry should be on relational issues.

How are you organized? Are you an unstructured person who prefers options and flexibility? Or are you a structured person who prefers to plan and bring order to life? If you are unstructured, then your ministry position should be *generally* described. Your relationships with others should be spontaneous. If you are structured, then your ministry position should be *clearly* described. Your relationships with others should be consistent.

This way of looking at our personality preferences provide us with four personal style quadrants.

1. Task/unstructured. You should consider a ministry position that needs you to fulfill a wide variety of responsibilities.
2. Task/structured. You should consider the kind of ministry position that allows you to know clearly what the goals are and how the task is to be accomplished.
3. People/unstructured. You should consider the kind of ministry position that gives you the freedom to respond to people spontaneously.
4. People/structured. You should consider the kind of ministry position that will enable you to interact with people in a more stable and defined setting.

Please put a double circle around the number that you think best describes you. Place a single circle around the one that you think describes you second-best.

Note: *Personal style explains* our behavior, but it doesn't excuse it!

To know more regarding your personal style, you may want to visit a DISC personality assessment link.

E – EXPERIENCES

And we know that for those who love God all things work together for good, for those who are called according to his purpose (Romans 8:28).

I want you to know, brothers, that what has happened to me has really served to advance the gospel (Philippians 1:12).

One of the most overlooked factors in determining the ministry God has for you is your past experience, particularly the hurts and problems you've overcome with God's help. Since our greatest life messages come out of our weaknesses, not our strengths, you should pay close attention to what you've learned in the "school of hard knocks."

God never wastes a hurt. He wants you to be open to ministering to people who are going through what you've already been through.

Praise be to the God and Father of our Lord Jesus Christ, the Father of compassion and the God of all comfort, who comforts us in all our troubles, so that we can comfort those in any trouble with the comfort we ourselves have received from God (2 Corinthians 1:3,4).

In the space provided, record the following experiences . . .

Your Educational Experiences: What were your favorite subjects in school? Where have you gone to school? What did you study?

_____
_____
_____
_____

Your Vocational Experiences: What have been some significant and relevant experiences as you consider your job history?

_____
_____
_____

Your Ministry Experiences: Where and how have you served in the past?

_____
_____
_____

Your Painful Experiences: What are the problems, hurts, trials—that God has used to shape you, grow you, teach you?

_____
_____
_____
_____
_____
_____

Now, spend some time in prayer asking God for clarity and focus. Use the following as a guide for your prayer:

Lord, I know You made me on purpose for Your purpose. I know I have a unique contribution to make in building Your Kingdom. Please show me my SHAPE. Because my time on earth is so limited, I want to serve You in the most strategic and fruitful way possible. Help me invest my time, my talent, and my treasure to the best of my ability. Give me clarity concerning my SHAPE so I can love, serve, and please You with all my heart, soul, mind, and strength. In Jesus' name, Amen.

Use the following space to create a summary for what you have discovered about yourself over the last few days. You will use this summary as you consult with your LifeGroup leader about being placed in a volunteer position in the life of CVC.

My top 3 spiritual gifts are:

1. _____
2. _____
3. _____

I have a heart for:

_____
_____

My top 3 abilities I feel God may want me to use are:

1. _____
2. _____
3. _____

My personal style is:

_____

_____

My top 3 experiences that I believe God may want me to leverage for Him are:

1. _____
2. _____
3. _____

Please write an email, send a text, or make a phone call to set up an appointment with your LifeGroup leader to pray over and discuss your next step.

What was one of the most helpful insights that you received during this lesson?

_____

_____

_____

WEEK 9, DAY 5: GIFTS FOR THE BENEFIT OF THE BODY

Sometimes, people call those on the pastoral staff their "ministers." A wise staff member won't let anyone introduce "the" minister. Staff members are ministers, but not "the" minister. We're all ministers. Every follower of Jesus is supposed to use his/her gifts to minister to others in the body of Christ.

Some of us choose a church like we choose a cruise line, "What's comfortable for me?" We look for a church and ask, "How can this church serve me and my family?" That's understandable. And our leaders pray and serve so that there is something good at CVC for you.

But we have to ask another question that's even more important. We need to choose a church like it's a battleship. We agree on the mission, the vision, the values, and the strategy. And then everyone plays his/her part.

We must learn to ask, "What can I do to serve others at this church?" We have to move from a consumer-centered faith to a Christ-centered faith.

We ask, "How can I serve?" and "How can I help?" That's what makes us like Jesus. Look up and highlight or underline Matthew 20:26-28.

You want to be like Jesus? Serve others.

You might be thinking, "I've tried serving. I served until I was drained dry. I'll never do that again." That's not how it should be. We don't want the few serving the many. We want the many serving the many.

If every person serves, then the burden won't be overwhelming for anyone. No one person has *all* the gifts. No one has *no* gift. We need each other.

One of the most unloving things we can do as believers is to neglect the use of our gift. It cripples the church when people say, "It seems like they don't really need me. Everything is getting done pretty well."

In the space below, describe what damage can occur in an organization with that kind of thinking.

_____

_____

_____

You might be failing to realize that some people are doing too much and they are on the edge of burnout. When you fail to live out your responsibility, then you aren't loving the person who has to fill in for you while you sit and soak it in.

No one should have too much to do. No one should have nothing to do.

YOUR GIFTS AND GOD'S COMMUNITY

We Americans tend to be individualists. Our typical western hero is the Lone Ranger. We are the champions of individual rights. We own personal computers. And when we read the Bible we think in very individual terms. But often the "you" in the Bible is plural.

Day 1's study began by saying, "You are gifted." But the gifting is not primarily for you. The subject of spiritual gifts must be understood in the context of the Christian community or the Body of Christ.

Paul makes this very clear in his first letter to the church in Corinth. He is writing to a deeply divided church. They are divided socially, theologically, and morally. They are even taking one another to court. Early in the letter, Paul makes reference to the fact that they are not "lacking in any gift" (1 Corinthians 1:7). But these spiritual gifts became a source of contention and superiority among them. They were grading each other spiritually on the basis of who had which gifts. It was as if they were saying, "If you don't have my gifts, you are a second-class citizen of the Kingdom of God."

Read 1 Corinthians 12:21-26.

In the space below, write down some thoughts about the purpose of spiritual gifts in the body of Christ.

_____

_____

_____

Now, read 1 Corinthians 12:31-13:3.

In the space below, explain what damage can occur when love is not the environment in which spiritual gifts are being exercised.

_____

_____

_____

This is not the only place in the New Testament that we find this emphasis on using our God-given gifts to benefit the Community.

Match the truths below with the appropriate verses.

1. Gifts are given for the common good.   A. Ephesians 4:11-12
2. Gifts are to be used to serve one another.   B. 1 Corinthians 12:7
3. Gifts are given to equip the saints for ministry. C. 1 Peter 4:10

We are to use our gifts to serve God in ministry and to serve each other so we will mature. Gifts are given so we can build each other up rather than tear each other down. In the Corinthian church, members were using their gifts like clubs to beat each other up. Ego, rather than the Spirit of God, was in control. Pride, rather than love, was at work among them.

Write out some thoughts about how you think gifts should be used to build each other up.

_____

_____

_____

_____

_____

ACCOUNTABILITY

Now, turn in your Bible to Matthew 25:14-30. It's a story Jesus told about accountability. The word "talent" in the story is a monetary term, but could be understood simply as "something to be invested." As you read this story, think about how you are investing your SHAPE for the Master's service.

What is the moral of this story? Given that more is expected from the one who has been given more (Luke 12:48), what does God expect you to do with what He's given to you?

_____

_____

_____

_____

Imagine yourself investing your SHAPE in powerful ways as you minister. Imagine yourself standing before the Lord giving an account of your life after a lifetime of faithful service. This is good news for those who have been transformed by the gospel! Match the following truths to the correct verses:

1. God will give to each of us according to our works.
2. God will give to us according to the fruit of our deeds.
3. God will repay us according to what we have done.

A. Matthew 16:27
B. Psalm 62:11-12
C. Jeremiah 17:10

One day Jesus said, *If anyone would come after Me, let him deny himself and take up his cross and follow Me. For whoever would save his life will lose it, but whoever loses his life for My sake and the gospel's will save it* (Mark 8:34-35). In Jesus' economy, keepers are weepers and losers are finders.

At CVC we are passionate about Missional Living—losing our lives, inviting people to new life in Christ, and discipling people to be committed followers of Christ. It's not a task that can be accomplished by the church staff alone. It's the call of God on each and every member and attender. The task is too big for a cadre of paid professionals. There is a world to win. It is God's call on you to lose your life and invest your God-given gifts not just on your own well-being, but in other people as well.

Close your time this week by reading through and verbalizing a prayer:

Dear heavenly Father, Help me stop playing it safe with my life. Help me begin to act more and more in faith. Help me get lost in investing what You have given to me for Your ministry. I want to become a working, serving saint. Lead me to understand more clearly what I am passionate about. I want to present it to You for You to use so I can make a difference for You in this world. I know that I am not called to simply occupy a seat in worship once a week. I thank You that I have been called and equipped to serve You by serving and loving others. Remind me often that Jesus said: "For even the Son of Man came not to be served but to serve, and to give His life as a ransom for many" (Mark 10:45). Help me become more and more like Him. In Jesus' name, Amen.

What was one of the most helpful insights that you received during this lesson?

_____

_____

_____

Serve in your area of giftedness, in your SWEET SPOT!

For additional study on this topic, you may want to watch/listen to message from CVC's 2013 series titled "Common Good." These messages may be found at: https://vimeo.com/album/2266332

Week 10

GENEROSITY: INCREASING AS AN INVESTOR

M EMORY VERSE
For where your treasure is, there your heart will be also.
Matthew 6:21

An Investor is someone who joyfully and sacrificially shares time, talent, and treasure to advance the cause of Christ in the world. In this week's lessons, we are focusing primarily on investing our treasure to honor Christ and grow His church. A biblical word for this is stewardship. To steward means to manage.

Sadly, most of us are aware of people who in the name of God have manipulated ministries and stewardship out of greed and in essence, have spiritually extorted money and possessions from people. One day, they will answer to a holy God for that sin. But in the Scriptures, God stresses stewardship not because He wants something FROM us, but because He wants something FOR us—freedom, joy, relationship, and abundant treasure in heaven.

> **Jesus is not calling men away from treasure.**
> **He's calling them to treasure.**
> *David Platt, President - International Mission Board*

WEEK 10, DAY 1: GOD OWNS EVERYTHING.
Think about it. Our souls don't have pockets!

We too easily forget that we are born into this world with empty hands and that we will leave this world with empty hands. We brought nothing with us into the world and we will take nothing with us out of the world (1 Timothy 6:7). The inescapable conclusion, then, is that we actually possess nothing and that God owns everything. While we are on this planet, our responsibility is to be managers of His possessions.

Look up the following verses and match the truths with the correct references.

1. Everything on earth belongs to God.
2. All the land on earth is God's land.
3. All the silver and the gold belong to God.
4. The power to gain wealth comes from God.
5. Everything under heaven is the Lord's.

A. Haggai 2:8
B. Deuteronomy 8:18
C. Job 41:11
D. Leviticus 25:23
E. Psalm 24:1

Take some time to read through the five statements above out loud. In the space below, write down one or two observations or implications of these truths. How might these truths change something about how you have been thinking or living?

_____
_____
_____

John Wesley said, "When the Possessor of heaven and earth brought you into being, and placed you in this world, He placed you here not as a proprietor, but a steward. As such, He entrusted you, for a season, with goods of various kinds; but the sole property of these still rests in Him nor can be alienated from Him . . . as you yourself are not your own, but His . . ."
("The Use of Money," in *Sermons on Several Occasions*, by John Wesley, p.446).

Read and highlight or underline 1 Corinthians 4:2.

Skim Matthew 25:14-30 and answer the following: What are some distinguishing characteristics between unfaithful stewards and faithful stewards?

An unfaithful steward   A faithful steward

_____   _____
_____   _____
_____   _____
_____   _____

A steward is a manager. We are called to manage God's treasures for God's glory, in God's way, and for God's purposes. We begin life with our hands wide open and nothing in them. Over time, as we live in His world, God places certain things into our hands. He shares His property with us. Everything we have is a gift from God. And we must remember that He owns it all. It's all His. We are called to be caretakers of what He owns.

We are responsible for what He entrusts to us as stewards, not as owners. We dare not think of gripping the things He entrusts to us. We must seek to hold everything loosely. We simply manage the treasures He entrusts to us, never forgetting that any way He directs us to share, to save, or to spend, it's His sovereign right.

Why? God owns it all. Understanding this fact and living in light of it will revolutionize our thinking when it comes to finances. What if "God owns it all" appeared on your checkbook, your wallet, your pocketbook, your income tax returns, your stock transaction, your credit cards, your home mortgage, your car title, your real estate contract, and your every business deal?

Good stewardship is not just releasing a few dollars here and there to a church. We start by surveying all that we have and remember how everything that we have—EVERYTHING, kept or released—should be used in the light of eternity. God is not asking us just to share our resources. He is asking us to recognize that all our resources belong to Him. His desire is that we use what we need and then give the rest away.

Bill and Vonette Bright were used by God to found and lead a worldwide evangelism and discipleship movement called Cru, formerly Campus Crusade for Christ. Since 1951, the influence of Cru has spread across the globe. Billions of people have been exposed to the gospel of Christ through the organization the Brights established.

Early in their marriage, the Brights created a contract with God that they felt became a defining moment for them and turned out to be a significant reason that God was able to use them in such amazing ways.

Bill and Vonette each took a sheet of paper and wrote a list of all the things they wanted out of life. Looking at their lists, they could see how materialistic their desires were. They had dreamed of owning beautiful cars, and a home in the upscale Bel-Air district of Los Angeles. Now they were convicted by Scriptures such as Mark 8:36: *For what does it profit a man to gain the whole world and forfeit his soul?*

They decided to draft and to sign a contract, completely surrendering their lives, their marriage, their possessions, and their futures to the Lord Jesus Christ.

From this day, Lord, we surrender and relinquish all of our past, present, and future rights and material possessions to you. As an act of the will, by faith, we choose to become Your bondslaves and do whatever You want us to do, go wherever You want us to go, say whatever You want us to say, no matter what it costs, for the rest of our lives. With Your help, we will never again seek the praise or applause of men or the material wealth of the world.

Signed _____
Date _____

Read through the Bright's contract again carefully and prayerfully. Is there any reason why you could not or would not personalize a similar commitment?

Using the Brights' contract as inspiration, in the space below, create your own contract with God as you recognize that all that you possess is actually owned by God.

_____
_____
_____
_____

Signed _____

Date _____

Use the words from a hymn of surrender, "Take My Life and Let It Be," by Frances R. Havergal, as a guide for your closing prayer today. Take special note of the words in the 4th verse.

> *Take my life and let it be consecrated, Lord, to Thee.*
> *Take my moments and my days, let them flow in endless praise.*
>
> *Take my hands and let them move at the impulse of Thy love.*
> *Take my feet and let them be swift and beautiful for Thee.*
>
> *Take my voice and let me sing, always, only for my King.*
> *Take my lips and let them be filled with messages from Thee.*
>
> *Take my silver and my gold, not a mite would I withhold.*
> *Take my intellect and use every pow'r as Thou shalt choose.*
>
> *Take my will and make it Thine, it shall be no longer mine.*
> *Take my heart, it is Thine own, it shall be Thy royal throne.*
>
> *Take my love, my Lord, I pour at Thy feet its treasure store.*
> *Take myself and I will be ever, only, all for Thee.*

What was one of the most helpful insights that you received during this lesson?

_____
_____
_____

It's a contradiction to say, "Lord, you can have my heart but keep Your hands off of my wallet.
Chad Allen, Lead Pastor - Cuyahoga Valley Church

WEEK 10, DAY 2: GENEROSITY AS A GLAD RESPONSE TO GOD'S GRACE

You matter to God—and so do your finances. God knows that your finances are an important part of your life. He understands this so much that in the Bible there are 2,350 verses that deal with money or finances. In fact, Jesus talked about money more than He did about heaven, hell, or love. He talked about it more than any other subject.

Why does the Bible talk so much about money? Because He understands how much power money can have over our lives if it's not managed rightly. Does God need our money? No. Does God want your money? Not primarily. What He's really after is your heart.

WHERE YOUR TREASURE IS, THERE YOUR HEART WILL BE.

Read and highlight or underline Jesus' words in Matthew 6:19-21.

Pay special attention to verse 21.

Please answer the following questions:

Where have we been told not to lay up treasures? (v. 19a)

_____

Why is it foolish to lay up treasures there? (v. 19b)

_____

Where have we been told to lay up treasures? (v. 20a)

_____

Why is it wise to lay up treasures there? (v. 20b)

_____

The location of your treasure will tell you what's in your_____. (v. 21)

Jesus is saying, "Show Me your checkbook, your MasterCard statement, your online banking account, and your receipts, and I'll show you where your heart is." If you know, love, and appreciate Jesus, your giving will not be a duty-driven drudgery; it will be a heart-felt delight.

Think about a husband and a wife celebrating a wedding anniversary. Imagine the husband wanting to do as little as possible to celebrate. Picture him saying to his wife, "What do I have to do to satisfy you? OK, already, I'll get you a present. Or, I'll take you out to eat. What's it going to take to get you off my back?" That kind of attitude would tell you a little about the husband's heart toward his wife. It's not good.

But if a husband is passionate about his wife—if his heart is for her and with her, if he's proud of her and about the relationship—he'd say, "I can't wait to go out with you, to sit and talk with you, to buy you the best meal I can afford, to buy you a present that will let you know how much I care about you. I wish I could do more. But what I'm going to do is to show you how much I adore you." That kind of attitude would tell you something else entirely. The husband who wants to do as much as possible has a heart full of love for his wife.

The same principles are true in our relationship to God. Are we seeking to get Him off our backs and do just as little as possible? Or are we seeking to give Him gifts of time, talent, and treasure that are worthy of Him and seeking to be just as generous as we can possibly be?

GOD'S GENEROSITY MOTIVATES OUR GENEROSITY.

It's receiving and meditating on the grace of God in Christ that enlarges our hearts and motivates our generosity. Once we grasp the magnitude of God's infinite grace that we have received through Christ, we will find ourselves becoming increasingly generous.

Jesus gave His all for us. He became poor so we could become rich. Read and highlight or underline 2 Corinthians 8:9.

What were some riches that Jesus possessed in eternity past—before He came to earth?

_____

_____

Describe the poverty that Jesus experienced as a result of His birth, life, and death.

_____

_____

Explain something about the spiritual poverty that you knew before you came to know Christ.

_____

_____

What are some of the riches that you now possess because of your relationship with Jesus?

_____

_____

Jesus loved us so much that He gave up His riches to become poor. Through His life, death, and resurrection, He made it possible for us to trade in our poverty for true wealth. He gave us what money cannot buy and death cannot take away—forgiveness of sin, freedom from guilt and shame, a rescue from hell, a home in heaven, a purpose for living, and a friendship with Him that changes everything.

TREASURING JESUS

One reason we are not rich toward God is because we simply don't value Jesus enough. Read two little parables Jesus tells in Matthew 13:44-46.

The kingdom of heaven is like treasure hidden in a field, which a man found and covered up. Then in his joy he goes and sells all that he has and buys that field. Again, the kingdom of heaven is like a merchant in search of fine pearls, who, on finding one pearl of great value, went and sold all that he had and bought it (Matthew 13:44-46).

Christ Himself is the treasure hidden in a field; He is the pearl of great price. He has infinite worth and value. Do we treasure Him above all?

The combined worth of all hidden treasure and all the gemstones that have ever existed do not even remotely compare with the unsearchable riches that are found only in Jesus. He became sin for us that in Him we might become the righteousness of God. Because of Christ, judgment day has been defanged for us. Christ's cross was our judgment day. Jesus ought to become increasingly precious to us. The riches of the gospel make all the glittering wealth of this world look incredibly dim and distasteful to us. Possessing Christ makes us less greedy and more giving.

When Jesus has become our greatest treasure, when He is more precious than gold, when the gospel of Christ's death in our place is the most prized news in the world to us, when we have learned to deny ourselves short-term pleasures for the sake of long-term joy, when we count everything as loss compared to the supreme value of knowing Christ, then our attitude toward accumulating worldly wealth radically changes.

If we will treasure Christ, the trinkets of this earth will grow strangely dim. If we will truly treasure Christ, we won't have a problem giving Him our money. So, it makes sense for us to give Him our hearts. If we will do that, we won't have a problem giving Him anything else.

The hymn "Be Thou My Vision" demonstrates how our values change once we come to have Christ. Use the words to this hymn to inspire your closing prayer.

Riches I heed not, nor man's empty praise,
Thou mine Inheritance, now and always:
Thou and Thou only, first in my heart,
High King of Heaven, my Treasure Thou art.

What was one of the most helpful insights that you received during this lesson?

_____
_____
_____
_____
_____

Jesus had put before us a choice: we can spend our resources on short-term pleasures that we cannot keep, or we can sacrifice our resources for long-term treasure that we'll never lose.

David Platt - Counter Culture, p.52
President, International Mission Board

WEEK 10, DAY 3: TREASURE IN HEAVEN

Yesterday, you read Matthew 6:20 where Jesus says, *Lay up for yourselves treasures in heaven.* But exactly how do we do that? Today, read the insights Jesus gives us about becoming eternally rich in Luke 16:1-9. As you read, put question marks by parts of the passage that you have questions about or don't understand.

He also said to the disciples, "There was a rich man who had a manager, and charges were brought to him that this man was wasting his possessions. And he called him and said to him, 'What is this that I hear about you? Turn in the account of your management, for you can no longer be manager.'

And the manager said to himself, 'What shall I do, since my master is taking the management away from me? I am not strong enough to dig, and I am ashamed to beg. I have decided what to do, so that when I am removed from management, people may receive me into their houses.'

So, summoning his master's debtors one by one, he said to the first, 'How much do you owe my master?' He said, 'A hundred measures of oil.' He said to him, 'Take your bill, and sit down quickly and write fifty.' Then he said to another, 'And how much do you owe?' He said, 'A hundred measures of wheat.' He said to him, 'Take your bill, and write eighty.'

The master commended the dishonest manager for his shrewdness. For the sons of this world are more shrewd in dealing with their own generation than the sons of light. And I tell you, make friends for yourselves by means of unrighteous wealth, so that when it fails they may receive you into the eternal dwellings (Luke 16:1-9).

This manager is in charge of all the rich man's possessions. He's a trusted servant who transacts the business for the rich man, taking care of the house, the bank account, and the property. He's kind of a CFO/COO combo. But this corporate executive isn't getting the job done for his boss.

In Jesus' story, the manager is getting fired. His boss says, "Wrap up the loose ends. Before I give you your last check, finish a few things you've started." The manager is probably used to a pretty good lifestyle. He has soft hands and a weak back. He's not used to physical work. So, after he loses his job, what's he going to do?

He figures out a way to make sure he has friends who will help him make a living after he's no longer working for his current boss. So, in his last few moments as manager, he designs a plan to gain the favor of a few people who owe his boss. He comes up with a scheme to protect himself in the future. He wants a few people to open up their resources to him someday.

His plan is to reduce the amount of money that two debtors owed the boss. He goes to the best customers and gives them deep discounts on what they owed his boss. Both the bills would have amounted to about 500 denarii, which is a year and a half of salary. That's a significant savings for the people who owe the boss.

Why would he do this? After he's kicked out of his company for mismanagement of funds, he wants to go to one of those customers who "owes him a favor" and hopefully they would pay him back. It's an

"I'll-scratch-your-back-today-and-you-can-scratch-mine-someday" scheme. Do something nice for someone and they'll say, "Hey, I owe you one!"

The manager figures out how to end up with a golden parachute. Even his boss smiles at how shrewd he is. When it's time to settle accounts, his boss laughs, "You know how to take care of yourself, don't you? You still lost your job. But I've got to hand it to you, you figured out a way to leverage the past and the present for your future. Now, get out of here!"

The last part of verse 8 contains a key point in Jesus' story, *For the sons of this world are more shrewd in dealing with their own generation than the sons of light.*

The word *"shrewd"* in the Greek New Testament means intelligent, wise, prudent, astute, clever, and cunning. Jesus is *not* saying, "Be a crook! Be dishonest." What He *is* saying is that we ought to be clever—that we can learn something from the astute way this man operated. The crooked manager had great foresight to anticipate his financial needs after he was fired. He used his financial leverage now to make friends for himself later.

Jesus is saying that every believer ought to be as shrewd as that guy—as shrewd as a pagan! Jesus is saying, "Don't let the sons of this age—those who are not Christ-followers— 'out-shrewd' you. After all, you are sons of light."

The master praised the clever, cunning manager. Why? Because he knew how to look after his future self. Jesus says that the people who don't even belong to Him are better at looking out for their future selves than the people who do belong to Him.

What can we learn from this shrewd manager? As Pastor Andy Stanley once said, "He knew he was facing a deadline; he formulated a plan, and he acted before the opportunity was gone" ("God's Kingdom, Our Stuff," message preached at Northpoint Community Church, by Andy Stanley, 1997).

We are also facing a deadline. It's death. Do you have a creative plan to gain treasure in heaven before that deadline? Are you acting before the opportunity is gone?

So how do we leverage this opportunity? Re-read and highlight or underline Jesus' words in Luke 16:9.

Giving our wealth to kingdom causes is an investment that will be used to reach people for Christ who will become our friends for all eternity.

Christian music artist Ray Boltz once wrote a song entitled "Thank You." It starts out with him having a dream of being in heaven and you are standing beside him. One of the verses says, "Then another man stood before you; He said, 'Remember the time a missionary came to church? His pictures made you cry. You didn't have much money, but you gave it anyway. Jesus took that gift you gave and that's why I'm in heaven today.' Thank you for giving to the Lord.

I am a life that was changed. Thank you for giving to the Lord. I am so glad you gave."

As you think back about how you came to faith in Christ, who are 3-5 people who influenced you?

_____
_____
_____
_____
_____

Spend some time speculating how they may have used their financial resources to help reach you. Use the space below to record a few ideas. (For example, if you were reached for Christ at a church service, their giving to the general fund helped pay for the staff, the ministries, and the facility that God used to reach you.)

_____
_____
_____

Money reveals our character, our motives, and our true values. Maybe that's one reason why this is such a sensitive area for most of us. Most of us have had a good 10, 20, or 30 years of earning behind us. Some more.

We're either leveraging our finances for God's purposes or not. We've either made the most of our money or not. We've either laid up treasure in heaven or not. Whether we have or haven't actually boils down to our character. We have made the choices. We are responsible for either applying God's principles or not.

Do you want to lay up treasure in heaven? Give a portion of your resources away. Write some checks to kingdom causes! Never squelch a generous impulse. God commands us to use our money to win the lost (Luke 16:9), to care for those in need (Galatians 2:10; 1 John 3:16-18), and to support leaders in ministry (1 Corinthians 9:4-14, Galatians 6:6).

When we do that, we are laying up treasure in heaven.

Imagine a clothesline stretched all the way out into infinity and beyond. That represents eternity. Now, imagine holding a sharpie and placing a little dot on the line. That represents your life on this earth.

Randy Alcorn, author of _The Treasure Principle_ says, "Our lives have two phases: one, a dot, the other a line extending out from that dot. Right now, we are living in the dot. But what are we living for? The shortsighted person lives for the dot. The person with perspective lives for the line. The person who lives for the dot lives for treasure on earth that ends up in junkyards. The person who lives for the line lives for treasure in heaven that will never end"
(_The Treasure Principle_, by Randy Alcorn, pp.48-49).

Alcorn encourages us to ask ourselves a question, "Am I living for the dot or living for the line?"

197

In the space below, describe some changes that might be necessary to take place in your life to live for the line, not the dot.

_____
_____
_____

What was one of the most helpful insights that you received during this lesson?

_____
_____
_____

If we are not investing our time, our talent, and our treasure in helping men, women, boys, and girls spend their eternity with Christ, then we are not only not getting rich, we are impoverishing ourselves and our souls forever.

What would happen if we all locked into God's principle? There would be an explosion of generosity and out-reach through our church that someone would write about someday. What if we totally yielded everything to the Lord and His purposes?

As you close your time today, pick 2 or 3 people from your list above who invested and influenced you to come to Christ. Thank God for them, and write them a quick note of appreciation.

Money reveals our character, our motives, and our true values.

WEEK 10, DAY 4: A PRACTICAL PLAN

Sound Christian financial planners/counselors teach a money management plan that is rooted firmly in the Scriptures. It's called the 10–10–80 plan. This simple budget isn't expressed explicitly in the Bible. But it follows the principles taught in God's Word.

Some people are intimidated by just the *thought* of a budget. But a budget is just a tool to help you plan ahead, to help you save for anticipated expenses, to enable you to be prepared for unanticipated (but inevitable) emergencies, and to insure that you live within your means.

SHARE 10%: ONE TENTH GOES TO GOD FIRST.

The 10-10-80 plan starts with the simple yet powerful premise that everything belongs to God. Even though God owns everything, God encourages us to give 10% back to His causes. Read and highlight or underline Leviticus 27:30.

The word "tithe" means 10 percent. That might seem like a lot, but think about it. If someone gave you a $10 bill and just asked for $1 back, you'd say that person was a very generous and reasonable person. When it's all said and done, we're still blessed to have $9!

If we remember that all we possess actually belongs to God and that the power we have to earn wealth comes from God, then giving back 10% to Him is something we ought to be willing (and even eager) to do.

In the space below, describe the practice of your parents (your family of origin) when it came to generosity.

_____

_____

_____

In Old Testament times, God's people were commanded to contribute at least a tenth of their income to God's work (Numbers 18:28, Deuteronomy 14:22, 2 Chronicles 31:5-6, Nehemiah 13:12, Malachi 3:8-10). Although the New Testament is not as explicit about the tithe, Jesus endorses the tithe (Matthew 23:23). Today, many spiritual leaders consider the tithe to be a guideline goal for every believer.

God invites us to test Him regarding the tithe. Read and highlight or underline Malachi 3:8-10.

If you are married, your spouse may not be where you are in his/her commitment to Christ. You may not have been used to giving a significant portion of your income to the church. You may be in debt and trying to get out. Ask God to enable you to move toward the tithe—even though a full tithe might not seem realistic to you at this time.

The tithe reflects a level of giving that is doable, yet one that will require faith. No matter where you are in your giving, the New Testament norm is to surrender all you own to God and then to express that by growing in how much you give to God through the church and other missions and ministries. Giving is not to be based on legalistic calculations of a grudgingly given percentage. Giving flows from a grateful heart in response to God's grace, mercy, and love.

For Christ-followers who have a limited income, the tithe may be a goal to attain. For more affluent believers whose income exceeds their needs, the tithe can become limiting. The tithe can be seen as a guideline goal that, when reached, becomes a starting point for even greater generosity.

Circle the words that describe your personal feelings and attitudes as you consider the biblical practice of tithing: irritated, peaceful, offended, bothered, excited, suspicious, hopeful, defensive, pensive, trusting, perplexed, uncertain, joyful, skeptical, relaxed, panicked, confused, thankful, anxious, delighted, threatened, confident, ashamed, calm, doubtful, _____.

In the space below, describe why you feel this way.

_____

_____

_____

SAVE 10%: ONE TENTH GOES TO YOUR SAVINGS SECOND.
You worked hard for your paycheck. Pay yourself by putting some earnings into savings! This is not to be vacation fund money. It's not a "mad-money" fund. This is to be put somewhere so you will earn some interest. The Bible teaches us to save.

Wealth gained hastily will dwindle, but whoever gathers little by little will increase it (Proverbs 13:11).

A good man leaves an inheritance to his children's children (Proverbs 13:22).

Precious treasure and oil are in a wise man's dwelling, but a foolish man devours it (Proverbs 21:20).

Too many people work 30-40 years and spend everything that they ever earned. They enter into their latter years with nothing. They spent it all. How tragic. Don't let that happen to you. Pay yourself!

You might consider setting aside the second 10 percent of your income to establish 3 savings accounts. The first savings account is your Emergency Fund. That savings account is at least three months' living expenses to give you a cushion when the unexpected happens.

The second savings account is planning ahead for the expenses you know are going to happen: insurances, car repairs, health care co-pays, vacation, cash for the next car (to avoid having to take out a loan to buy a depreciating asset), weddings, school, etc.

The third savings account is for your investments. A little saved early and consistently adds up over time. You'll be glad you did.

SPEND 80%: THE REST OF YOUR INCOME GOES FOR YOUR LIVING EXPENSES.
You already honored God from the first of your wealth, and then you paid yourself. Now, with God's guidance and for His glory, enjoy using the remaining money to meet your needs.

What do you do if you can't live on the 80 percent (while giving the first 10% and saving the second 10%)? That's when you have to take a hard look at your standard of living. You have two choices. One, simplify your lifestyle by living in a less expensive apartment or house, eliminating the cable bill, eating out less often, buying less clothes, etc. Two, consider how to increase your income.

Why do people share so little and save so little? Most people want to be generous. And they want to save. But very few do. Why? It's mainly because we like to spend!

We have an almost uncontrollable urge to spend! We have a budget-busting urge to buy. We like the thought of wearing something new, of going somewhere exciting, of driving something better, of living somewhere nicer.

When we are sad, we spend. When we are glad, we spend. When we are bored, we spend. When we work hard, we reward ourselves and spend. When it's cold, we spend. When it's hot, we spend.

If there is no spending plan in place—no formula we are following—then the average person won't control the desire to spend.

A budget is extremely helpful in managing expenses. For help on establishing a budget, consider the following recommendations:

daveramsey.com (Financial Peace University - FPU)
http://www.daveramsey.com/specials/mytmmo-gazelle-budget/

crown.org
https://planner.crown.org/Secure/Account/Login.aspx?ReturnUrl=%2fSecure%2fBudget%2fNewBudget.aspx

familylife.com
http://www.familylife.com/~/media/Files/FamilyLife/Generic/SIMPLEBUDGETWORKSHEET.pdf
Debt obviously limits our financial freedom to share and to save. For help on eliminating debt, consider utilizing:

Dave Ramsey's Debt Snowball tool
https://www.mytotalmoneymakeover.com/index.cfm?event=displayDebtSnowballLanding

Are you currently using a spending plan?   ☐ Yes   ☐ No

If you don't currently have a budget, take some time over the next few days to develop a spending plan by using one of the tools listed above.

If you practice the 10-10-80 plan, you'll probably be better off than the vast majority of Americans. You'd certainly be among the top tier in both giving and saving if you put 10% towards each. The keys?
1) Spending less than you earn (not spending all of your pay raises).
2) Working hard to maximize your income.

It's that simple. But it's not that easy.

The 10-10-80 plan will require courage, tenacity, and discipline.
But if you stick with it, the results will be worth the effort.

Is the 10-10-80 plan the only way to do it? No. There are lots of good budget plans out there. But 10-10-80 is a good place to begin to learn the three key financial disciplines of planning, giving, and saving.

Close this time in prayer by asking God to help you develop a sharing, saving, and spending plan so you can become a better steward of His resources.

After prayerfully digesting what you have read and learned, what are 3 things you can do to a better inventory of God's resources?

1. _____

2. _____

3. _____

What was one of the most helpful insights that you received during this lesson?

_____

_____

_____

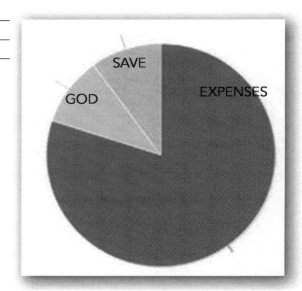

WEEK 10, DAY 5: THE LAW OF THE HARVEST

God's Word makes it clear that we are to give our treasure to support His work in this world. Read and underline or highlight 2 Corinthians 9:6-8.

The point is this: whoever sows sparingly will also reap sparingly, and whoever sows bountifully will also reap bountifully. Each one must give as he has decided in his heart, not reluctantly or under compulsion, for God loves a cheerful giver. And God is able to make all grace abound to you, so that having all sufficiency in all things at all times, you may abound in every good work (2 Corinthians 9:6-8).

The Law of the Harvest is taught in these verses. Use the following three words to complete the three statements below: more, what, later.

We reap _____ we sow.
We reap _____ than we sow.
We reap _____ than we sow.

The Law of the Harvest works on the farm. If you sow a kernel of corn, at a later time, you'll get several ears of corn. This law also works in your relationships. If you sow some love today, you'll reap more love tomorrow. This same law also works in your finances.

If we sow just a little → give just a little → then we can only hope for a meager harvest = skimpy reaping. But if we sow a lot → give bountifully = then over time, we can expect God to reward our consistent generosity. That means that one of the worst things we can do for our spiritual and financial futures is fail to sow. Conversely, one of the best things we can do for our spiritual and financial futures is to grow in generosity.

Over and over, the Scriptures are clear that God rewards generosity. Read the following statements and match the appropriate verse references.

1. The Lord blesses those who give to the poor.
2. God waters those who water others.
3. God blesses those who share their bread.
4. Whoever gives to the poor will not want.
5. Heaven's windows open to bless those who tithe.
6. When we give in secret God rewards us.
7. Givers receive back in a "running over" way.
8. Giving to the needy stabilizes our moneybags.

A. Luke 12:33
B. Luke 6:38
C. Matthew 6:3-4
D. Proverbs 22:9
E. Proverbs 28:27
F. Malachi 3:10
G. Proverbs 11:25
H. Deuteronomy 15:10

Bottom line? We cannot out give God. That's the Law of the Harvest.

Don't mistake this for a "name-it-and-claim-it" theology or a "give-to-get" motivation. The Law of the Harvest doesn't mean that if you put $10 in the offering basket at church, then you'll have $100 in your mailbox by the time you get home. What God's Word is telling us is that over time, God rewards consistent generosity. If you want to have an abundance, then sow bountifully.

PRIORITY GIVING

Write your check to the Lord first. Don't give God leftovers. Read and highlight or underline Matthew 6:33.

Jesus is saying to seek God first. And then all these things—the food, the clothes, the shelter, the things you need to make it in your culture—will be added to you. Seeking first His kingdom means a lot of things. But don't miss this: one thing it means for sure is to seek Him first with your finances.

Jesus knew something about the Jewish principle of giving the firstfruits to God. Read and highlight or underline Proverbs 3:9-10.

When harvest time came, the ancient Jews would bring to the Temple or to the synagogue the first grapes, the first wheat, the first olives. Why? To support God's work and to care for the poor. It was a way to demonstrate to God that He comes first—that He is the priority.

God is responsible for giving us the opportunity, the energy, and the creativity to earn. When we honor Him first, we are saying that God is number one in our lives. Plus, we set in motion God's blessing and interaction in our financial lives. We open ourselves up to God's supernatural activity to provide for us in ever-increasing ways.

Some of us have been praying more than ever for God to bail us out of tough economic times. We want God involved in our finances. In Matthew 6:33 Jesus is saying, "Here's the way to get God involved. Seek Him first."

We pay for the mortgage, transportation, taxes, insurance, food, clothing, utilities, cell phones, medical, entertainment/recreation, and education. What does God's kingdom too often get? Leftovers.

Seek His kingdom with your leftovers and it's as though God is saying, "You're tying My hands here when it comes to My personal activity in assisting you financially. But if you will seek Me first, then you need not worry and be driven by fear—even in tough economic times—because I will see to it (sometimes in miraculous ways) that your needs will be met. When everything is crashing down in your culture, you'll be crash proof. You'll have whatever you need to do My will."

What if your first transaction out of every paycheck was to support God's work? It's a way to obey Matthew 6:33.

God gets the first transaction after we get paid, not the last. To make sure that happens, some people set up an automatic bank withdrawal to go straight to their church to eliminate the temptation to withhold or delay their tithe. CVC's website and app also provide easy access to electronic giving. This keeps us from giving God "leftovers."

In the following space, share how you feel about setting up an automatic bank withdrawal to make sure that your giving to the Lord is priority giving.

_____

_____

PERCENTAGE GIVING

God gives us everything we have—the ability to think and work and earn. He gives us a whole pie. And then he asks us for a portion to do His work in the world. When it comes to your giving, just settle on some percentage. As we learned yesterday, the Bible says 10% is a good place start. It's an amount observed in the Old Testament in Malachi.

Some godly parents teach their children to give a dime out of every dollar to God. You say, "I can't give ten percent!" Start somewhere. Start at 3% or 5% or 8%.

Committing to a percentage is important because it helps us with the fear and the emotions that flare up throughout the course of a year that can keep us from giving like we know we should give.

What percentage can you see yourself giving? How about 5 percent? Pastor Andy Stanley in Atlanta says, "Even if your knees are quivering and you can only muster 1 percent, I urge you to commit to something and stick to it."

Whatever percentage you choose, have a target you can aim for no matter how much your emotions fluctuate. Try it for thirty or sixty days and watch what happens.

Fill in the following blank. At the present time, here is the percentage that I feel led to give to God and His work. _____ %

PROGRESSIVE GIVING

This means progressively increasing the percentage you give over the years. You might be thinking, "You've got to be kidding me!"

Grow in grace (2 Peter 3:18).

Shouldn't we grow in the grace of love, the grace of joy, and the grace of peace? Of course. Why shouldn't we grow in the grace of giving?

Think about it this way: God intends for us to grow spiritually. We all know we should be growing in our self-control, our gentleness, and our patience. That's what we pray for and work toward. God's agenda for your life is that you be gradually transformed, little by little, to the likeness of Christ. We are supposed to grow spiritually. So, why should it be any different in our giving?

We should also grow in our giving. But you can't grow as a giver if you don't also increase your giving. If you've been giving 10% for twenty years and you've never increased your percentage of giving, you haven't grown.

If you've been giving 3 percent for 5 years, maybe it's time to move up to 5 percent. If you've been giving 5 percent for 10 years, maybe it's time to move up to 8 percent. If you've been giving 10 percent for 20 years, maybe it's time to move up to 11 percent or 12 percent or 15 percent. Some families increase their percentage by 1/2 percent every year.

Giving should be an exciting, close-encounter-with-God experience. So if your giving has become a mundane routine, then maybe it's time to stretch your financial faith a little. Increase the percentage. And then trust God to provide for you just like you did when you first started to give.

What is one minor adjustment you can immediately make to grow as a steward and investor of what God has given you?

Close out your time this week in prayer. Use the following prayer as a guide for your own.

"Lord, You are the Giver of life. All I have is from your hand. You have called me to be a steward of Your abundance, a caretaker of all You have entrusted to me. Help me to always use your gifts wisely and teach me to share them generously. Send the Holy Spirit to work through me, bringing Your message to those in my sphere of influence. May I be a faithful steward out of my love of Jesus.

Take, Lord, and receive all my freedom, my memory, my intelligence, and my will—all that I have and possess. You, Lord, have given those things to me. I now give them back to you, Lord. All belongs to you. Dispose of these gifts according to your will.

I ask only for your love and your grace, for they are enough for me. Dearest Lord, teach me to be generous. Teach me to serve you as you deserve; to give and not to count the cost; to fight and not to heed the wounds; to toil and not to seek for rest; to labor and not to seek reward, save that of knowing that I do your will" (*The HarperCollins Book of Prayers*, by Ignatius Loyola, Robert Van de Weyer, ed., p.206).

What was one of the most helpful insights that you received during this lesson?

_____

_____

_____

COMMON QUESTIONS AND ANSWERS ABOUT THE TITHE

Malachi 3:7-12 teaches us how and why God opens the windows of heaven and blesses His people. The passage speaks of tithes and offerings, giving 10% and beyond of our income to God's work in the world. It's helpful to address some important questions and issues. So, here goes!

Common Questions about tithes and offerings . . .

1. Isn't the tithe an Old Testament law that Jesus never taught?

Jesus criticized the religious leaders of His day. They tithed, but neglected justice, mercy, and faithfulness.

You are careful to tithe even the tiniest income from your herb gardens, but you ignore the more important aspects of the law—justice, mercy, and faith. You should tithe, yes, but do not neglect the more important things (Matthew 23:23, NLT).

It's not either "give the tithe" or "act with justice." It's both/and. Do both. The New Testament (NT) standard is always higher than the Old Testament (OT) standard. When Jesus talked about OT principles, He always raised the bar. He said, "Adultery isn't just the deed; it's the thought." Jesus raised the bar over and over. Why would we think He would lower the bar when it comes to our giving?

2. So, are New Testament believers supposed to tithe?

We're saved by grace through faith, and we ought to give by grace through faith. We should give out of a heart of joy and gratitude. If you can't give that way, then don't give. But ask God for the grace to give out of a grateful heart. And realize if you don't give, you are not tapping into the Law of the Harvest, the Law of Reciprocity. If you don't give generously, then you really can't claim the promise from Malachi 3 about the windows of heaven opening up for you.

Having said that, we must keep in mind NT teaching:

On the first day of every week, each one of you should set aside a sum of money in keeping with his income (1 Corinthians 16:2, NIV).

He's saying, "Give individually, regularly, methodically, proportionately."

Whoever sows sparingly will also reap sparingly, and whoever sows bountifully will also reap bountifully. Each one must give as he has decided in his heart, not reluctantly or under compulsion, for God loves a cheerful giver (2 Corinthians 9:6-7).

He's saying, "Give bountifully, intentionally, willingly, cheerfully."

Whatever you decide to do about the tithe, make sure you give individually, regularly, methodically, proportionately, bountifully, intentionally, willingly, and cheerfully. Don't give because it's a rule.

The NT pattern is to recognize that all that we have belongs to God. We are managers of His money. If we're 2% givers, maybe we should ask God for the grace to go to 4. If we're 5% givers, maybe we should ask God for the grace to go to 8. If we're 10% givers, maybe we should ask God for the grace to go beyond. And some people who have extra, should grow way beyond the 10%.

If you aren't giving 10%, then the tithe is a good goal to aim at. If you are giving 10%, then the tithe is a great pad to launch from. We're supposed to grow in giving just like we're supposed to grow in other areas of our lives. We're supposed to grow in love, in service, in devotion, in the fruit of the Spirit, right? Well, shouldn't we also grow in giving, in generosity? If you have been giving 10% since you were 5 (giving from an allowance) and you're still giving 10% 50 years later, then something's wrong with your growth in this area of your life.

3. Where should I give the tithe?

Remember that Malachi 3:10 says, *Bring the whole tithe into the storehouse.* So, another way to ask this question is, "What is the storehouse?"

The storehouse in OT times was the place in the Temple where products were stored. The people were supposed to bring their goods—the produce from their fields, the grain, the olives, the olive oil—and it would be stored in rooms, in a kind of warehouse in the temple. The resources were then used to support full-time servants of God—the Levites, prophets, and priests, to meet the expenses for worship at the Temple, and to bless the lives of the needy. So, basically, the people are being told, "Bring the whole tithe to the Temple."

Are we supposed to follow this practice of storehouse giving?

CVC's Founding Pastor Rick Duncan says, "I can just talk about what I've seen and practiced over the years. Even before I became a pastor, Maryanne and I gave 10% to our local church. And we supported other ministries after we gave to the church first. We trusted the leadership of the church to use the money to pay salaries of missionaries, of pastors, of leaders in our church, to meet the spiritual and physical needs of people in our community and world.

"I used to serve on staff in a para-church ministry for four years—the Fellowship of Christian Athletes. And we always told people, 'Give first to your church. If you have available funds to give after that, then support this ministry as God leads.' The best para-church ministries say the same thing."

There was not a needy person among them, for as many as were owners of lands or houses sold them and brought the proceeds of what was sold and laid it at the apostles' feet, and it was distributed to each as any had need. (Acts 4:34-35)

If you are involved in a good local church with a variety of ministries that engage in evangelism and discipleship and missions and that cares for the poor and needy, then give to your church first. Trust and invest in what God is doing through your leaders.

4. Isn't tithing your time and talent enough?

Suppose a husband said to his wife, "I'm going to give you my time. I'll talk to you all day and all night. I'll listen to you. We'll take walks together. My time is yours. And I'm going to give you my talent. I'll fix things around the house. I'll write you songs and poetry and love letters. My talent is yours. But, you know, you can't have any of the money. That's for me." Would she feel honored with that?

This is one area where we have to be "all in." Time. Talent. And Treasure. Like a three-legged stool, you need to have all three to function as designed and to be effective.

5. Should I tithe on my gross or my net?

It all depends on whether you want God to bless your gross or you want God to bless your net! Remember 2 Corinthians 9:7, *Let each one do just as he has purposed in his own heart, for God loves a cheerful giver.* The <u>cheerful</u> giver says, "How much can I give?" The <u>fearful</u> giver says, "How little can I give?"

6. Should I tithe if my spouse says no?

1 Peter 3:1-6 gives instruction to wives with non-Christian husbands. They are to win their husbands by their chaste, respectful, and submissive behavior. A Christian wife who insists on tithing when her husband says no may actually be setting up an obstacle in keeping her husband from being open to the gospel. ("All that church wants is your money.")

Respect your spouse's position. Don't force the issue. God knows your heart.

Larry Burkett was a Christian financial consultant. Here's his suggestion: "Ask your spouse if you could give something, maybe $50 a month. Then, as a couple, evaluate whether or not you're better off or worse off financially. If you're worse off, you'll stop. If you're better off, you'll give more." Who knows? You may ultimately end up tithing. Burkett said that he found this was the first step in many unbelieving spouses coming to the Lord.

Some would say, "Well we are not under law. We are under grace." True. But who should be the most grateful and, therefore, the most generous? Those under the law or those under grace?

We should want to go beyond the tithe.

R.G. LeTourneau was the father of the modern earthmoving industry. He was responsible for 299 inventions—like the bulldozer, portable cranes, logging equipment, mobile sea platforms for oil exploration, etc. During World War II, his company produced 70% of all the army's earth-moving machinery. He called God the Chairman of his Board. His life's verse was Matthew 6:33: *Seek first the kingdom of God and His righteousness and all these things shall be added unto you.* LeTourneau went way beyond the tithe. He gave 90% of his profit to God's work and kept only 10% for himself. LeTourneau was convinced that he could not outgive God. "I shovel it out," he would say, "and God shovels it back, but God has a bigger shovel."

The cheerful giver says, "How much can I give?"
The fearful giver says, "How little can I give?"

Week 11

SPIRITUAL MULTIPLICATION: REPRODUCING AS A DISCIPLER

MEMORY VERSE

Go therefore and make disciples of all nations, baptizing them in the name of the Father and of the Son and of the Holy Spirit, teaching them to observe all that I have commanded you. And behold, I am with you always, to the end of the age.

Matthew 28:19-20

WEEK 11, DAY 1: THE CALL TO DISCIPLESHIP

At Cuyahoga Valley Church, we explain our mission, the big picture, this way: We are inviting people to new life in Christ. We say, "Everyone. Live new. Everyday."

In a word, a person who is experiencing new life in Christ is a disciple. The Greek word for disciples is *"mathetes."* It means "a learner, a pupil." Our goal is not decisions for Christ, but disciples of Christ. We aim to produce disciples, not decisions.

Being a disciple is not optional. It's essential. Read the words of Jesus in Matthew 28:19-20.

Go therefore and make disciples of all nations, baptizing them in the name of the Father and of the Son and of the Holy Spirit, teaching them to observe all that I have commanded you (Matthew 28:19-20a).

The word "go" in Matthew 28:19-20 is actually a participle in the Greek language like the words "baptizing" and "teaching." It could be accurately translated "as you are going." The actual command from Jesus in the passage is to "make disciples." Whatever a church does, the first priority must be to make disciples.

In ancient Jewish life, a disciple was sometimes referred to as someone who had been covered in the dust from a teacher's feet. There is a passage in the Mishna, the ancient record of the oral law of the Jewish people that says, "Let your house be a gathering place for the sages. And wallow in the dust of their feet. And drink in their words with gusto" (The Neusner version of the *Mishnah*, p.673).

A disciple was a person who would sit at the feet of a teacher and be so attentive that he would, figuratively speaking, be covered in dust from the teacher's feet. That is how close a disciple wanted to be to his sage—his teacher. This is how close we should want to be to our Teacher, Jesus. And why would a disciple want to be that close? So he or she could "drink in their words with gusto."

As you think about yourself as a disciple of Jesus, on a scale of 1-10 (10 being high) how would you rate yourself?

_____ Covered in the dust of His feet.
_____ Drinking in His words with gusto.

Describe in the space below what needs to change in your life so you can grow in these areas?

_____
_____
_____
_____

It can sometimes feel like church leaders are focused on getting people to come to the church a lot. Sunday School. Worship services. Training events. Prayer meetings. Service projects. Building and property maintenance. Meeting after meeting after meeting . . .

It's tempting for leaders to measure the effectiveness of church the old fashioned way: the ABCs—Attendance, Buildings, and Cash. As long as attendance is strong, the buildings are in good shape (or new ones are being built), and cash is in the bank, then leaders can feel like they are winning.

But if you hang around church for awhile, you will notice that some of the people who show up at all these meetings and activities can be as mean as snakes. Some of the most faithful attenders are the people who cause others in the church the most sleepless nights. The so-called pillars of the church can often be immature, petty, selfish, loveless, joyless, angry, and divisive.

Use the space below to joy down a few thoughts (no names please!) about a person you know who attended church faithfully but who did not faithfully exhibit Christ-like characteristics. Why do you think it possible to attend church a lot but never experience new life in Christ?

_____
_____
_____
_____

Going to church a lot doesn't necessarily make anyone a mature follower of Jesus. We can multiply the number of our meetings and events as a church. We can enlarge and modernize our buildings. We can congratulate ourselves that we are meeting and exceeding the budget. But if people are not growing as disciples, then we have missed the mark! Organizational growth is not necessarily an indicator of spiritual growth. (Organizational decline is not necessarily an indicator of spiritual growth, either!)

Therefore, our goal must be to help people advance, to progress, to keep on moving one step forward from where they are now. Our ultimate goal is not to build attendance, get more people into our LifeGroups, or expand the budget (as important as these things might be). These can be means to our ultimate goal. But they can't replace the ultimate goal: To make disciples—to develop people to be mature in Christ, who then develop others to be mature in Christ.

Read the following ways Jesus describes a maturing disciple and match them to the appropriate verses.

1. Bears a cross and follows Jesus	A. Matthew 28:19-20
2. Loves Jesus even more than family	B. John 8:31-32
3. Has a love for others	C. John 15:8
4. Has yielded control of possessions to Christ	D. Luke 6:40
5. Learns to observe all Jesus' commands	E. Luke 14:26
6. Abides in the Word of Christ	F. John 13:34-35
7. Is trained to be like Christ	G. Luke 14:27
8. Glorifies the Father by bearing fruit	H. Luke 14:33

Colossians 1:6 says that the gospel is "bearing fruit and increasing" in the lives of the believers at Colossae. When the spiritual leader, Paul, prays for the Colossians in verse 10, he prays that they may be *walking in a manner worthy of the Lord, fully pleasing to Him, bearing fruit in every good work and increasing in the knowledge of God* (Colossians 1:10).

So, we have asked a follow-up question, "What does a disciple—a person who is bearing the fruit of New Life in Christ, someone covered in the dust of Jesus, someone who is drinking in Christ's words with gusto—look like? Combining biblical teaching and simplicity, one way to describe a disciple living a new life in Christ is that they see themselves as:

1) Beloved Child
2) Self-feeder
3) Servant
4) Investor
5) Discipler
6) Missionary

What was one of the most helpful insights that you received during this lesson?

_____
_____
_____

Close your time in prayer and use the following as a prayer guide:

Lord Heavenly Father, I do not want to be a person who attends meeting after meeting at church but never changes. I want to be a true disciple of Christ. Help me be covered in the dust of my teacher, Jesus. May I drink in His words with gusto. Help me to experience continuous growth as a Beloved Child, a Self-feeder, a Servant, an Investor, a Discipler, and a Missionary. May I bear the Fruit of New Life as a maturing disciple of my Lord and Savior, Jesus Christ. In His name, Amen.

Only a disciple can make a disciple.
A. W. Tozer

WEEK 11, DAY 2: BEING DISCIPLED

It's important for a disciple to get a snapshot of the spiritual life of the person who is going to be discipled.

The following questionnaire is helpful in assessing areas of focus if you are seeking to be discipled, or if you are seeking to disciple someone else. (If you are seeking to be discipled, share the questionnaire with your discipler, i.e., your LifeGroup or HuddleGroup leader. If you are seeking to disciple someone, give him or her the questionnaire so you will have better insight about areas of focus for his/her growth.)

Please spend the time in this session taking a snapshot of your own spiritual life related to the Fruit of New Life.

24 QUESTIONS

Background information for an effective discipleship relationship

Name _____

Date _____

The following questions are not a test. There are no wrong answers. Please answer the questions honestly. This will help in the selection of discipleship materials most appropriate for you.

Beloved Child:

1. What is your spiritual age _____? (In other words, when did you receive Jesus Christ as your personal Lord and Savior—how long have you been a Christ-follower?)
2. How assured are you that you are headed to heaven when you die?
    A) Very sure
    B) Fairly sure
    C) Fluctuating between certainty and doubt
    D) Uncertain
3. How often do you spend time in daily prayer?
    A) Often
    B) Regularly
    C) Occasionally
    D) Seldom
4. How often do you have the sense that you are truly loved by God—that your relationship with Him is not based on your performance, but on His grace, forgiveness, and unconditional love which is found in Christ.
    A) Consistently
    B) Regularly
    C) Sporadically
    D) Rarely

Self-feeder:

5. Do you have some problems with reading the Bible? If so, what kind of problems?

_____

_____

_____

6. To what extent did you understand the teaching of the Bible before you became a believer?
   A) Very Much   B) Much   C) Little   D) Very Little
7. How frequently do you read the Bible for yourself?
   A) Daily   B) 2-3 times/week C) Weekly   D) Occasionally
8. How often do you find spiritual truths in the Bible and apply them to your life?
   A) Often   B) Regularly   C) Occasionally   D) Seldom

Servant:

9. Does your family support you in your efforts to serve Christ?
   Please explain their level of support, or their lack of it.

_____

_____

_____

10. Briefly describe your past and/or current service in the life of a church or ministry.

_____

_____

_____

11. How consistent are you to pursue the filling of the Spirit as you seek to serve Christ?
    A) Very consistent   B) Somewhat consistent   C) Erratic   D) Unsure

Briefly share some insights/processes that you would use to teach someone how to be filled with the Holy Spirit.

_____

_____

12. What spiritual gift or gifts has the Lord placed in your life?
    (See your results from Week 8.)

_____

_____

_____

Investor:

13. Please describe what you consider to be the spiritual strengths you can invest in the lives of others.

   _____

   _____

   _____

14. How satisfied are you about being someone who holds loosely to material things so that you can give away your possessions to help others?
   A) Very satisfied
   B) Somewhat satisfied
   C) Sometimes satisfied
   D) Not satisfied
   Please explain your answer:

   _____

   _____

   _____

15. Before you spend money on a daily basis, how frequently do you think about the fact that God actually owns everything you possess?
   A) Often   B) Regularly   C) Occasionally   D) Seldom

16. Which of the following statements best describes your level of generosity to your church?
   A) I have not yet begun to give consistently.
   B) I am giving regularly and moving toward the tithe, 10% of my income.
   C) I am currently tithing.
   D) I give a tithe and also offerings over and above the tithe.

Discipler:

17. In your own words, describe what a mature follower of Jesus looks like.

   _____

   _____

   _____

18. How confident are you that you can honestly say to others, "Imitate me like I imitate Christ"?
   A) Very confident
   B) Confident
   C) Somewhat hesitant
   D) Unsure
   What needs to change in your life so you can say, "Follow me like I follow Jesus?"

   _____

   _____

   _____

19. How are you taking advantage of opportunities (reading, groups, listening, accountability, classes, seminars) to be equipped as a disciple so you can, in turn, disciple others?

_____
_____
_____

20. Will you commit to spend time equipping other followers of Jesus in order to encourage them to follow Christ more closely?

☐ Yes   ☐ No   ☐ Unsure

What might hold you back?

_____
_____
_____

Missionary:

21. How regularly do you see yourself as a "missionary cleverly disguised" at work, in your neighborhood, at school, in your family, and with your friends?

A) Constant awareness
B) Often
C) Sometimes
D) Rarely.

What is it that keeps you from caring about others as souls that will spend eternity in either heaven or hell?

_____
_____
_____

22. Briefly share when and how you have served outside the church to help reach the last, the least, and the lost.

_____
_____
_____

23. Have you shared with someone your story of how Christ saved you and/or how Christ is working in your life?

☐ Yes   ☐ No

If so, briefly share about that experience.

_____
_____
_____

24. Have you explained the gospel (the plan of salvation) to anyone?

☐ Yes   ☐ No | Please explain.

_____
_____
_____

After completing this assessment, what areas did you observe or sense a need to grow in? Discuss with your LifeGroup leader steps you can take to greater develop those traits of discipleship.

For a more detailed evaluation, we have developed a helpful online tool for you to use to assess your spiritual life. You will be able to identify areas of strength and areas of opportunity for growth. Please use the following web address to access the Fruit of New Life inventory. http://cvconline.org/FONL2/fruit.html

Close your time in prayer today and ask God to help you grow as a disciple of Jesus. Spend time praying that God will enable you to grow as a disciple in the six areas of the Fruit of New Life: Beloved Child, Self-feeder, Servant, Investor, Discipler, and Missionary.

What was one of the most helpful insights that you received during this lesson?

_____

_____

_____

Most people in America, when they are exposed to the Christian faith, are not being transformed. They take one step into the door, and the journey ends. They are not being allowed, encouraged, or equipped to love or to think like Christ. Yet in many ways a focus on spiritual formation fits what a new generation is really seeking. Transformation is a process, a journey, not a one-time decision.

David Kinnaman, Author of Unchristian

WEEK 11, DAY 3: ENVIRONMENTS FOR DISCIPLESHIP

What do clubs in a golf bag have to do with discipleship?

A golf bag has lots of clubs. The best golfers master them all to become winners. The driver is for the longest distance off the tee. The fairway woods are for longer distances off the fairways. The irons are for landing shots on the green with accuracy. The wedges are for moving the ball near the hole with, hopefully, pinpoint precision. The putter closes out the scoring.

Now, compare Jesus' disciple-making strategy to the use of the clubs in your golf bag.

The driver: Jesus spoke to the thousands (Matthew 5).
The fairway woods: He appeared to 500 (1 Corinthians 15).
The long irons: Jesus had a loyal following of 120 (Acts 1).
The mid-range irons: He sent the 72 out two-by-two (Luke 10).
The wedge: Jesus chose the 12 to be with Him (Matthew 10).
The putter: Jesus majored in a one-on-three "huddle" relationship with Peter, James, and John (Matthew 17).

Jesus discipled people in multiple environments—by the thousands, and the threes, and everything in between. He used every club in His bag! In golf, if you want to win, you'd better become proficient in using every club in the bag! In the spiritual life, if we want to experience discipleship the Jesus way, we'd better have access to many differing discipling contexts/environments/group sizes.

As you think about your spiritual life, which environments so far—worship services, large groups, LifeGroups, huddles, personal conversations—have most helped you grow as a disciple? How have these environments helped you grow?

_____

_____

_____

It's right to think of every single God-honoring relationship, practice, experience, and learning environment as part of your discipleship journey. God sovereignly arranges all your opportunities in life to help you become increasingly like Jesus. You just have to take advantage of the opportunities He provides. Everything from listening to a sermon, to having a cup of coffee with a Christian friend can be part of God's discipleship plan for you.

But connecting intentionally in smaller group settings is the environment where discipleship growth can happen more rapidly and intensely. Golfers sometimes say, "You drive for show but putt for dough." It's what they do around the greens with the short irons, wedges, and putters that turns average pros into great ones.

Jesus focused on and excelled in up-close and personal disciple-making. He could preach and teach powerfully to the crowds, but He knew how to prioritize disciple-making in the 1 on 12 group, and in the 1 on 3 huddle.

A church with a disciple-making culture will use lots of environments to accomplish disciple-making. But effective disciple-making churches make great use of up-close and personal settings. You can impress people from a distance, but you impact them up close. This is why Jesus invested in groups, particularly the 12 and the 3.

This is why you will often hear how important it is for you to be connected in a LifeGroup, a small group of 8-12 people that mirrors Jesus' relationship with His 12 disciples. But it's also important to go further if we really want to follow the Jesus model. Intense discipling, deep-dive discipleship, for Jesus, seems to have happened best in what could be called a huddle—an intimate group of 3 followers: Peter, James, and John.

THE 3: PETER, JAMES, AND JOHN

These three always head the list of the 12 disciples (Mark 3:16, 17; Acts 1:13; sometimes with Andrew and Matthew 10:2; Luke 6:14). These three had been among the first ones chosen by Christ to make up the twelve. They had been previously associated in the fishing trade (Luke 5:10). Repeatedly, they are mentioned as the threesome who accompanied the Lord in unique situations (Matthew 17:1-9; Mark 5:35-43; Mark 14:32-42).

Peter, James, and John appear together five times in the gospels. Match the following descriptions with the appropriate verses.

1. Mark 1:29-31   A. Jesus' message about the last days
2. Mark 5:37   B. The Garden of Gethsemane
3. Mark 9:2   C. The raising of Jairus' daughter
4. Mark 13:3   D. The healing of Peter's mother-in-law
5. Mark 14:33   E. The Transfiguration

If we are going to experience discipleship environments like Jesus, then huddles are vital. Think about it. Jesus spent most of His time with twelve and the majority of that time with three.

DISCIPLESHIP IN A HUDDLE
So, what is a huddle? What happens in a huddle?

1. Huddles are groups of 3 people plus the leader that imitate Jesus' discipling relationship with Peter, James, and John.
2. Huddles are formed through a natural affinity between the leader and the members.
3. Huddles are environments that are caring, open, honest, confidential, accountable, challenging, relaxed, and fun.
4. Huddles are established for a one-year commitment that can be renewed as needed.
5. Huddles ask and answer 2 primary questions in a meeting: 1) What is God saying to me? and 2) What am I going to do about it?
6. Huddles are focused on helping one another produce the Fruit of New Life.
7. Huddles are effective because they utilize the wisdom, insights, and challenges of every group member rather than the leader only.
8. Huddles are less curriculum-based and more Spirit-led as the leader evaluates the needs of the group and needs of the individuals.

9. Huddles maximize a leader's time in that he/she disciples 3 at a time rather than just one.
10. Huddles are able to multiply organically over time (*Building a Discipleship Culture*, by Mike Breen)

Who are 3-5 followers of Christ that you greatly respect and who are accessible to you? These could be people who are currently in your LifeGroup. Write their names in the space provided.

_____
_____
_____
_____
_____

Follow me as I follow Christ.

Think about how you might ask one of the persons listed above to disciple you in the context of a huddle. Write down some talking points in the space below.

_____
_____
_____
_____
_____
_____
_____

Now, would you craft an email or make a phone call to ask someone to disciple you?

☐ Yes   ☐ No   ☐ Maybe later

If you won't craft the email or make the phone call, what is holding you back?

_____
_____
_____
_____

What was one of the most helpful insights that you received during this lesson?

_____
_____
_____

Close your time in prayer asking God to give you a desire to be discipled and to give you a desire to also be a discipler.

WEEK 11, DAY 4: CURRICULUM FOR DISCIPLESHIP

In a very real sense, Jesus has already defined our discipleship curriculum. It's described in Matthew 28:20. Look up the verse in your Bible and circle the word "all."

We are to teach every follower of Christ to observe *all* that Jesus commanded. Someone said, "All means all and that's all all means." Teaching another person to observe *all* that Jesus commanded is a daunting task!

But making disciples is far more than a program.
It is the mission of our lives. It defines us.
A disciple is a disciple maker.
Francis Chan - Multiply: Disciples Making Disciples

One of the greatest disciplers ever, the Apostle Paul, talked about the goal of discipleship in Colossians 1. Look up Colossians 1:28-29 and highlight or underline the verses in your Bible.

When it comes to discipleship, who are we to proclaim?
(Hint: Look at Colossians 1:27.)

_____

Although we know that as individuals we can't do everything, who should we want to be discipled? Who should be warned and taught?
(Hint: The word appears 3 times in verse 28.)

_____

What is the goal of our discipleship?
(Hint: It occurs in the last part of verse 28.)

_____

How hard should we work to disciple others?
(Hint: 2 words in verse 29 answer this question.)

_____

What must our perspective be if we ever feel like we don't have the resources, wisdom, or strength to disciple others?
(Hint: The last part of verse 29 provides the answer.)

_____

So, the goal is to help followers of Jesus observe all He commanded so that they become mature in Christ. Read 1 John 2:12-14 and underline the levels of maturity mentioned.

John refers to his readers as little children, children, young men, and fathers.

Most would agree that he is referring not to their physiological ages, but to their levels of spiritual growth. In some ways spiritual growth is analogous to physiological growth.

Spiritual babies	→	Spiritual children
Spiritual children	→	Spiritual adolescents
Spiritual adolescents	→	Spiritual young adults
Spiritual young adults	→	Spiritually reproducing parents

If you consider yourself a spiritual child, you obviously have lots of growing to do. But you can still have an influence on others. You can be a discipler of a spiritual baby. If you consider yourself to be a spiritual young adult, you can still be a discipler of a spiritual adolescent. All that's necessary is that you stay several steps ahead of the one(s) you are discipling. Pray. Who might God want you to influence for Christ?

If you are growing as a disciple, then you can disciple others who may not be as far along as you are. Others will see your growth in Christ. They will sense your credibility. They will grab your arm and say, "Let us go with you, for we have seen that God is with you" (Zechariah 8:23).

It seems clear that God is looking for spiritual parents who will purpose to help other believers grow as disciples. It is wrong for parents to neglect the training of their children. In a similar way, it's wrong for believers to neglect the development of spiritual babies, children, adolescents, and young adults. Everyone needs a discipler. But, practically speaking, just how do we do this?

WHAT'S OUR CURRICULUM?
We produce discipleship curricula at CVC that helps people grow: *Your New Life*, a 3-week booklet; *Watermark*, a booklet on baptism; *Taproot*, a 6-week study for discipleship huddles; *Living New*, a 12-week LifeGroup curriculum (that's what you're completing now!); a Missional Living booklet; a LifeHouses booklet; a yearly Bible reading and Bible memory plan; a Live New Journal; weekly sermon-based LifeGroup study guides; and more.

In addition to CVC-produced materials, we can recommend CBMC's *Operation Timothy*, The Navigator's *2:7 series*, Cru's *10 Basic Steps to Christian Maturity*, Lifeway's *MasterLife* and Francis Chan's *Multiply*.

All these tools are helpful. But we cannot rely on programs and materials to do the job. A discipling ministry must be carried out in the context of community. Discipleship happens best when it is relationship-based, not curriculum-focused. Discipleship happens through people, not programs. Disciples cannot be mass produced.

We cannot drop people into a curriculum-based program and see disciples emerge at the end of a production line. It takes time to make disciples. It takes patient personal attention. It takes hours of prayer. It takes patience and understanding to teach people how to get into the Word of God for themselves, how to feed and nourish their souls, and how to become reproducers for Christ.

THE DNA OF LIFE TRANSFORMING HUDDLES

Discipleship is really about life transformation. We've already seen from the life of Jesus that Jesus had close ties with Peter, James, and John. It seems that life change happens best in a group of 3-4. Some people call them Life Transformation Groups. Others call them Huddles.

But how do they work? What is the DNA of a life transforming huddle?

Life transformation simply will not happen if all we do is get together and share life's challenges in a sympathetic way. And life transformation won't happen if all we do is get together and unsympathetically challenge each other to do more and try harder.

Disciples are people who are learning to *be* and to *do*. Disciples learn to *be* like Jesus. That's an internal change involving our attitudes and desires. And disciples learn to *do* what Jesus did, and would do, if He lived in our bodies in our cultural and relational context. Discipleship is the process of becoming who Jesus would be if He were you.

How did the church grow from 120 people in an upper room to more than 50% of the Roman Empire in about 250 years? They had a way of reproducing the life of Jesus in disciples (in real, flesh-and-blood people) who were able to do the things we read about Jesus doing in the gospels.

The acronym DNA can help us keep a discipleship huddle focused and moving forward so that each individual is growing spiritually.

Look up John 14:6. The DNA of a life transforming huddle comes from Jesus Himself who said, *I am the way, the truth, and the life* (John 14:6). If you haven't already, circle the words "way," "truth," and "life."

D – DIVINE TRUTH
Jesus said that He is the Truth. Foundational huddle question

#1: What are you reading and applying from God's Word and what are you doing about it?

N – NURTURING RELATIONSHIPS.
Jesus said that He is the Life. Foundational huddle question

#2: How are you encouraging and bonding with others in Christ, especially the significant others in the circle of your family and close friends?

A – APOSTOLIC MISSION.
Jesus said that He is the Way. Foundational huddle question #3: Who are you focused on reaching for Christ, and what are your next steps in seeking to reach them?

A life transforming huddle meets together regularly and discusses, encourages, and monitors DNA each time they meet. As issues, challenges, and opportunities arise, the discipler can choose podcasts, blog posts, articles, books, and booklets in order to customize the discipleship content for the individuals in the huddle. (Other helpful discipleship questions are included as an appendix at the end of this week's materials.)

Using the DNA approach helps to keep the discipling organic, personal, and relational rather than content-oriented and curriculum-based. It's what helps keep the discipling transformational rather than informational.

As you close your time today (and as an extension of yesterday's application), ask God to show you three things:

1. A leader who might have the desire and the time to disciple you in a huddle context.
2. 2 others who might want to join your huddle.
3. 2 or 3 people who need to be discipled, and who might be open to being discipled by you.

What was one of the most helpful insights that you received during this lesson?

_____
_____
_____

WEEK 11, DAY 5: FINDING THE RIGHT PEOPLE TO DISCIPLE

Everyone is called to be a growing disciple. But not everyone wants to grow. Since we have a limited amount of resources—time, talent, and treasure—we ought to be careful about how we invest our resources in discipleship. In the gospels, we see Jesus being extremely careful about choosing those whom He would mentor, train, and develop.

Before calling His disciples, Jesus took time to go off by Himself and pray. Read Luke 6:12-16.

Take some time to do a little speculation. Based on what you know about Jesus, the disciples, and the mission, what are a few characteristics you think Jesus was looking for when He chose the 12?

_____

_____

_____

Jesus' 12 disciples were from all walks of life: fishermen, political activists, tax collectors, common people, strong leaders, rich, poor, educated, and uneducated. They obviously met Jesus' qualifications, but many of us might have overlooked them.

Many years ago, Tim Hansel wrote an imaginary letter to Jesus from "Jordan Management Consultants" about the qualifications of the 12. It illustrates that the qualifications Jesus looked for were different than what we might be seeking. Jesus chose the ones the world considered unlikely, marginalized, and ill-equipped.

To: Jesus, Son of Joseph
Woodcrafter's Carpenter Shop
Nazareth 25922

From: Jordan Management Consultants

Dear Sir:

Thank you for submitting the resumes of the twelve men you have picked for managerial positions in your new organization. All of them have now taken our battery of tests; and we have not only run the results through our computer, but also arranged personal interviews for each of them with our psychologist and vocational aptitude consultant.

The profiles of all tests are included, and you will want to study each of them carefully.

As part of our service, we make some general comments for your guidance, much as an auditor will include some general statements. This is given as a result of staff consultation, and comes without any additional fee.

It is the staff's opinion that most of your nominees are lacking in background, education, and vocational aptitude for the type of enterprise you are undertaking. They do not have the team concept. We would recommend that you continue your search for persons of experience in managerial ability and proven capability.

Simon Peter is emotionally unstable and given to fits of temper. Andrew has absolutely no qualities of leadership. The two brothers, James and John, the sons of Zebedee, place personal interest above company loyalty. Thomas demonstrates a questioning attitude that would tend to undermine morale. We feel that it is our duty to tell you that Matthew had been blacklisted by the Greater Jerusalem Better Business Bureau; James, the son of Alphaeus, and Thaddaeus definitely have radical leanings, and they both registered a high score on the manic-depressive scale.

One of the candidates, however, shows great potential. He is a man of ability and resourcefulness, meets people well, has a keen business mind, and has contacts in high places. He is highly motivated, ambitious, and responsible. We recommend Judas Iscariot as your controller and right-hand man. All of the other profiles are self-explanatory.

We wish you every success in your new venture.

Sincerely,
Jordan Management Consultants

Taken from *Eating Problems for Breakfast*, by Tim Hansel, pp.194-195.

Jesus saw potential in His first followers that the world would tend to overlook and He invited them into a discipling relationship. When we are looking for people to disciple, we should not always choose who the world might choose. The world's best and the brightest don't always meet God's qualifications.

Let's fast-forward to learn how another discipler made his decisions about who are the best candidates for discipling.

The Apostle Paul once gave his protégé, Timothy, instructions about the kind of people he ought to be discipling. Read and highlight or underline 2 Timothy 2:2, one of the most important verses in the Bible about discipling.

Describe what you see in the verse about the characteristics we ought to look for in the lives of someone we may want to disciple.

_____

_____

_____

LOOKING FOR FIT PEOPLE

The Apostle Paul's first qualification was that the people we choose to disciple would be Faithful. These are people who are reliable, dependable, and trustworthy. The second and third criteria come from the phrase *"will be able to teach others also."* They must be Intentional about reproducing what you have taught them. Finally, they must be Teachable since people who teach others must be people who have previously been taught.

When you are looking for someone to disciple, you are looking for someone who is Faithful, Intentional, and Teachable. This reflects our desire to develop spiritually FIT disciples who will reproduce in the lives of others.

How do we determine faithfulness, intentionality, and teachability? By observation. Implied in the ability to make this kind of assessment is a relationship. You have to be close enough to observe the person in a variety of settings over time.

Do you see someone who is growing to be an example to others in the disciplines and habits that will help people grow closer to Christ? Do you see evidence of faithful commitment to personal devotions, regular church attendance, involvement in a LifeGroup, or in serving? Are they intentional in inviting others to serve with them in areas where they have volunteered? Do you see someone who asks questions, who is humble enough to admit that he/she doesn't have all the answers, and who is hungry to learn even through painful experiences?

A FIT person takes steps to get involved in the opportunities presented through the church. A FIT person is someone you've connected with relationally and had the opportunity to observe his/her attitudes, behaviors, and choices.

We need to engage in loving relationships with other Christians, always having our radar on, looking for those who are FIT. To follow the biblical pattern of discipleship, we must prayerfully and intentionally select FIT people to disciple who will go on to disciple others.

Who are 3-5 people who come to your mind as you think about someone the world might neglect or ignore, but who shows signs of being Faithful, Intentional, and Teachable? Write a few names in the space below.

_____
_____
_____
_____
_____

Now, ask God for wisdom over the next few weeks and months to determine if these people are the ones that He would call you to disciple.

REPRODUCING DISCIPLES: MULTIPLICATION, NOT ADDITION
Look very carefully once again at 2 Timothy 2:2. How many generations of disciples do you see?

Do you see in this verse a progression—from 1) Paul, to 2) Timothy, to 3) faithful men, to 4) others? That's four generations.

Paul introduces the concept of multiplication in this verse rather than mere addition. He's encouraging Timothy to impact men (not one man) who will, in turn, impact others.

> **One indispensable requirement for producing godly,**
> **mature Christians is godly, mature Christians.**
> *Kevin DeYoung*

Do the math. If you were to lead one person to Christ every day for 30 years you would end up with 10,950 people who were on their way to heaven because of your evangelistic efforts. But how many of us lead someone to Christ every day?

But what happens if you lead someone to Christ and then disciple that person for a year? What if you help that person become a mature follower of Jesus and teach him/her to lead others to Christ? At the end of the year, there would be 2 of you. That may not sound like much. But keep reading.

Suppose the two of you each win one person to Christ and take them through a discipleship process? At the end of the next year, there would be 4. Do it again the following year and there would be 8. Then 16, 32, 64, 128, 256, 512, 1,024 . . . You get the idea. What if the process went on and on and on? In 30 years, the number of disciples would be 536,870,912. Those are amazing numbers.

What if you became the first in a multiplying chain of discipleship in your family, in your neighborhood, or at your workplace? Imagine what God might be able to do in, through, with, and for you? What if God literally changed the world through you?

WHO ME? A DISCIPLER?
Yes, you! You might be thinking, "God couldn't use me. I'm too young in the faith. My past sins are too ugly. I'm not holy enough yet. I've wasted too much time."

Please don't disqualify yourself. Read about Peter's failure and restoration in John 18:15-17 and John 21:15-17. After Peter denied Christ, Jesus restored him and said, "Feed My sheep." If Jesus restored and used a person like Peter, then He can restore and use you, too.

How might you get started?

What if you took 1, 2, or 3 people through this same curriculum you are currently using? All you need to be is a few steps ahead of the people you are discipling. Who in your family, in your neighborhood, in your church, or in your workplace also needs to know what you have been learning?

How do you ask? Ask one-on-one, face-to-face, "You know, I've been encouraged and helped in my relationship with Christ through a study I've done at church. It takes about 15 minutes a day, 5 days a week. Then, we meet with a leader for an hour or so to discuss what we're learning. I've been encouraged to help others grow. I would love the privilege of helping you grow in your relationship with Christ, too. Are you interested?"

It's that simple. If you disciple others using this material, then please let our staff at CVC know and someone on our team can help you reproduce copies. Email CVC at connect@cvconline.org.

Close your time today by asking God to help you be a discipler.

What was one of the most helpful insights that you received during this lesson?

_____

_____

_____

Christianity without discipleship is always
Christianity without Christ.
Dietrich Bonhoeffer - German Pastor, Theologian, Martyr

Appendix A

DISCIPLESHIP HUDDLE QUESTIONS

Questions can be a great tool to use in discipling people if they are asked with the right heart. Some people can ask questions in a demanding, judging, or punishing way. The discipler must see himself as a Beloved Child and must see others in the huddle as Beloved Children.

True disciplers connect with the hearts of others. They give and receive God's grace so everyone in the huddle can connect authentically in order to be transformed by God's grace and truth (John 1:14). It's in this context that the following questions might be used.

The following questions have been compiled from a variety of sources including John Wesley's "Small Group Questions," "Renovare Questions," "Questions from The Highway"—Community in Palo Alto, "Florent Varak's Questions," "Neil Cole's Questions," "Dave Guiles' Questions," "Paul Klawitter's Questions," and "Richard J. Kejcir's Questions."

Before you meet with your huddle, you might want to scan this list of questions and ask God to help you choose one or two to supplement your regular DNA questions. This is a "shopping list" of questions. It's helpful to get the questions in front of the huddle members before you meet.

QUESTIONS RELATED TO BEING A BELOVED CHILD

- What are the secrets, the sins, and the wounds of your past that still haunt you—that keep you from believing you are a Beloved Child?
- What are some of the reasons why you sometimes doubt the wisdom, goodness, and power of God?
- What are the recurring idols in your heart that pull you away from your New Life in Christ?
- When and how have you been self-conscious, self-pitying, or self-justifying?
- Are you doing anything about which your conscience is uneasy?
- How did you practice *joy* this week? Have you had a thankful attitude toward God? Have you struggled with anger toward God? How so? What can you do about it?
- Did you struggle with a disappointment this week? How did you handle it?
- What disappointments did you face? Did they consume your thoughts? What did you do about it? What can you learn?

QUESTIONS RELATED TO BEING A SELF-FEEDER

- In what ways did God make His presence known to you since our last meeting? What experiences of prayer, meditation, and spiritual reading has God given you?
- In what ways did you encounter Christ in your reading of the Scriptures since our last meeting? How has the Bible shaped the way you think and live?
- What errors or lies that you once believed have now been corrected by your reading of the Scriptures?
- What do you need to ask the Spirit of God to reveal to you that you have not yet understood?

QUESTIONS RELATED TO BEING A SERVANT

- Are you consciously or unconsciously creating the impression that you are better than you are? In other words, where and how are you tempted to be a hypocrite?
- Is there anyone you fear, dislike, disown, criticize, hold resentment toward, or disregard? If so, what are you going to do about it?
- Are you too frequently grumbling or complaining?
- Have you become critical, irritable, or touchy? Why have you allowed yourself to be this way?
- What difficulties or frustrations did you encounter? What joys or delights?
- What spiritual gifts did the Spirit enable you to exercise? What was the outcome?
- What opportunities did God give you to serve others since our last meeting? How did you respond?
- Have you demonstrated a servant's heart? How so? What have you done for someone else this week?
- Did you express a forgiving attitude toward others?

QUESTIONS RELATED TO BEING AN INVESTOR

- In what ways has God blessed you this week? How have you shared your blessings?
- What are the specific places, times, or situations where you are especially susceptible to temptation to act in sensual, selfish, or materialistic ways?
- How are you growing in your generosity? What is keeping you from being as generous as you would like to be? What will you do about that?

QUESTIONS RELATED TO BEING A DISCIPLER

- Did you give the proper quality/quantity of time in your most important relationships in order to help others grow?
- What blocks your growth in Christ? What is blocking your growth in your relationships and is keeping you from becoming more mature and effectual?
- Who is someone that God has put on your heart that you could help grow in Christ?

QUESTIONS RELATED TO BEING A MISSIONARY

- Have you encountered injustice, or any oppression of others? Were you able to work for justice?
- Is God putting a particular burden on your heart about a cause, a problem, or an issue? What is a Global Goliath that you would like to defeat? What brings a tear to your eye or makes you pound the table? What makes you think, "That needs to change"?
- What lost person(s) has God particularly burdened you about this week? What will you do about seeking to reach him/her with the good news of Jesus?

GENERAL QUESTIONS

- How have you sensed any influence or work of the Holy Spirit in your life since our last meeting?
- What fruit of the Spirit would you like to see increase in your life? What disciplines might be useful in this effort?
- Specifically, what area of your life do you feel that God most wants to change? Have you taken specific steps to make those changes?
- What good habit do you feel God wants to form in your life? Have you taken specific steps to develop that habit?
- Did your life reflect verbal integrity this past week?
- Did you practice any undisciplined or addictive behavior this past week?
- What have you held back from God that you need to surrender?
- Is there anything in your life that has dampened your zeal for Christ?
- What worries or other issues are you currently facing?
- What do you see as your number one need or struggle for this next week?
- How can this huddle help you?

Appendix B

THE LEADERSHIP GREENHOUSE

Although not every follower of Christ has the spiritual gift of leadership (Romans 12:8), every follower of Christ has been called to lead at some level. For example, we've all been called to lead ourselves.

In addition, we all are called to influence others to some degree: friends influencing friends, parents influencing children, big brothers and sisters influencing little brothers and sisters, etc.

So, while we all may not have the leadership gift with a capital "L," we all have leadership opportunities and responsibilities with a little "l." This means we need to grow as leaders. Leadership development is a unique aspect of discipleship.

Do you see yourself as a capital "L" leader or a little "l" leader? Why do you answer the way you do? Is it possible that you have put a lid on your leadership potential?

At CVC, we call our leadership development process a Leadership Greenhouse. A greenhouse, of course, is an environment where plants are grown. Incoming sunshine is absorbed inside the structure, which allows for greater opportunity to influence the growth of plants. Light, shade, watering, fertilizing, and humidity are engineered to facilitate growth. Greenhouses enable the plants to overcome poor exterior growth environments such as poor land, light, or water. Particular attention is paid to the control of pests, diseases, heat, humidity, and irrigation. Plants can be grown at any time during the year. Usually, the end aim is that the plants leave the greenhouse to be a source of blessing to the world outside.

"Leadership development is an intentional process in which a potential, new, or growing leader interacts with an experienced leader producing transformation in the character and competencies that increase their ability to influence people, outcomes, and culture" (*Leadership Pipeline Development*, by Mac Lake).

It's helpful to think of leadership development as movement along a continuum. Or we could think of leadership development as movement in the Leadership Greenhouse from one table or section to another.

Leading Self → Leading Others → Leading Leaders → Leading Departments → Leading Organizations

Everyone is called to lead self. And to some degree, everyone is called to lead others. But not everyone is called to lead leaders, to lead a department, or to lead the organization.

For example, if a person's primary spiritual gifts are mercy and service (Romans 12:7-8), they will be called to lead self and lead others. But they likely will not be called to lead beyond leading others. It's important to remember, though, that the person with service/mercy gifting can be a totally-mature, absolutely-committed, fully-pleasing, top-of-the-line disciple without ever leading leaders or leading a department.

Some people, however, have been gifted in different ways. Their leadership capacity is greater. God's calling for them is not higher or better. It's simply different. Part of their discipleship journey must include leadership development at the level of leading leaders, and perhaps even leading departments and leading organizations.

It's important that we provide a discipling pathway that allows people to grow in their ability to lead at whatever the next level might be for them.

> **Leadership is all about taking people on the journey.**
> **The challenge is that most of the time, we are asking people**
> **to follow us to places we ourselves have never been.**
> *Andy Stanley - Lead Pastor, North Point Community Church*

Week 12

WITNESS: LIVING AS A MISSIONARY

MEMORY VERSE
but in your hearts honor Christ the Lord as holy, always being prepared to make a defense to anyone who asks you for a reason for the hope that is in you; yet do it with gentleness and respect,
1 Peter 3:15

WEEK 12, DAY 1: WHY LIVE MISSIONALLY?

The short answer? Because Jesus is the only way. Turn in your Bible and highlight or underline John 14:6.

Jesus taught that there is a real heaven and a real hell. Everyone we know, love, and care about will spend eternity in one place or the other (Matthew 25:34, 46; Hebrews 9:27). And Jesus made an audacious claim about Himself. He said, *I am the way, and the truth and the life. No one comes to the Father except through Me* (John 14:6). Jesus boldly claims to be the only way to heaven.

This is why we must be on mission to share with others the good news that Jesus saves.

THE WAY. THE TRUTH. THE LIFE.

It's significant that in the Greek language the definite article for the word "the" in John 14:6 precedes each word— "way," "truth," and "life." Jesus is not claiming to be *a* way, *a* truth, or *a* life. He's claiming to be *the* way, *the* truth, and *the* life.

Imagine that you have a life-threatening illness. You know you need to get to a hospital. But you are in a strange town. You ask for directions. Suppose a person says, "Take the first right here, then go left at the next intersection. Veer right at the 3rd street you cross. When you come to a Y in the road, turn left. Go through an intersection with a 4-way stop sign . . ." Chances are you'd get lost halfway there.

But suppose a person says, "Get in my car. I'll take you to the hospital. You can trust me. I know the way and the truth about the medicine you need. See, I am the only doctor in town. No one else can prescribe the meds for you. Only me." In that case, the person is, temporally speaking, the way, the truth, and the life.

And that's precisely the case with Jesus. He doesn't point the way or draw some impersonal map. He *is* the way, the truth, and the life. The *only* way, truth, and life. For everyone.

In just a few words, explain what Jesus means when He says He is *the* way.

_____

_____

_____

In just a few words, explain what Jesus means when He says He is *the* truth.

_____

_____

_____

In just a few words, explain what Jesus means when He says He is *the* life.

_____

_____

_____

In just a few words, explain what Jesus means when He says that no one comes to the Father except through Him.

_____

_____

_____

ARROGANT? NARROW-MINDED? INTOLERANT? JUDGMENTAL? DOGMATIC?

Many people in the Western world consider Jesus' words in John 14:6 to be arrogant and narrow-minded. They find it difficult to believe there is only one way to God because they know kind, respectable people who do not believe in Jesus.

Skeptics say that it is intolerant, judgmental, and dogmatic to believe that the only way for anyone to be saved is through Jesus. In fact, many of our friends believe the opposite—namely, there are many ways to God, a view called religious pluralism. Because our culture values tolerance, cynics say, "Who do these Christians think they are? Who are they to judge everyone else? How dare they say that Jesus is the only way?" They believe there are many ways to God, not just one way, because it seems more enlightened, humble, and tolerant.

But Christ-followers did not invent this claim that Jesus is the only way. This is not the church's claim. According to John 14:6, it's Christ's claim. Believers are merely relating His claim and the claim of the writers of the New Testament. Turn in your Bible and highlight or underline Acts 4:11-12.

Please fill in the blanks below based on Acts 4:11-12.

_____ is the stone that was rejected.

There is salvation in _____ _____ _____.

There is _____ _____ _____ under heaven given among men by which we _____ be saved.

Let's bring this close to home—close to your home. You have family members, friends, co-workers, and neighbors who don't know Christ. Because all people are born sinful and without a saving relationship with Jesus Christ, they will experience an eternity separated from Him.

As beloved children of God, we have a unique opportunity to be a part of His plan to reconcile broken people to Himself. It is an honor that God chooses to use us in being a part of this amazing journey to make his transformational truth known to the world! There is no plan B. God intends for us to be the ones sharing the exciting truth of His love with each man, each woman, and each child all across the planet, regardless of race, culture, or background.

In the space provided below, make a list of people you know who do not yet know Christ as personal Lord and Savior.

Family	Friends	Co-Workers	Neighbors
_____	_____	_____	_____
_____	_____	_____	_____
_____	_____	_____	_____
_____	_____	_____	_____
_____	_____	_____	_____
_____	_____	_____	_____
_____	_____	_____	_____

Why should we be passionate about Missional Living—about sharing our faith with others? Dr. Grey Allison, Founder and former President of Mid-America Baptist Theological Seminary, gives 4 reasons. Match the following reasons we should have a burden to share the gospel with the appropriate verses:

1. The cry from without; apart from Christ, people are hurting.   A. Matthew 28:19
2. The cry from within; God puts His love in our hearts.   B. Acts 16:31
3. The cry from beneath; those in hell would warn others.   C. Luke 16:27-28
4. The cry from above; God Himself has commanded us to witness.   D. 2 Corinthians 5:14, 20

If we listen carefully, we'll hear the heart cries of those who are lost around us. Deep down, they know something is wrong. They know their lives are not right. But they don't know why. They don't know how to be restored. They don't know how to gain new life. They would listen if we would lovingly build bridges and share the good news.

If we will listen to our hearts, we'll be motivated by our love for Jesus. See, we live on mission because we have come to know and love Jesus. We just naturally talk about what we love. When we fall in love with Jesus, nobody will have to twist our arms to get us to share Christ with others. We'll want everybody to know and love Him just like we know and love Him.

If our spiritual ears are open, we would be able to hear the cries of those who are in hell, "This torment is unbearable. This agony is awful. Can someone dip his finger in water and cool my tongue? Please warn my family members and my friends! Warn them so they won't end up here in this place of torment!" (Luke 16:24, 27-28).

If we are listening to the Lord, we will hear Him commanding us to share our faith in Christ. That's really all we need to know. If we've surrendered to Him and if He is our Lord, then when He says witness, we should witness. Jesus literally, personally tells us to go make disciples, to go win the lost. Why witness? It's not because we feel like it. It's because we've been commanded by God to share Christ.

Which of the 4 reasons above is the most motivating to you today? Why?

_____

_____

_____

_____

Use the following prayer as inspiration for your own:

Lord God, help me see people the way You see them. Help me be broken-hearted for those who need Christ and Your restoration. Thank You that Jesus is the way, the truth, and the life. Thank You that you have given me a New Life in Christ to share with others. Help me to invite people to Jesus, the One who saves everyone who calls on Him. Please work powerfully to draw my family, my friends, my co-workers, and my neighbors to Christ. In Jesus' name, Amen.

Ask God many times throughout your day today to see people as He does, and take the time to reach out past your comfort zone to care for someone who may not know Jesus, especially someone of a different culture, race, or background.

What was one of the most helpful insights that you received during this lesson?

_____

_____

_____

_____

If sinners be damned, at least let them leap to Hell over our dead bodies. And if they perish, let them perish with our arms wrapped about their knees, imploring them to stay. If Hell must be filled, let it be filled in the teeth of our exertions, and let not one go unwarned and unprayed for.
Charles H. Spurgeon

WEEK 12, DAY 2: ME, A MISSIONARY?

What does the word "missionary" mean to you? How would you define the term? _____

_____

_____

_____

_____

Match the following terms that describe our identity as missionaries with the appropriate verses.

1.	Ambassador	A.	Matthew 28:19
2.	Witness	B.	2 Corinthians 5:20
3.	Discipler	C.	Acts 1:8
4.	Fisherman	D.	Psalm 126:5-6
5.	Sower	E.	Matthew 4:19

As followers of Jesus, we are ambassadors—authorized representatives of the King of heaven while living here on this earth. We are witnesses—empowered people who testify to what we have seen Christ do in our lives. We are disciplers—commissioned followers of Jesus who teach others to follow Jesus, too. We are fishermen—equipped people who cast nets and catch people for Christ. We are sowers—generous people who scatter the seeds of the gospel to as many people as possible.

Which calling makes you feel most comfortable? Least comfortable? Why?

_____

_____

_____

_____

YOU ARE A MISSIONARY FOR GOD!

At CVC one of our passions is Missional Living. We see ourselves as God's agents of restoration in the relationships and community around us. We want to change the world and restore the broken.

That's why we focus on building bridges of friendship to reach our family members, our neighbors, and our communities. That's why we use our time and resources to serve, bless, and reach out to those who don't know Christ. Lost people matter to God, and, therefore, they matter to us. We want the New Life God has given us to be abundantly fruitful for His Kingdom.

Write the following statement somewhere and post it in a prominent place, perhaps in the flyleaf of your Bible:

WE WANT TO GO TO HEAVEN AND TAKE AS MANY PEOPLE WITH US AS WE POSSIBLY CAN.

MISSIONARY PRAYING

One ingredient that every missionary knows is vital for the success of his/her mission, is prayer. Prayer changes things. No missionary effort will have life-changing impact without passionate, prevailing prayer.

Think about the people you know who are far from God. Are you praying for them? Are their names written down on a prayer card or in a prayer journal so you are reminded to pray for them often?

Why do they need your prayers? They are blind, bound, and buried. Match the following verses with the appropriate description.

1. People far from God are blind.
2. People far from God are bound (captured).
3. People far from God are buried (dead).

A. Ephesians 2:1
B. 2 Corinthians 4:4
C. 2 Timothy 2:16

Apart from Christ, every person on the planet is in a spiritually helpless and hopeless state.

The Bible teaches that, temporarily, God has given Satan some "leash" as His enemy. In fact, Satan is called "the god of this world." And he works to make sure that our unsaved family members and friends cannot see the beauty and majesty of Jesus. *The god of this world has blinded the minds of the unbelievers, to keep them from seeing the light of the gospel of the glory of Christ, who is the image of God* (2 Corinthians 4:4).

The Bible teaches that Satan seeks to capture unsuspecting people in his traps. When people do come to faith in Christ, it's because they have been set free from the devil's snare. *And they may come to their senses and escape from the snare of the devil, after being captured by him to do his will* (2 Timothy 2:26).

The Bible teaches that people apart from Christ are spiritually dead. They may be alive physically, but they are dead spiritually. *You were dead in the trespasses and sins* (Ephesians 2:1). All around us people are dead men walking; dead women walking; dead boys, girls, and teenagers walking. This means that apart from Christ, no one is able to spiritually respond to God and to truth. A corpse doesn't hear conversations going on at a funeral home. It doesn't have an appetite. It's dead. This is also true when it comes to the spiritual life of people apart from Christ. They don't hear God. They don't have an appetite for the things of God.

Write down the names of some people you know who are blind, bound, and buried. You might list some of the same people you listed in the study for Week 5, Day 1. Or some new people might come to mind.

Blind	Bound	Buried
_____	_____	_____
_____	_____	_____
_____	_____	_____
_____	_____	_____
_____	_____	_____
_____	_____	_____

Question: Who gives sight to the blind? Who sets the captives free? Who raises the dead to life? That's right! Jesus!

And this is precisely why we should pray! Prayer is asking Jesus to do for us what we cannot do.

Lost people don't just need a new set of glasses, they need a new set of eyes. And that's what Jesus does. A blind person isn't just near-sighted or far-sighted. It's pointless to say to a blind person, "Just focus more!" Pleading with a spiritually blind person to try harder to see the gospel of Jesus won't work. Why not? They can't see.

Lost people don't just need a little more fresh air; they need to get out of jail. And that's what Jesus does. An imprisoned person isn't just in need of a little stroll in the jail yard. It's pointless to say to someone who is incarcerated to try harder to live free. Begging a spiritually entrapped person to kick his/her ungodly addictions won't work. Why not? He/She is in Satan's snare.

Lost people don't just need resuscitation; they need resurrection. And that's what Jesus does. A dead body cannot respond. It's pointless to shout at a corpse: "Hey! I know you are in bad shape. But pull yourself together and get up!" And making an appeal to a spiritually dead person won't work. We can't simply say, "Just try harder to be a good person." It won't work. Why not? They are dead.

A blind, bound, and buried person does not have the capacity to repent and believe the gospel. No preaching, no spiritual motivation, no psychological techniques, no positive thinking, no do-it-yourself schemes will help. So, what can help?

Prayer!

Maybe many of the people you know are messed up. You've been trying to fix it. You've tried everything: Threats. Manipulation. Intimidation. Cooperation. Counseling. Begging. Preaching. Church-going. Nothing is working.

Could it be that spouse, that child, that teen, that parent is blind, bound, and buried? Nothing is going to change until God intervenes. Start praying. Start hitting your knees.

To help you learn how to pray biblically, here is a prayer based on the truths we see in 2 Corinthians 4:4, 2 Timothy 2:26, and Ephesians 2:1.

> *Lord God Almighty, You are infinitely rich in mercy and You delight in making all things new. Please be merciful to _____ and make him/her into Your masterpiece. He/She is spiritually dead in trespasses and sins. So, please raise him/her to life. He/She has been held captive by Satan to do his will. Please set him/her free to do Your will instead. He/She has been blinded by the enemy and cannot see the grace of God in the face of Christ. Open his/her eyes to behold the glory of Your grace. Show off Your great power in saving him/her and giving him/her the gift of faith in Jesus.*
> *In Jesus' name, Amen.*

What if you began to pray this way for those you know who are lost? (For years if you have to.)

Today, use the 2 lists you've created in the lesson for Week 12, Day 1 and in today's lesson to make a prayer list of lost people. Keep your list in a visible place in your Bible or in a journal.

See, you can't raise the spiritually dead. You can't set a captive free. You can't make a blind person see. But you can talk to the One who can. You can pray. Will you?

What was one of the most helpful insights that you received during this lesson?

_____

_____

_____

_____

_____

Talk to God about your friend before you talk to your friend about God.

WEEK 12, DAY 3: HEARING THEIR STORIES

Everybody loves a good story. And everybody has a life story. To be effective in reaching people for Christ, it's helpful to use a 3 story approach: 1) Their story, 2) Your story, and 3) God's story. We need to hear the stories of those who don't yet know Christ, share our stories, and then point them to Jesus and His story.

Sometimes, we can be so interested in making our points that we fail to hear the stories of hurt and pain in the lives of other people. How do we handle things when someone far from God lives and acts in ways that we know displease Him? Too often, believers turn off non-believers with our attitudes, words, and actions.

Are we curious about the stories of other people? Or are we just wanting to make our points? We must develop friendships with people outside the church and <u>listen</u> to them, not just talk at them.

JESUS AND THE WOMAN AT THE WELL

Take a few minutes and read the story in John 4:4-42 about Jesus and a woman who was far from God.

This story about Jesus starts by saying that Jesus was traveling from Judea to Galilee. Verse 4 says He "had to" pass through Samaria. Those words mean that it was absolutely necessary for Jesus to follow the plan of God for His life, for that day. There was a Divine appointment ahead. And God has Divine appointments for us, too.

Jesus comes into a Samaritan village. A well called Jacob's well is there. Jesus is worn out by the trip. So, He sits down at the well at noon. He's alone. His disciples have gone to the village to buy some lunch. And an amazing conversation begins. This is a conversation that teaches us to be friends with outsiders—to hear their stories.

"IN, NOT OF"

One principle we see in the John 4 story is that although we are not to be "of the world" we are to be "in the world." Jesus connects with the woman. He asks for a drink of water. He's *in* her world, but not *of* her world. Describe in the space below what it means for you to be "in the world, not of the world."

_____

_____

_____

_____

Sometimes we can be too engaged with the world. There's not much real difference between our lifestyles and our non-Christian friends' lifestyles. We're "of the world." And that's not good. We are to be pure and holy. Other times we can be too disengaged from the world. No one would ever find us going through a place like Samaria. So, we live isolated lives. We listen only to Christian music, hang out with only Christian people, and go only to Christian places.

To be sure, our culture may be offensive, but we cannot take offense. We must live in a way that honors God, but we must do it in a way that can still influence outsiders. So, we talk to people. Anyone. Everyone. We ask questions—lots of them. Then, we listen closely to their answers.

"PERSONS, NOT PROJECTS"

There was a deep emptiness in the woman's heart. She had a sense of failure. She felt unlovable, perhaps even un-forgivable. She maybe even thought that God had forsaken her. Perhaps her family and friends had disowned her.

No respectable Rabbi would speak with a woman in public. But Jesus set all that aside. It didn't bother Him that she was a Samaritan. Jesus saw her as a person. He took the initiative in speaking to this woman because He cared about people.

What about us? We can want so much for people to come to Christ that, if we're not careful, we'll treat them like projects, not persons.

Describe a time in your life (perhaps at the Bureau of Motor Vehicles or a doctor's office) when someone made you feel like a project, not a person. Then write down how you wish you had been treated.

_____

_____

_____

_____

"CONVERSATION, NOT CONDEMNATION"

Jesus knew that the woman had 5 divorces and was living with a man who was not her husband. Jesus knew that she had broken God's law. She was living with the sin of adultery staining her past and present. She was an outcast of society—someone dirty.

If anyone had a right to condemn her, Jesus did. After all, He was the sinless Son of God. But Jesus chose to offer her a chance to taste living water! And a chance to worship. Jesus didn't act shocked by her lifestyle. He didn't condone it, but He didn't condemn her. He conversed with her.

Be honest. What are some sinful behaviors in the lives of others that make you pull back from engaging in a relationship?

_____

_____

We all probably see some sins in the lives of others that might make us want to condemn them. But if someone is far from God, why should we expect them to live like someone who is not? We should not be offended when non-Christians lie and cheat and steal, when they commit adultery, do drugs, or get drunk. Our faith sometimes seems too focused on other people's faults.

One unbelieving young adult said, "Christians talk about hating sin and loving sinners, but the way they go about things, they might as well call it what it is. They hate the sin and the sinner" (*Unchristian*, by David Kinnaman, p.181).

Most of us would be quick to say, "I don't hate the sinner!" But our actions might communicate otherwise. Be sure you don't act in ways that might make someone *think* you hate the sinner.

Think about it. There is someone you love even though you don't approve of what he or she does. There is someone you accept even though some of his or her thoughts revolt you. There is someone you forgive, even though he or she hurts the people you love the most. Do you know who that person is? That person is . . . you. There are plenty of things about you that you don't like, but if you can love yourself without approving of all you do, you can love others without approving of all they do. Don't label. Don't condemn. Be a friend with no strings attached.

"FOR, NOT AGAINST"

Jesus didn't launch into a big tirade about how He was against divorce and how He was against couples living together prior to marriage. Instead, He was for something better. He said to the woman, "If your relationships haven't been very satisfying, I have something infinitely more satisfying for you: Living water. And true worship."

He's saying to this woman, "God is seeking you. He's for you, not against you. I'm for you, not against you. When you start to worship Him truly, you'll find a satisfaction, a joy, a peace that nothing else will give you." Jesus knew that when she found satisfaction in Him, she would be set free. Jesus is for, not against this woman.

Sometimes, people will want to drag us into conversations about lifestyle, "What do you think about this . . . or that?" And we have to stand where God stands on issues. We need to know what God's Word says about morality and ethics and lifestyle. The law of God never changes and He uses the law to bring conviction of sin to people so that they long for a savior.

But our job is not to police or monitor morality. The law of God is not only in the Bible, but it is also written on people's hearts. Deep, deep down inside, we all know—insiders and outsiders—that left to ourselves, we're not right with God. Most people don't need you to bring the hammer down on this moral issue or that moral issue. What they need is for you to just keep pointing them to Jesus, to the One who can forgive and satisfy their deepest longings.

In the space below, make a list of people you know who are far from God—people that are difficult for you to love and engage but easy to avoid or condemn.

_____

_____

_____

_____

_____

_____

_____

ARE WE LISTENING?
Are we engaging with and interested in the stories in people's lives?

"Christians . . . so often think they must always contribute something when they are in the company of others, that this is the one service they have to render. They forget that listening can be a greater service than speaking. Many people are looking for an ear that will listen. They do not find it among Christians, because these Christians are talking when they should be listening" (*Life Together*, by Dietrich Bonhoeffer, pp.97-98).

Jesus didn't tell the Samaritan woman to get her life straightened out and *then* they would talk. He accepted her. He didn't approve of her sin. But He loved her in spite of it.

We must learn to accept people where they are, not approving their sin or enabling their sin, but loving them in spite of their sin—because God loved us in spite of ours.

The Samaritan woman's life changed that day when she met Jesus. She experienced healing in her life that day, when she met the One who loves the unlovable, who restores the broken.

Jesus shows us how to engage with people who are far from God. We can be friends with people outside the church. We can and must hear their stories.

QUESTIONS TO ASK TO HELP YOU LISTEN BETTER
If you are interested in another person, the questions ought to flow naturally. But here are a few questions that might encourage a meaningful conversation between you and a pre-Christian friend.

General questions:

* What are your sources of strength in your day-to-day living?
* What have been a few of your most memorable experiences so far in life?
* What do you consider to be major turning points or defining moments in your life?
* What gives you joy in your life?
* What do you value most in life?
* What would you say you are living for?
* When you have problems or crises, how do you manage to get through them?
* What have you found to be the best way of dealing with disappointment and discouragement?
* How do you handle being hurt by life and being wounded by others?
* How do you handle pressure, i.e., when the pressure is really on, what do you need most?

Spiritual questions:

- Do you think much about spiritual things?
- What do you think is a person's greatest spiritual need?
- Do you feel close to or far away from God?
- What do you imagine that God is like?
- Have you ever been mad or upset with God?
- Have you ever done something for which you feel God could not forgive you?
- Do you feel there are barriers of some type separating you from God?
- When did you feel closest to God?
- How do you see yourself moving closer to God?
- When you get to heaven, what will be the first three questions you will ask God?

In the space below, write a few questions of your own:

_____
_____
_____
_____

Close your time today praying for the people listed above. Ask God to give you the opportunity to ask one of those persons a question or two this week. Ask God to help you give someone an opportunity to share their story. And then . . . listen!

Pick 1-2 people from the list above. Write one of questions next to that name and look for an opportunity to ask them that question this week.

Name

_____

Question

_____
_____

What was one of the most helpful insights that you received during this lesson?

_____
_____
_____
_____
_____

WEEK 12, DAY 4: SHARING YOUR STORY

Think of a person who would relate to your journey to faith in Christ. Who do you know who might connect with your story? In the space below, describe the kind of people who would resonate with the storyline of your life.

_____

_____

_____

_____

God tells us we are forever on "standby." We are always ready to share with others what Christ has done in our lives with gentleness and respect.

But in your hearts honor Christ the Lord as holy, always being prepared to make a defense to anyone who asks you for a reason for the hope that is in you; yet do it with gentleness and respect, (1 Peter 3:15).

Again, we are always ready to share with others what Christ has done within us.

We all have a story—a testimony. Some are glamorous, some are difficult, and some seem plain. If you have a New Life in Christ, you have an amazing story to tell.

When we say, "I don't have much of a story," in essence what we're saying is that Christ loving me, dying for me, and rising from the dead for me isn't much of a story!

In God's eyes, it's epic! God is the Author of your story. That means it has eternal proportions and ramifications! God has taken you from death to life, from darkness to light, from bondage to freedom, from brokenness to restoration.

Your story is absolutely amazing. Your life experiences, background, how you became drawn to Christ, as well as your personal decision to follow Him, give you a unique and powerful story of a new life in Him. You are a new creation in Christ and this wonderful story needs to get put to work. If you have your testimony carefully reviewed and written down, you will be able to share it comfortably in day-to-day situations.

AN OUTLINE FOR SHARING YOUR STORY

Today, we will have a different kind of time with God. Today, we will examine the example of how Paul shared his story with King Agrippa and use it as a template to tell our own story of grace.

As you read Acts 26 in your Bible, take note of the outline Paul used to share his story. In the margin of your Bible, write down the following outline beside the appropriate verses.

Your life before Christ

A gracious introduction:	Acts 26:2-3
The good in Paul's past life:	Acts 26:4-5
The sinfulness of Paul's past life:	Acts 26:9-11

How you came to Christ

The circumstances of conversion:	Acts 26:12-15

Your life after Christ

The changes after conversion:	Acts 26:19
The gospel message:	Acts 26:23
A personal appeal:	Acts 26:29

GUIDELINES FOR WRITING YOUR STORY

Today, use Paul's outline to craft your own testimony. But before you do, here are a few guidelines for writing your story:

Do:

...ask God to give you wisdom.

...keep your story to a 3-5 minute limit—about 700 words.

...be realistic.

...include the gospel. Say something like, "I realized Christ died for my sins and rose again. I turned from my sin, received the gift of salvation, and trusted Jesus as my personal Lord and Savior. He has given me New Life."

Don't:

...make statements that reflect negatively on any church organization.

...make statements that reflect negatively on any individual.

...mention denominations or church names.

...speak or write in a preachy manner.

...use religious terms like saved, sin, or convicted without explaining them.

...spend a lot of time on your past sins—your old life—and only a little bit of time on your new life/change.

...glorify the church or people. Instead, glorify Christ!

PRAY BEFORE WRITING YOUR STORY

Before you begin to write, you might want to use the following prayer as inspiration for your own:

Father, thank You for saving me and for being with me now. Fill me with power from Your Holy Spirit. Thank You that my story is the one You gave me to share with others. I know that it represents the power of a transformed life. Help me write it in a way that honors You. I pray that You will give me opportunities to share this wonderful story with others so that they could be drawn to a New Life in Christ. In Jesus' name, Amen.

WRITING YOUR STORY

Now, write down your personal story using Paul's example found in Acts 26.

A gracious introduction:

_____

_____

_____

_____

_____

_____

_____

The good in your past life (what you are grateful for):

_____

_____

_____

_____

_____

_____

_____

_____

The sinfulness of your past life (thoughts, actions, and attitudes unpleasing to God):

_____

_____

_____

_____

_____

_____

_____

The circumstances of conversion (when, who did God use and how, the moment you said "I do" to Jesus):

_____

_____

_____

_____

_____

_____

_____

The changes after conversion (description of your New Life / transformation):

_____
_____
_____
_____
_____
_____
_____

The Gospel message (the basics of the death and resurrection of Jesus):

_____
_____
_____
_____
_____
_____
_____
_____

A personal appeal (Invitation to respond):

_____
_____
_____
_____
_____
_____
_____

STRENGTHEN THE TELLING OF YOUR STORY

This week, share your story with a believing friend so that he or she can celebrate your testimony and give you some feedback. After getting some feedback, rewrite your story and be ready to share it with your LifeGroup. Always ask permission to share your story.

In the space below, brainstorm some ways that you might be able to share your story with others.

_____
_____
_____
_____

Which of these outlets will you use in the days ahead?

_____

_____

What was one of the most helpful insights that you received during this lesson?

_____

_____

_____

_____

_____

Telling your story without asking permission can be awkward and rude. Ask, "May I share with you . . ."
Chad Allen, Lead Pastor - Cuyahoga Valley Church

WEEK 12, DAY 5: TELLING HIS STORY

Week 5, Day 3 was about "Hearing their stories." Week 5, Day 4 was about "Sharing your story." Once you've heard their story and shared yours, the people you care about may be open to hear more—to hear about His story—the story of Jesus. It's important that you know how to share the story of Jesus.

But lots of us don't share His story. Maybe we don't know how.
Or maybe we're ashamed.

Open your Bible and highlight or underline Romans 1:16. Paul was probably in Greece leading the church in a city called Corinth when he wrote this letter to the Roman Christians. He's especially concerned that they not be ashamed of the story of Jesus.

Christ-followers were not honored in Rome. They had no political power or cultural influence. So, it would be tempting for them to be ashamed of the story of Jesus.

In the space below, share some reasons why you think followers of Jesus are sometimes ashamed of telling the story of Jesus.

_____

_____

_____

_____

Paul says in Romans 1:16 that the good news about Jesus is nothing to be ashamed of. The story of Jesus has power. It changes everything. Everyone who trusts in Jesus is rescued in this life and in the life to come.

Out there in the marketplace, on your team, at school, in your family, and neighborhood, lots of people will ignore you, laugh at you, and marginalize you if you speak up for Jesus.

So, how can we not be ashamed? Think about the power. When the story of Jesus intersects our story, there is a power—a force, strength, energy, might, and muscle—to transform hell-bound sinners into heaven-destined saints.

Nothing in the world can do this except the story of Jesus. Judaism can't do it. Buddhism can't do it. Hinduism can't. Islam can't. None of these have a Savior who can solve the problem of the sin that separates us from a holy God. None of these offer us hope by grace through faith rather than by works. Only one story has the power to save. It's the story of Jesus.

Can you share His story? Heaven and hell hang in the balance for some of the people you love. And you may be one of very few people—maybe the only one—who has the relational credibility to share His story with them.

If you can remember 3 circles, and some profound concepts related to each circle, you can tell His story.

3 CIRCLES: LIFE CONVERSATION GUIDE

GOD'S DESIGN

We live in a broken world, surrounded by broken lives, broken relationships, and broken systems.

This brokenness is seen in suffering, violence, poverty, pain, and death around us.

Brokenness leads us to search for a way to make life work.

In contrast to this brokenness, we also see beauty, purpose, and evidence of design around us.

The Bible tells us that God originally planned a world that worked perfectly—where everything and everyone fit together in harmony.

God made each of us with a purpose—to worship Him and walk with Him.

The Bible says:

God saw all that He had made, and it was very good (Genesis 1:31).

The heavens declare the glory of God, and the sky proclaims the work of His hands (Psalm 19:1).

In the space provided below, please write a summary in your own words of "God's design" aspect of His story.

_____

_____

_____

_____

_____

_____

_____

_____

BROKENNESS

Life doesn't work when we ignore God and His original design for our lives.

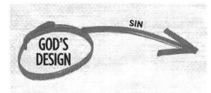

We selfishly insist on doing things our own way. The Bible calls this sin. We all sin and distort the original design.

The consequence of our sin is separation from God—in this life and for all of eternity.

The Bible says:

All have sinned and fall short of the glory of God (Romans 3:23).

For the wages of sin is death (Romans 6:23a).

Sin leads to a place of brokenness. We see this all around us and in our own lives as well.

When we realize life is not working, we begin to look for a way out. We tend to go in many directions, trying different things to figure it out on our own.

Brokenness leads to a place of realizing a need for something greater.

The Bible says:

They exchanged the truth of God for a lie, and worshiped and served something created instead of the Creator (Romans 1:25).

There is a way that seems right to a man, but its end is the way to death (Proverbs 14:12).

In the space provided below, please write a summary in your own words of the "brokenness" aspect of His story.

_____
_____
_____
_____
_____
_____
_____
_____
_____
_____

Because of His love, God did not leave us in our brokenness.
Jesus, God in human flesh, came to us and lived perfectly according to God's Design.

Jesus came to rescue us—to do for us what we could not do for ourselves. He took our sin and shame to the cross, paying the penalty of our sin by His death. Jesus was then raised from the dead—to provide the only way for us to be rescued and restored to a relationship with God.

The Bible says:

For God loved the world in this way; He gave His One and Only Son (John 3:16a).

He erased the certificate of debt . . . and has taken it out of the way by nailing it to the cross (Colossians 2:14).

Christ died for our sins according to the Scriptures . . . He was buried [and] raised on the third day according to the Scriptures (1 Corinthians 15:3-4).

Simply hearing this Good News is not enough.

We must admit our sinful brokenness and stop trusting in ourselves. We don't have the power to escape this brokenness on our own. We need to be rescued.
We must ask God to forgive us—turning from sin to trust only in Jesus. This is what it means to repent and believe.

Believing, we receive a new life through Jesus and God turns our lives in a new direction.

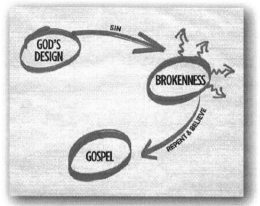

The Bible says:

Repent and believe in the good news (Mark 1:15b).

For you are saved by grace through faith, and this is not from yourselves; it is God's gift—not from works, so that no one can boast (Ephesians 2:8-9).

If you confess with your mouth, 'Jesus is Lord,' and believe in your heart that God raised Him from the dead, you will be saved (Romans 10:9).

When God restores our relationship to Him, we begin to discover meaning and purpose in a broken world. Now we can pursue God's Design in all areas of our lives.

Even when we fail, we understand God's pathway to be restored—this same Good News of Jesus.

God's Spirit empowers us to recover His Design and assures us of His presence in this life and for all of eternity.

The Bible says:

For it is God who is working in you, enabling you both to desire and to work out His good purpose (Philippians 2:13).

For we are His creation, created in Christ Jesus for Good works, which God prepared ahead of time so that we should walk in them (Ephesians 2:10).

In the space provided below, please write a summary of the 3 Circles Life Conversation in your own words.

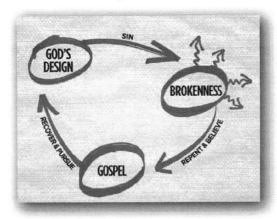

_____

_____

_____

_____

_____

_____

_____

_____

_____

_____

You can also weave in/share your story through the 3 Circles guide:

- What did brokenness in your life look like?
- When and how did you hear the Gospel?
- When did you repent and believe?
- How have you experienced God's restoration and recovery in your life?

Today, practice the 3 Circles with someone who is already a follower of Jesus. And then ask them to pray with you and for you to have the opportunity to tell His story to someone you listed in your Week 5, Day 1 and Week 5, Day 3 lessons.

Pray and ask God what person on your prayer list is most ready to hear His story. Write his/her name on the space below. Now, write down when, where, and how you will be a missionary to that person by sharing His story with him/her?

_____

_____

_____

_____

_____

What was one of the most helpful insights that you received during this lesson?

_____

_____

_____

_____

_____

Week 13

SPIRITUAL WARFARE: BATTLING AS A MISSIONARY

MEMORY VERSE
Finally, be strong in the Lord and in the strength of his might. Put on the whole armor of God, that you may be able to stand against the schemes of the devil. For we do not wrestle against flesh and blood, but against the rulers, against the authorities, against the cosmic powers over this present darkness, against the spiritual forces of evil in the heavenly places. Ephesians 6:10-12

WEEK 13, DAY 1: THE INVISIBLE WAR

We all have parts of our lives where obeying God seems really hard. Have you ever wondered why you still want to sin? You know you have been chosen by God, adopted into His family, redeemed by the blood of Christ, forgiven of all your sins, and sealed by the Holy Spirit.

But you also know that you're still tempted to get angry. You're tempted to waste time, eat too much, or shop too much. You find yourself wanting to get drunk, look at pictures of naked people, lie, gossip, sleep with your boyfriend, or cuss up a storm.

Or maybe you seem morally upright on the outside, but inside you know you lack any real passion for prayer or God's Word. You feel spiritually lazy and sluggish. Or you lack compassion or genuine care for others. Or your heart is filled with pride.

What's wrong with us? We are in an invisible war. In the Bible it's called spiritual warfare. If you lose this war, you will pay a steep price. Your family will pay a price. Your friends will pay a price. Your church and ministry will pay a price.

Read and highlight or underline Ephesians 6:10-12 and fill in the blanks below.

We do not struggle against _____ and _____.

We do struggle against the _____, the _____, the _____ _____ over this present darkness, and the _____ _____ of evil in the heavenly places.

When the devil rebelled, in those ancient days, a host of angels rebelled with him. And there are names for these rebellious angels, these evil spirits and demons. "Rulers" and "authorities" and "powers" point to the fact that demons have a measure of control in a world that is dark in its rebellion against God. These are "spiritual forces of evil"—an army of wicked spirits waging war in heavenly realms.

It's not a reach to think that an evil spirit has been assigned to tempt you and me. You are in an invisible war.

Some people think of the devil as a childish superstition or as an outdated myth. They reject the foolish man-made caricature of a sinister-looking tempter with horns, a pointed tail, and a pitchfork. But the Bible presents the devil as real. He appears in Genesis 3 and is defeated in Revelation 20. Jesus Himself experienced real encounters with a real devil (Matthew 4:1-11).

We are mistaken if we either minimize or maximize the devil's existence or influence. "There are two equal and opposite errors into which our race can fall about the devils. One is to disbelieve in their existence. The other is to believe, and to feel an excessive and unhealthy interest in them. They themselves are equally pleased by both errors and hail a materialist or a magician with the same delight" (*The Best of C. S. Lewis, The Screwtape Letters*, by C.S. Lewis, p.13).

It is a terrible mistake to think that after we come to Christ all our troubles in life are over. That fight that you had at work, that trouble you're having at home, that conflict you're in with a Christian friend? We don't wrestle (or struggle or fight) against mere flesh and blood. There is a spiritual struggle behind and beyond the relational struggle.

One of the enemy's schemes is to make you think that the battle is only against flesh and blood. Don't say, "My spouse is my problem (or my kids, or my boss, or my friends)." Satan's scheme is getting us to focus on people, not on the real battle.

Our spiritual warfare is against supernatural evil powers. We have to know that whenever we are seeking to do God's will and someone attacks us, or someone gets really angry with us, or someone stands in our way, something else is also going on—something deeper, bigger, more terrible, more sinister, and more destructive than meets the eye. This doesn't mean that flesh and blood can't hurt or hinder the cause of Christ. But the spiritual forces of evil are more dangerous and must be overcome in every conflict or the battle is lost.

The invisible war often shows up in a skirmish with flesh and blood. But that can't become the focus of the fight. You are in an invisible war.

All of your life in Christ is a war. From the cradle to the grave, your life is war. The devil and his followers hate God. The devil and the demons want to keep you from knowing God, loving God, serving God, or honoring God. The devil and his minions want to destroy your love, your joy, your peace, your family, your career, your church. And until we get to heaven, we will be in an invisible war.

The Bible uses many names and descriptors for the devil. Match the appropriate verses with the name or descriptors.

1. Satan
2. Destroyer
3. The adversary
4. The deceiver of the whole world
5. The father of lies
6. The god of this world
7. The tempter
8. The one who disguises himself as an angel of light

A. John 8:44
B. Revelation 12:9
C. Matthew 4:3
D. 2 Corinthians 4:4
E. Revelation 9:11
F. Revelation 12:9
G. 2 Corinthians 11:14
H. 1 Peter 5:8

One of the devil's schemes is to convince us that he's not real—that his followers, the fallen angels, aren't real. He wants us to be oblivious to the fact that there is an invisible war going on around us. You are in an invisible war.

Open your Bible to Isaiah 14 and Ezekiel 28 to read how the devil, once an angelic being, led a rebellion against God. He's been seeking to destroy God's kingdom ever since. In the space below, list some of the facts you find in Isaiah 14:12-15 and Ezekiel 28:14-19 about Satan's fall.

_____

_____

_____

"Satan was the originator of sin. Satan sinned before any human beings did so, as is evident from the fact that he (in the form of a serpent) tempted Eve (Genesis 3:1-6; 2 Corinthians 11:3) . . . The devil's characteristic has been to originate sin and tempt others to sin" (*Systematic Theology*, by Wayne Grudem, p.415).

When the devil rebelled, a number of angels rebelled with him. We now call them "demons." In Ephesians 6, they are referred to as "rulers," "authorities," and "powers." These titles indicate that demons have influence in the world. These are "spiritual forces of evil"—an army of wicked spirits waging war in heavenly realms. It's not a reach to think that perhaps specific evil spirits have been assigned to tempt individual believers.

We need to think of the devil and demons as spiritual bullies, even spiritual terrorists capable of great harm, but using fear as their #1 tactic. Our victory depends on understanding and depending on God's authority and power.

What was one of the most helpful insights that you received during this lesson?

_____

_____

_____

As we close our time today, use the following as a guide for your prayer.

Heavenly Father, I know that the devil is prowling around like a roaring lion wanting to devour me. He and his demons are seeking to steal, kill, and destroy everything good and godly that I hold dear. Help me today to trust in You, to win today's spiritual battles, and to bring glory and honor to Your name (1 Peter 5:8; John 10:10b; Ephesians 6:12; Luke 10:18).

Sovereign God, protect me from the enemy: the evil one, the tempter, the accuser. Guard me against the schemes of his followers, fallen angels who are now the evil spirits who are seeking to minimize and neutralize my life in Christ. Lead me not into temptation, but deliver me from the evil one (Revelation 12:7-9; Matthew 6:13; 1 Thessalonians 3:5; Revelation 12:10, Leviticus 17:7; Luke 8:30; Luke 7:21). *In Jesus' name, Amen.*

We are mistaken if we either minimize or maximize the devil's existence or influence. We dare not underestimate our spiritual enemies.
Chad Allen - Lead Pastor, Cuyahoga Valley Church

WEEK 13, DAY 2: GOD IS SUPREME OVER THE DEVIL'S SCHEMES.

We dare not underestimate or overestimate our spiritual enemies. The devil and his demons are very, very clever. They have been causing believers to fall for centuries. We don't stand a chance of winning this war on our own. It's why we need to depend on God's strength.

Finally, be strong in the Lord and in the strength of His might (Ephesians 6:10).

When we engage in spiritual warfare in the Lord's strength, we will find that the enemy is no match for the Lord Jesus. Jesus is the Creator. The devil is His creature. Jesus and the devil are not equal forces.

Read the Old Testament story about a man named Job in Job 1:6-12.

What are the indicators in this story that the Lord clearly is authoritatively superior to Satan?

_____

_____

_____

The devil can't do anything unless God in His providence allows him to do it. In fact, Martin Luther once called the devil "the Lord's devil." It might be helpful to think of the devil as being on a leash, God's leash. This invisible, spiritual war is not a battle between two equal forces—between good and evil, between light and darkness. The devil is not omnipotent. He's not omniscient. He's not omnipresent. All that the devil does is done only by God's permission and ultimately will be used by God for His own purposes.

This means that our God is supreme over the devil's schemes. Read and highlight or underline Colossians 2:14b-15.

Jesus has disarmed, shamed, and triumphed over the devil and his demons. Jesus has already won the war and the devil has already lost.

How can knowing that the devil is no match for God bring encouragement to your life?

_____

_____

_____

The Bible teaches that while Jesus has won the war, battles still remain.

Spiritually speaking, we are living in an in-between time. We are between the 1st and 2nd comings of Christ. Jesus accomplished our salvation when He came the first time. He will complete our salvation when He comes the second time. Theologians call this in-between time the "already" and the "not yet" aspects of our salvation.

The victory won by the Allied Forces in World War II can be an analogy of what has happened. The cross was D-Day in our spiritual warfare. It was the decisive invasion that sealed the doom of the devil. The final victory, like VE-Day, will happen at the final judgment when the devil is cast into hell.

Christ-followers today live in between D-Day and VE-Day. During this time, the army of Christ advances against the devil and his demons slowly but surely. It will be a spiritual war until Jesus Christ wins fully and finally. One day every enemy will be placed under His feet (1 Corinthians 15:27, Ephesians 1:22, Hebrews 2:8). "Some days see advances while other days see retreats, but overall there is an advance until the last day, the day of the enemy's complete surrender" ("Our Ancient Foe," by Keith Mathison, www.ligonier.org).

Why doesn't God just squash this rebellion? Donald Grey Barnhouse wrote, "Although the Lord had the power to destroy Satan with a breath, He did not do so. It was as though an edict had been proclaimed in heaven: 'We shall give this rebellion a thorough trial. We shall permit it to run its full course. The universe shall see what a creature, though he be the highest creature ever to spring from God's Word, can do apart from Him . . . And the wreck and ruin which shall result will demonstrate to the universe, and forever, that there is no life, no joy, no peace apart from a complete dependence upon the Most High God . . ." (*The Invisible War*, by Donald Grey Barnhouse, p.51).

God is allowing this rebellion by Satan to play itself out to prove for all eternity to all creation, that rebelling against a loving, sovereign Creator is foolish, futile, and devastating.

JESUS MAKES US STRONG.
We shouldn't be surprised that even though we are saved, we still struggle with the enemy. But our struggle can be victorious if we stay strong. Look again at Ephesians 6:10.

"Be strong" is a present passive verb in the Greek language. A literal translation might go like this: ". . . keep on being made strong . . ." By ourselves, we can't work up the strength to win this war. We don't have the strength to win. We need to let Jesus make us strong. And we can't let our guard down. We must keep on being strong in the Lord. We always have to be vigilant to get strength from the Lord for this fight.

How does Jesus strengthen us? Read and highlight or underline Luke 22:31-32 where Jesus once spoke to a follower, Peter.

While we are on this side of eternity, temptations will come. And, no doubt, Satan and his demons seek to sift all of us. But Jesus, as Hebrews 7:25 tells us, is our great High Priest and is praying for us that our faith will not fail. Jesus is our strength.

Since Jesus is praying for us, then why would we be afraid of the devil or his demons? Look up and highlight or underline Romans 8:37-39.

Even though the devil and the rest of his wicked spirits are powerful when compared with us, they stand no chance against Jesus. They can go only as far as He allows them and no farther. When it comes to spiritual warfare, we have to learn to focus on the power of Jesus more than the ploys of Satan.

You are in an invisible war. You can't win without Jesus and His strength. So, stay close to the Lord. Abide in Jesus. Stay connected to Christ. Be filled with His Spirit. Pray without ceasing.

JESUS HELPS US STAND.

There is a very real danger that we might fall in this invisible war. But in Christ, we can stand. Read Ephesians 6:11.

We're to stand—to dig in, to not run. We are to stand in Christ. Three times in the Ephesians 6 verses, Paul tells us to make sure that we stand—that we not fall. He writes about standing here in verse 11. And he writes about standing again twice in verses 13 and 14.

Take up the whole armor of God, that you may be able to withstand in the evil day, and having done all, to stand firm. Stand therefore . . . (Ephesians 6:13-14a).

The "standing" is not that we're like brick walls that are passive. No. We have the battle gear on. We're ready to fight. We're both defending and attacking. We're standing our ground. We're withstanding the enemy's attacks. We resist his onrushing attacks. And we even gain ground.

Stand. But we can't stand on our own. We need Jesus to help us stand. I love what the Bible book, Jude, says about this:

[Jesus] is able to keep you from stumbling and to present you blameless before the presence of His glory with great joy (Jude 1:24).

Why is it important for believers to understand that the outcome of this invisible, spiritual war is already determined?

_____

_____

_____

What was one of the most helpful insights that you received during this lesson?

_____

_____

_____

Close today's time by using Martin Luther's classic hymn
"A Mighty Fortress Is Our God" as a basis for your prayer:

> A mighty fortress is our God, a bulwark never failing;
> Our helper He, amid the flood of mortal ills prevailing:
> For still our ancient foe doth seek to work us woe;
> His craft and power are great, and, armed with cruel hate,
> On earth is not his equal.
>
> Did we in our own strength confide, our striving would be losing;
> Were not the right Man on our side, the Man of God's own choosing:
> Dost ask who that may be? Christ Jesus, it is He;
> Lord Sabaoth, His Name, from age to age the same,
> And He must win the battle.
>
> And though this world, with devils filled, should threaten to undo us,
> We will not fear, for God hath willed His truth to triumph through us:
> The Prince of Darkness grim, we tremble not for him;
> His rage we can endure, for lo, his doom is sure,
> One little word shall fell him.
>
> That word above all earthly powers, no thanks to them, abideth;
> The Spirit and the gifts are ours through Him Who with us sideth:
> Let goods and kindred go, this mortal life also;
> The body they may kill: God's truth abideth still,
> His kingdom is forever.

***There will be times we may lose a battle, but we
need to remember and be encouraged by the fact
that the devil has already lost the war. So we don't
fight for victory, we fight from victory.***
Chad Allen - Lead Pastor, Cuyahoga Valley Church

269

WEEK 13, DAY 3: THE SCHEMES OF SATAN

When it comes to spiritual warfare, Jesus is our strength (Ephesians 6:10) and Jesus helps us stand (Ephesians 6:11). That brings up some questions. Why do we need His strength? What do we need to stand against? Read Ephesians 6:11 and 2 Corinthians 2:11.

Satan has his schemes. The word "schemes" in the Greek language is *methodia*. It could be translated methods, strategies, or deceits. We are to stand against the devil's methods and strategies that are designed in a diabolical way to make us fall. And, sadly, we can be too ignorant of his tactics.

Satan has his designs. The word "designs" in the Greek language is *noema*. It could be translated devices, intentions, or evil purposes. It's the word used for the minds that are blinded or corrupted by Satan (2 Corinthians 3:14; 4:4; 11:3). And, tragically, we can be too ignorant of the way Satan blinds our minds to his tactics.

In war, generals will study the strategies and tactics of the enemy leaders so they can anticipate an attack. You have to know some things about your enemy or you are doomed to lose the battle. We need to do a little recon. We need some intelligence. We need to know more about our enemy than we do. What are the devil's tactics, strategies, and methods?

How does this war work? The enemy uses the influences of the world and the desires of our own flesh against us. And the battlefield is our mind. He leverages the world and the flesh against us. He lies to us about the world and the flesh. The more we listen to the lies, the bigger the world gets to us, and the more power our flesh has over us. The enemy's scheme is to get us to feed our own flesh and to allow the world to overcome us. When that happens, we've been overcome by darkness.

But the Bible teaches us that we can stand against the enemy's schemes. How? We believe the truth of God's Word rather than the lies. Read and highlight or underline 2 Corinthians 10:4-5.

The implication here is that the devil and his followers have access to our minds. They can't read our minds, but they can influence our thoughts.

An ungodly thought can be planted by the enemy. The Bible tells us that spiritual warfare is the battle for your mind.

The more we choose to reject the lies of the enemy and believe the truth—what God says about Himself and about us—then the less and less influence the world will have, and we will desire to satisfy our flesh less and less.

THE ENEMY'S MAIN SCHEMES

ISOLATION

One of the devil's schemes is the age-old divide and conquer. You see predators do it in the animal kingdom. And remember, the enemy is a predator. Read and highlight or underline 1 Peter 5:8.

Lions don't attack the animals in the middle of the herd. They pick out a prey that is weak and alone. Then they attack and devour. The devil is going to tell you that you don't need a community—that you don't need to be held accountable, that you don't need anyone asking you the tough questions. Why? He wants to isolate you to devour you.

Describe a time in your life or in the life of someone you know when isolation resulted in a spiritual downfall. Why do you think isolation can become such an effective temptation?

_____

_____

_____

Followers of Christ need each other. Don't try to live your Christian life outside of community. Don't battle alone. Once you are alienated and divided and alone, you are susceptible to attack and defeat. We must move heaven and earth to stay in community and stay in accountability with other believers! We have forgotten that we are in an invisible war.

A lone soldier defeating an army of enemiesmakes for a great movie but a terrible reality.
Chad Allen- Lead Pastor, Cuyahoga Valley Church

DECEPTION

The devil makes sin look good. The enemy presents the bait and hides the hook. He knows our weaknesses. He knows what trips us up. Read and highlight or underline John 8:44.

The enemy will try to convince us that we can get away with our sin. The enemy says things like, "Go ahead and marry that non-Christian," or "It won't hurt to look at that website," or "You deserve to party hard tonight," or "A little cheating never hurt anybody," or "Everybody else is sleeping around; you might as well, too," or "You'll be better off by lying about that to your spouse."

Put a star by the lies that you have been tempted to believe or write down some other lies you've been tempted to believe:

* God will cut you some slack; you might have to pay a little price but it's really no big deal.
* You can always sin today and be OK because you can stop the sin tomorrow.
* One more time won't hurt you.
* The consequences of sin aren't always so bad.
* God loves you so much, He won't make you answer for your sin.
* It's not hurting anyone.
* No one will ever find out.
* After all, God is all love and all grace.

_____

_____

The truth is that God's love is a holy love, a righteous love. And we will reap what we sow (Galatians 6:7-8). The truth is that if we sow to our flesh, we will reap corruption. Remember: sin will take you further than you want to go, keep you longer than you want to stay, and cost you more than you want to pay.

ACCUSATION

We often find ourselves in a cycle of temptation and accusation. Once we commit a sin, the devil will then tell us that we are failures or frauds as followers of Christ. We fall to the temptation and then he beats us up with accusation. Read and highlight or underline Revelation 12:10.

When we sin, the Holy Spirit convicts us so we will repent. Then, He comforts us and reminds us that we are forgiven, accepted, and beloved. The Spirit convicts us to comfort us (John 16:7-8).

But the enemy accuses us to condemn us. When we sin, the enemy wants us to wallow in our guilt and self-condemnation. He whispers, "How could you do that? How could you say that? You can't serve Christ. You must not be a real Christian at all. How could God love you? You're a loser. You're no good." These are lies from the accuser of the brothers and sisters.

What are some specific lies and accusations the enemy has tempted you to believe?

_____

_____

_____

We have to learn to discern the voice of the Spirit who convicts us to comfort us from the devil who accuses us to condemn us.

What is the difference between conviction from the Holy Spirit and condemnation from the devil?

_____

_____

_____

Use the following verses to help you understand what the Holy Spirit might say to you to convict and then comfort you: John 5:24, Romans 8:1, and 1 John 1:9.

_____

_____

_____

OVERCOMING ISOLATION, DECEPTION, AND ACCUSATION

In 2007, Pastor John Piper was speaking at a Passion Conference to an audience of young adults. He was concerned that the devil was accusing many of them because of their sexual sins in the past and was sidelining them from future service to Christ. He said to them:

"What . . . breaks [my heart] today is not mainly that you have sinned sexually, but that this morning Satan took your [sexual sin] . . . and told you: 'See, you're a loser. You may as well not even go to worship. No way are you going to make any serious commitment of your life to Jesus Christ! You may as well go back to school and get a good practical education, and then a good job so you can buy yourself a big wide screen and watch sex till you drop'" ("How to Deal with the Guilt of Sexual Failure for the Glory of Christ and His Global Cause," by John Piper, www.desiringgod.org).

Piper used verses from the Old Testament prophet, Micah. Read and highlight or underline Micah 7:8-9.

Then, based on the truths of this Scripture, Piper shared how to talk to the enemy when he is accusing you:

"You make merry over my failure . . .? Yes, I have fallen. And I hate what I have done. I grieve at the dishonor I have brought on my king. But hear this, O my enemy, I will rise. I will rise. Yes, I am sitting in darkness. I feel miserable. I feel guilty. I am guilty. But that is not all that is true about me and my God. The same God who makes my darkness is a sustaining light to me in this very darkness. He will not forsake me. O yes, my enemy, this much truth you say, I have sinned. I am bearing the indignation of the Lord. But that is where your truth stops and my theology begins: He—the very one who is indignant with me—He will plead my cause. You say He is against me and that I have no future with Him because of my failure. . . . That is a lie. And you are a liar. My God, whose Son's life is my righteousness and whose Son's death is my punishment, [is] for me. For me! FOR me! And not against me" ("How to Deal with the Guilt of Sexual Failure for the Glory of Christ and His Global Cause," by John Piper, www.desiringgod.org).

As you close your time today, think about some condemnation and accusation that the devil has used to neutralize you. Creatively think of a way to personalize Piper's words as a way for you to resist the devil so he will flee from you (1 Peter 5:8-9).

_____
_____
_____
_____
_____
_____

What was one of the most helpful insights that you received during this lesson?

_____
_____
_____

WEEK 13, DAY 4: THE ARMOR OF GOD (1)

God has all power and can do anything He desires. He can command Satan not to even touch you. God can remove the devil any time He wants.

And that's what some of us want. We just don't want anything bad to happen to us. We want God to insulate us from any demonic attack. Some believers blame a lost filling or a broken water heater or a flat tire on spiritual warfare. We want to get spiritual warfare tools to keep bad stuff from happening.

But it appears that God does not completely limit Satan's access to our lives. His hand-cuffing the devil is not what God wants to be the basis of our victory. Instead, God wants us to draw strength from Him for the fight. It connects us with Him. And when we win in His strength, He gets greater glory.

One of the things He gives us in our battle is battle-gear. The Lord has not left us defenseless. Ephesians 6 talks about the gear. Read Ephesians 6:13-17. Highlight, circle, or underline the 6 metaphors that are used to describe the spiritual warfare resources that we have in Christ.

In the space below, write down the armor/weapons from head to toe as a way to help you remember each piece.

Head: _____

Chest: _____

Waist: _____

Feet: _____

Left Hand: _____

Right hand: _____

Over the next 2 days, we will take a look at each piece—each spiritual resource that we have in Christ.

THE HELMET OF SALVATION
And take the helmet of salvation . . . (Ephesians 6:17a).

Many scholars believe that for all these pieces of armor, the emphasis is not on the noun, but on the object of the preposition. Place the emphasis, then, on the reality of our salvation, not on the metaphor of the helmet.

Jesus Himself is our salvation. An angel said about Mary, the mother of Jesus, *She will bear a son, and you shall call his name Jesus, for he will save his people from their sins* (Matthew 1:21).

Jesus saved us from the penalty of sin. That's justification. He is saving us from the power of sin. That's sanctification. He will save us from the presence of sin. That's glorification. Jesus saves. And knowing that makes a difference when we are attacked by the enemy.

The helmet of salvation helps us stand firm against all the devil's schemes and enables us to look beyond death, doubt, and disappointments toward our destiny. Because we know that we are saved, we won't as easily fall into despair and defeat in the midst of hardship and difficulty. It's no wonder so many Christians doubt their salvation. It's a "head shot" from the enemy. But we know we are saved. So, we continue to fight the fight with a "blessed assurance" of our salvation.

THE BREASTPLATE OF RIGHTEOUSNESS
Stand therefore . . . having put on the breastplate of righteousness . . . (Ephesians 6:14).

Righteousness is being right with God and living the right kind of life. But if we are honest, we have to say, "That's not me. I have sinned." However, when we trust in Jesus and His work on the cross on our behalf, He makes us righteous. Read 2 Corinthians 5:21.

In Jesus, we are righteous. God looks at us just as if we had never sinned. We are clothed in the righteousness of Christ. That's called positional righteousness.

And positional righteousness must lead us into practical righteousness. Remembering who we are (positional righteousness) will fuel what we do (practical righteousness). We are to live out a life of righteousness. Daily righteous living ought to be the norm for us. When we fail to live righteously, we give the devil an opportunity to defeat us. Unrighteous living gives Satan a foothold in our lives (Ephesians 4:27).

What are some sins that might give the devil a foothold in a believer's life? How does a failure to pursue righteousness give the devil an opportunity to tempt a believer into further unrighteousness?

_____

_____

_____

THE BELT OF TRUTH
Stand therefore, having fastened on the belt of truth . . .
(Ephesians 6:14a).

The belt of a Roman soldier was a wide leather belt designed to hold the soldier's clothing in place. The soldier tucked his outer garment under the belt so that it wouldn't hinder his fighting. When his belt was tightened, a Roman soldier was ready for battle.

In the same way, God's truth makes us ready for the fight against Satan, who is a liar (John 8:44). The best defense against his lies is the truth of God. God's Word is the truth. Jesus once prayed to His Father, *Sanctify them in the truth; Your word is truth* (John 17:17).

What truths have helped you have victory in spiritual warfare?

_____

_____

_____

What are some practical ways for you to get the truth of God's word into your life as a defense against the enemy's lies? (This might be a good opportunity to review the lessons on Bible Intake from Weeks 1 and 2.)

_____

_____

_____

THE SHOES OF THE GOSPEL OF PEACE
And, as shoes for your feet, having put on the readiness given by the gospel of peace (Ephesians 6:14).

The Roman soldier usually wore strong boots with heavy soles for protection and studded nails for traction. Because the soldier often fought in hand-to-hand combat, his footing had to be sure. A soldier who lost his footing would be vulnerable to the enemy.

In the same way, when we face spiritual battles, standing firm requires the right footwear. If we are going to "stand" and "withstand," then we need the shoes of the gospel of peace.

The gospel is the good news about Jesus. He died in our place for our sin so we could have peace—peace with God, peace in our hearts, and peace with each other.

We take ground spiritually when our feet, shod with the good news of the Gospel, advance and take back territory the devil has acquired.

Often, the devil seeks to use conflict and controversy with other believers to steal, kill, and destroy our witness and influence. But focusing on our common ground—the gospel that saved all of us by grace through faith in Jesus—will help us protect our relationships. "An unwillingness to think badly of any Christian is a sandal most easy to the foot. . ... Wear it in the church, wear it in all holy service, wear it in all fellowship with Christians, and you will find your way among the brethren greatly smoothed. You will before long win their love and esteem and avoid a world of jealousy and opposition that would otherwise have impeded your course" (*Spiritual Warfare in a Believer's Life*, by Charles Haddon Spurgeon, p.141).

In the space below, name someone with whom you are not at peace. How could this conflict be evidence of spiritual warfare in your life? How might pursuing peace with that person defeat the work of the devil and advance the Kingdom of Christ?

_____

_____

_____

What was one of the most helpful insights that you received during this lesson?

_____

_____

_____

WEEK 13, DAY 5: THE ARMOR OF GOD (2)

Yesterday, we explored 4 pieces of spiritual armor in Ephesians 6: the helmet of salvation, the breastplate of righteousness, the belt of truth, and the shoes of the gospel of peace. Today, we will study the two spiritual resources for spiritual warfare that God has given us to hold in our hands.

THE SHIELD OF FAITH

In all circumstances take up the shield of faith, with which you can extinguish all the flaming darts of the evil one (Ephesians 6:16).

"The shield for the Roman soldier was large, usually about four feet by two feet, made of wood, and covered with tough leather. The soldier would hold it up and be protected from spears, arrows, and 'fiery darts.' Arrows, dipped in pitch lit on fire, would be released. When the flaming darts collided with the shields, their flames were put out. In ancient warfare, the shield was prized by a soldier above all other pieces of armor. He counted it a greater shame to lose his shield than to lose the battle. The Roman soldier thought it would be an honor to die with his shield in his hand" (*The Covering*, by Hank Hanegraff, pp.70-71).

Faith is a defense. If you have the shield of faith, the enemy might scorch your shield but he won't sear your soul.

Think about it. If the shield is our faith, then the darts must be our doubts. Troubles come that we don't understand. That's when our faith is challenged. The devil wants us to doubt God.

A mother contracts breast cancer. A dad has a stroke. A young adult struggles with rheumatoid arthritis. Empty nesters find themselves struggling to care for an elderly parent. A husband loses a job. A couple goes through a difficult divorce. All are tempted to ask, "Why? Why us? Why me? Why would a good God allow such tragedy to happen?"

This is when our faith is tested. This is when we must trust. When we cannot trace His hand, we trust His heart. We keep on trusting God in the midst of our questions. Instead of asking, "Why? Why me?" we ask, "What? What now – how do You want to use this?"

What is a difficult situation you are currently experiencing that is tempting you to doubt God? How might those doubts be darts from the enemy? How can you fortify your faith?

THE SWORD OF THE SPIRIT

And take . . . the sword of the Spirit, which is the Word of God (Ephesians 6:17b).

It's clear here. We can't miss it. The sword of the Spirit is the Word of God. One ministry of the Holy Spirit to help believers to understand and apply the truths of the Bible. *The Spirit of truth… will guide you into all the truth . . .* (John 16:13).

The word "sword" here translates the Greek word *makaira*. It's a word used to describe a weapon as short as a 6-inch dagger or as long as an 18-inch sword. The makaira was put into a sheath or a scabbard by the side of the soldier and used in hand-to-hand combat. It's a shorter sword for up-close and personal, precision warfare. This sword was not only used to withstand an attack, but to make an attack, to pierce the enemy, to penetrate and cut.

All the other armor is defensive in nature, yet the sword is our <u>offensive</u> weapon. If we do not know the truths of God's Word and have them in our head and heart, then we are trying to fight while unarmed.

We must learn to skillfully use God's sword. We must learn what we have in God's Word. We must take it—welcome it, receive it.

We see an example of how to use this weapon in Matthew 4:1-11.
In the space below, record the temptation and how Jesus used the sword of the Spirit—how He used the Word of God to defeat the devil.

Satan's temptation #1: _____
Sword of the Spirit #1: _____

Satan's temptation #2: _____
Sword of the Spirit #2: _____

Satan's temptation #3: _____
Sword of the Spirit #3: _____

How will you take and hold the Word of God more firmly? Check which area needs the most increased attention in your life:

I will take a better hold of the sword of the Spirit by increasing my Bible intake through (check one) . . .

- ☐ hearing more of the Word of God
- ☐ reading more of the Word of God
- ☐ studying more of the Word of God
- ☐ memorizing more of the Word of God
- ☐ meditating more on the Word of God
- ☐ applying more of the Word of God

Write down an area where you are being attacked by the enemy:

_____

Use a search engine or a study Bible to find several verses from the sword of the Spirit so when the devil attacks you with temptation, you can attack back. List several references to those verses below and write out the verses:

_____

_____

_____

_____

_____

_____

_____

_____

_____

_____

_____

_____

_____

_____

A SUPERSTITIOUS RITUAL?

Being armored doesn't mean that we perform a superstitious daily ritual by repeating a rote prayer that will magically keep the devil away. Below is an example of how NOT to pray:

"Today, I put on me and on my family the helmet of salvation, the breastplate of righteousness, the belt of truth, and the shoes of the gospel of peace. We are holding the shield of faith and the sword of the Spirit which is the Word of God. Now, Jesus, keep the devil away from me and the people I love. Amen!"

We wish it were that easy. Wearing all the armor of God is not about finding some quick fix or immediate solution to our struggles in life.

- Being armored means that 24-7-365 we live in light of the fact that we are saved and sure of it.
- Being armored means that we are clothed in the righteousness of Christ and, therefore, living righteously.
- Being armored means that we know the truth so that every day we refuse to believe the devil's lies and choose to live according to God's truth.

- Being armored means that because of the gospel, we claim our peace with God and, so far as it depends on us, we live in peace with others.
- Being armored means that when the devil's darts of doubt fly against us, we trust in God, knowing that God is for us, not against us.
- Being armored means that we use the Word of God wisely.

Satan looks for that unguarded area where he can get a beachhead (Eph. 4:27). No one piece of God's armor is insignificant, and no one piece can be ignored. If any piece of the armor is missing, a gaping hole remains and we are vulnerable to the enemy. God has provided the "whole armor" for us, and we dare not omit any part.

Which piece of God's armor is most missing in your life? Where are you most vulnerable?

_____

_____

_____

What can you do to fortify yourself in this area?

_____

_____

_____

ARMED AND DANGEROUS

We have six pieces of spiritual armor and weaponry. How do we put it all together? Read and highlight or underline Ephesians 6:18.

Sometimes, the hardest thing to do is the best thing to do, like prayer. Prayer is a wartime walkie-talkie. "Dear God" is not a casual thing to say. We are engaging in spiritual battle when we pray. It is prayer that makes you armed and dangerous.

A battling Christian is a praying Christian. Prayer is our nuclear weapon. We have to hit our knees to win this spiritual fight.

A soldier of Christ prays at all times. We must learn to have ongoing conversations with God all day every day. When we are tested or tempted, we pray.

A soldier of Christ prays with alertness. One of our problems is that we have a peacetime mentality. We have to remember that there is a war waging spiritually all the time. The souls of our friends and family are at stake. If we aren't careful, we can slip into a non-alert state of life. In U.S. history, there were two times we weren't alert: 12/7/1941 and 9/11/2001. Do we need to experience a personal Pearl Harbor or a personal 9/11 before we realize that we have to pray? When it comes to spiritual warfare, we are always in a state of either yellow, orange, or red alert. Spiritually, we should always be on alert.

A soldier of Christ prays for his/her fellow soldiers of Christ. Often something takes place during a war so that a soldier's instinct for self-preservation is overridden to protect others. When we pray, we pray for the protection of our fellow soldiers.

We don't want to just be armed, but we want to be armed and dangerous . . . to the devil. And that's why we pray.

As you close your time today, scan Appendix A for this week's study and use it as fuel for your prayers.

What was one of the most helpful insights that you received during this lesson?

It cannot be stated too frequently that the life of a Christian is a warfare, an intense conflict, a lifelong contest. It is a battle, moreover, waged against invisible foes, who are ever alert, and ever seeking to entrap, deceive, and ruin the souls of men. The life to which Holy Scripture calls men is no picnic, or holiday junketing. It is no pastime, no pleasure jaunt. It entails effort, wrestling, struggling; it demands the putting forth of the full energy of the spirit in order to frustrate the foe and to
come off, at the last, more than conqueror. It is no primrose path, no rose-scented dalliance. From start to finish, it is war. From the hour in which he first draws sword, to that in which he doffs his harness, the Christian warrior is compelled to "endure hardness like a good soldier."
E. M. Bounds - *The Necessity of Prayer*

Appendix A

A SPIRITUAL WARFARE PRAYER

Our Father in heaven,

You are my Hope, my Victory, and my Peace. Because you are the only sovereign King who rules over all heaven and earth, I will be confident and unafraid today. My strength, my courage, and my joy come only from You, Lord. You alone are my Savior. (Matthew 12:20-21, Isaiah 9:6-7, 1 Timothy 6:15-16, Isaiah 41:10, Isaiah 12:2)

I come to You, Father, only through the merits of the Lord Jesus Christ, the One who died on the cross and shed His blood to forgive all my sins—past, present, and future—and who rose from the dead, ascended into heaven, and sent His Spirit to live in me. (Romans 5:8-10, 1 Corinthians 15:3-6, Acts 1:8-9)

I come to You, Father, through the power of the Holy Spirit who has caused me to be born again, who now lives in me, and who intercedes for me with groanings too deep for words. (John 3:3-8, John 14:16-17, Romans 8:26)

I come boldly to Your throne of grace to find Your help in my time of need. I need You today, Lord. I am desperate for You. I trust You, Lord God, to defeat my enemies—the world, the flesh, and the devil—that wage war against the physical, relational, emotional, and spiritual health of my family, my ministry, and my soul. (Hebrews 4:16, Psalm 63:1, Ephesians 6:10-18)

I ask You, Lord God, to demonstrate Your great power over the enemy. Win victories this day in, through, with, and for me. I realize that I am not wrestling against flesh and blood, but against the rulers, against the authorities, against the cosmic powers over this present darkness, against the spiritual forces of evil in the heavenly places. (Ephesians 6:10-12)

I am Your child, heavenly Father. Since I am Your child, then I am Your heir—an heir of God and a fellow heir with Christ. Because I am in Christ, I can now resist the devil. In Christ, I claim the promise that no weapon formed against me or my family shall prosper. (Romans 8:15-17, 1 Peter 5:8-9, Isaiah 54:17)

Holy Spirit, lead me and guide me today. Fill me. Bear Your fruit through me. Grant to me the ability to discern between righteousness and wickedness, and the wisdom to choose the path of righteousness. (Romans 8:13-14, Ephesians 5:18, Galatians 5:22-23, Ephesians 5:10, Joshua 24:14-15)

Thank You, Lord Jesus, for rescuing me from my sins and the devil's stronghold by going to the cross for me. You have disarmed the rulers and authorities and put them to open shame by triumphing over them through Your work on the cross. (Colossians 2:13-15, 2 Corinthians 2:14)

Thank You for clothing me in Your righteousness in Christ Jesus.
I am Your property. I belong to You, Lord. Grant to me Your prosperity as I delight in Your law and meditate on Your Word. (Isaiah 61:10, 1 Corinthians 6:19-20, Psalm 1:1-3, Joshua 1:8)

I know that the devil is prowling around like a roaring lion wanting to devour me. He and his demons are seeking to steal, kill, and destroy everything good and godly that I hold dear. Help me today to trust in You, to win today's spiritual battles, and to bring glory and honor to Your name. (1 Peter 5:8, John 10:10b, Ephesians 6:12, Luke 10:18)

When the enemy causes me to doubt my identity in Christ—telling me I'm a worthless sinner, a lost cause, an embarrassment to You—remind me of whose I am and who You say I am—a saint, a new creation, Your beloved child, living new in Christ. (Ephesians 1:1, 2 Corinthians 5:17, John 3:16)

Lord, please forgive me for the ways I have given the enemy opportunities to gain any foothold or stronghold in my life, my family, or my ministry. By Your grace and for Your glory, help me take back any ground he's gained in my life, in my family, or in my ministry. Help me to be aware of his schemes and to not be ignorant of his devices. (Deuteronomy 18:9-12, Psalm 139:23-24, Ephesians 4:27, Ephesians 6:11, 2 Corinthians 2:11)

Sovereign God, keep me from the enemy: the evil one, the tempter, the accuser. Protect me from his followers, fallen angels who are now the evil spirits who seek to minimize and neutralize my life in Christ. Lead me not into temptation, but deliver me from the evil one. (Revelation 12:7-9, Matthew 6:13, 1 Thessalonians 3:5, Revelation 12:10, Leviticus 17:7, Luke 8:30, Luke 7:21)

Help me to submit again today to Your authority, Your control, and Your will. May Your kingdom come and Your will be done in and through me. Lead me to say no to the devil and his temptations and yes to You and Your abundant life. By Your power, help me resist the devil and see him flee. (Matthew 6:10, Luke 9:23, John 10:10, James 4:7)

Lord Jesus, help me to live in the light of Your presence. Lead me in Your paths of righteousness and away from anything evil. (John 17:15, Ephesians 1:18-23, John 12:26, Psalm 23:3)

Mighty Lord, thank You for spiritual armor for the spiritual battle—the belt of truth; breastplate of righteousness; helmet of salvation; feet fitted with the readiness of the Gospel of peace; shield of faith; and the sword of the Spirit, the Word of God. By faith, I now put on each piece. Help me remain strong in Your mighty power and stand against the enemy's wicked schemes. (Ephesians 6:10-18)

Thank You for such spiritual weapons as faith, truth, and righteousness that demolish strongholds. Help me to keep my mind fixed on what is true, noble, right, pure, lovely, admirable, excellent, and praiseworthy. (2 Corinthians 10:3-6, Philippians 4:8)

Holy Spirit, I know my own actions can open the door to the enemy. Lead me to be humble, not prideful; forgiving, not holding grudges; content, not striving for what doesn't satisfy. (2 Corinthians 2:10-11, Galatians 5:22-23, Ephesians 4:27)

I recognize that the devil is attempting to incite me to sin—to prompt me to do evil. I'm desperately dependent on You to fight off the enemy's deceitful attacks. (1 Chronicles 21:1, John 13:2, Acts 5:3)

I pray as well for each member of my family and for my pastors, church staff, and fellow believers. May they also suit up in Your armor and experience victory by Your power. (Colossians 4:3; Thessalonians 5:25, Hebrews 13:18, 1 Peter 5:8-10)

Assist me now, Lord, as I exert my authority in Christ over the enemy. (Because we wrestle against demons—spiritual forces of wickedness—this is an opportunity to address and resist the evil spirit behind particular sins or temptations you or your loved ones are facing such as unbelief, depression, anger, lust, fear, greed, despair, pride, sloth, etc.)

In the name of the Lord Jesus Christ, the One who shed His blood on the cross and rose from the grave, I command you, evil spirit of _____, to leave me, my family, and my ministry. Because I am in Christ and stand in His victory over you, you must flee. Evil spirits, rulers, authorities, cosmic powers, spiritual forces of darkness, you are now bound from my family, my mind, my body, my home, and my finances. In the name of Jesus, I resist the devil and all demons.

Now, I ask You, Lord God, to build a hedge of protection around me and my loved ones throughout this day and night. I ask You, in the name of Jesus, to send angels to surround us and to protect us today and every day. Guard our souls, bodies, minds, wills, and emotions. May Your holy angels protect us from any and all harmful demonic attacks. Because the grace of the Lord Jesus Christ is with me, I live by faith and know that You, the God of peace, will soon crush Satan under my feet. I long to see Satan fall like lightning as I live in the authority You have given me over the power of the enemy. (Job 1:10, Psalm 3:3, Psalm 34:7, Romans 16:20, Luke 10:18-19)

Almighty God, use me as a soldier in Your spiritual battles. I need not live in fear because greater are You who lives inside me than the enemy who is in the world. Enable me to fight the good fight and advance Your Kingdom into the enemy's occupied territory. (Colossians 2:15, 1 John 4:4, 2 Timothy 4:6-8)

Father God, keep me alert to the evil one with spiritual eyes wide open as You use me to make a difference for eternity by helping other people come to know You, grow in You, and live for You. (1 Thessalonians 5:6, Proverbs 4:23, 1 Corinthians 10:12, Matthew 28:19-20)

O Lord, thank You that absolutely nothing—not even the spiritual forces of evil—can separate me from Your love. (Romans 8:38-39, Luke 4:1-13)

I ask all of this in the name of Jesus. Amen and Amen.

This prayer has been composed by Rick Duncan utilizing personal study and resources from Dean Ridings, author of the *Pray! Prayer Journal* (NavPress), and Wayne Grudem's *Systematic Theology.*

Appendix B

DEMON POSSESSION, "DELIVERANCE MINISTRY," AND CVC

*T*his position paper is designed to answer the question, "Can a Christian be demon possessed?" It also explains our position on a controversial and often divisive approach to spiritual warfare called "deliverance ministry."

The term "demon possession" is an unfortunate term that has found its way into some English translations of the Bible but is not really reflected in the Greek text. The Greek New Testament can speak of people who "have a demon" (Matthew 11:18; Luke 7:33, 8:27; John 7:20, 8:48-49, 52; 10:20) or it can speak of people who are suffering from demonic influence (Greek: *daimonizomai*), but it never uses language that suggests that a demon actually "possesses" someone.

It does not seem very helpful to attempt to define categories or degrees of demonic influence, as has sometimes been done, with words such as "depressed," "oppressed," "obsessed," etc., for Scripture does not define a list of categories like this for us to use, and such categories only tend to make complicated what is a simple truth that there can be varying degrees of demonic attack or influence in a person's life (see Luke 4:2, 2 Corinthians 12:7, Ephesians 6:12, James 4:7, 1 Peter 5:8).

An individual Christian's life can become influenced by demons, especially if that person does not know about or make use of the weapons of spiritual warfare that are taught throughout the Bible and emphasized in Ephesians 6:10-20.

It would seem that in some cases the degree of demonic attack or influence in a Christian's life could be quite strong. Yet the distinction between influence and control must be maintained. Repetitive sin puts people in moral bondage but not in bondage to indwelling spirits. The teaching of the Scriptures is that Christians cannot be controlled against their wills by demonic habitation. Followers of Christ have the King Himself dwelling in them (John 14:23, Romans 8:9-17) and the One who is in us is greater than the one who is in the world (1 John 4:4).

A believer's will cannot be completely dominated by a demon so that the believer has no power left to choose to do right and obey God. Scripture guarantees that sin shall have no dominion over us since we have been raised with Christ (Romans 6:14, see also verses 4 and 11).

When it comes to spiritual warfare, all Christians should believe in deliverance. We know that we have been delivered from the kingdom of darkness into the kingdom of the Son he loves (Colossians 1:13). Through the Holy Spirit, we are in Christ and Christ is in us and we are the freed captives of our King.

One real potential for problems in the Christian life is blaming things on the demonic, and neglecting normal Christian growth and maturity. Many Christians are looking for the quick fix of "casting out a demon" to help them overcome some sinful behavior rather than doing the hard work of consistently applying the classic spiritual disciplines over a long period of time. This can be a sign of a lack of maturity in the lives of many believers or a poor understanding of the biblical process of sanctification.

Our mode of warfare is best captured by Ephesians 6:10-20: reliance on the power and protection of God, embracing the Word of God, specific obedience, fervent and focused prayer, and the aid of fellow believers. Spiritual warfare with the power of evil is a matter of consistently and repeatedly turning from darkness to light by applying the classic disciplines of our faith. We resist the devil through disciplines such as prayer, reading Scripture, memorizing verses, meditating on the Word, repentance, faith, obedience, worship, service, stewardship, evangelism, fasting, accountability, and solitude. Following Jesus in this way releases the power of God in our lives.

Our enemy is real and tempts us in a myriad of ways. We stand upon the teaching of God's Word and Jesus who taught us to pray, "Lead us not into temptation, but deliver us from evil." Our warfare is focused on the power of God, rather than the devil's ploys. Ephesians 6:10-11 says, *Be strong in the Lord and in His mighty power. Put on the full armor of God so that you can take your stand against the devil's schemes.* Our enemy may prowl like a lion but he is on God's leash.

At CVC, we will not permit a ministry of "casting out spirits" from believers to function. Members and regular attenders who practice this kind of "deliverance ministry" will be instructed to stop. This is an unbiblical practice that hinders the process of biblical sanctification, confuses the saints, and divides the church.

(For further understanding of our position, please read *The Covering* by Hank Hanegraff, and *Power Encounters: Reclaiming Spiritual Warfare* by David Powlison.)

25 BOOKS FOR PERSONAL GROWTH
by Rick Duncan|Founding Pastor,
Cuyahoga Valley Church

THEOLOGY

1. Knowing God by J.I. Packer
2. The Holiness of God by R.C. Sproul
3. Seeing and Savoring Jesus Christ by John Piper
4. Systematic Theology by Wayne Grudem
5. The Reason for God by Tim Keller
6. Mere Christianity by C. S. Lewis

DEVOTIONAL

1. Pilgrim's Progress by John Bunyan
2. The Pursuit of God by A.W. Tozer
3. The Practice of the Presence of God by Brother Lawrence
4. Morning and Evening by Charles Haddon Spurgeon
5. My Utmost for His Highest by Oswald Chambers
6. Calvary Road by Roy Hession

DISCIPLESHIP

1. Spiritual Disciplines for the Christian Life by Donald Whitney
2. Radical and Follow Me by David Platt
3. Crazy Love by Francis Chan
4. The Master Plan of Evangelism by Robert E. Coleman
5. The Spirit of the Disciplines by Dallas Willard

LEADERSHIP

1. Spiritual Leadership by J. Oswald Sanders
2. The Making of a Leader by Robert Clinton

3. <u>Spiritual Leadership</u> by Henry and Richard Blackaby
4. <u>Courageous Leadership</u> by Bill Hybels

BIOGRAPHY

1. <u>George Muller of Bristol</u> by Arthur T. Pierson
2. <u>Shadow of the Almighty</u> by Elizabeth Elliot
3. <u>Jonathan Edwards</u> by Ian Murray
4. <u>Hudson Taylor's Spiritual Secret</u> by Dr. and Mrs. Howard Taylor

REFERENCES

BOOKS:

Akin, Daniel L. *A Theology for the Church*

Alcorn, Randy. *The Treasure Principle*

Barnhouse, Donald Grey. *The Invisible War*

Bauer, Walter. *A Greek English Lexicon of the New Testament*

Bloye, Brian. *It's Personal*

Bonhoeffer, Dietrich. *Life Together*

Bridges, Jerry. *The Pursuit of Holiness*

Chan, Francis. *Crazy Love*

Chan, Francis, *Forgotten*

Conner, W.T. *Work of the Holy Spirit*

Crabb, Larry. *Connecting*

DeMoss, Nancy Leigh. *Choosing Forgiveness*

Erickson, Millard. *Christian Theology*

Foster, Richard. *Celebration of Disciplines: The Path to Spiritual Growth*

Graham, Billy. *Just As I Am*

Graham, Billy. *The Holy Spirit*

Grudem, Wayne. *Systematic Theology*

Guthrie, Donald. *New Testament Theology*

Hanegraff, Hank. *The Covering*

Hansel, Tim. *Eating Problems for Breakfast*

Harris, R. Laird (edited by). *Theological Wordbook of the Old Testament*

Havergal, Frances, R. *Take My Life and Let It Be*

Hession, Roy. *The Calvary Road*

Hirsch, Alan. *The Forgotten Ways*

Keller, Tim. *The Reason for God*

Kinnaman, David. *Unchristian*

Lake, Mac. *Leadership Pipeline Development*

Lewis, C.S. *Mere Christianity*

Lewis, C.S. *The Best of C.S. Lewis, The Screwtape Letters*

Lewis, C.S. *The Last Battle*

Lewis, C.S. *The World's Last Night and Other Essays*

Lloyd-Jones, Martin. *Studies in Sermon on the Mount, Volume II*

Loyola, Ignatius. Van de Weyer, Robert, ed. *The HarperCollins Book of Prayers*

McGee. Robert S. *The Search for Significance*

MacArthur, John. *The Disciples' Prayer*

Morgan, G. Campbell. *The Spirit of God*

Owen, John. *Overcoming Sin and Temptation*

Packer, J.I. *Praying*

Packer, J.I. *Rediscovering Holiness*

Pink, A.W. *The Holy Spirit*

Piper, John. *Desiring God*

Piper, John. *When I Don't Desire God*

Powlison, David. *Per Encounters: Reclaiming Spiritual Warfare*

Propri, Joe. *The Peace and Joy Principle*

Ridings, Dean. *Pray! Prayer Journal*

Ryle, J.C. *Holiness*

Sire, James W. *The Universe Next Door*

Sproul, R.C. *The Holiness of God*

Spurgeon, Charles Haddon. *Spiritual Warfare in a Believer's Life*

Stanley, Andy. *God's Kingdom, Our Stuff, message preached at Northpoint Community Church, 1997*

Temple, William. *Readings in John's Gospel*

Thomas, Geoffrey. *Reading the Bible*

Tozer, A.W. *The Knowledge of the Holy*

Van de Weyer, Robert, Loyola, Ignatius. ed., *The HarperCollins Book of Prayers*

Waggoner, Brad. *The Shape of Faith to Come*

Wesley, John. *The Use of Money, in Sermons on Several Occasions*

Whitney, Donald. *Spiritual Disciplines of the Christian Life*

Whyte, Alexander. *Lord, Teach Us to Pray*

Willard, Dallas. *The Spirit of the Disciplines*

OTHER:

"The 1689 Confession: A Faith to Confess." (author unknown)

"The Westminster Catechism."

"The Neusner version of the Mishnah"

CBMC's Operation Timothy

The Navigator's 2:7 series

Cru's 10 Basic Steps to Christian Maturity

Lifeway's MasterLife

Piper, John. Message: Glorifying God... Period, July 15, 2013

WEBSITES:

Daveramsey.com
http://www.daveramsey.com/specials/mytmmo-gazell-budget/

crown.org
https://planner.crown.org/Secure/Account/Login.aspx?ReturnUrl=%2fSecure%2fBudget%2fNewBudget.aspx

familylife.com
http://www.familylife.com/-/media/Files/FamilyLife/Generic/SIMPLEBUDGETWORSHEET.pdf

Dave Ramsey's Debt Snowball tool
https://www.mytotalmoneymakeover.com/index.cfm?event=displayDebtSnowballLanding

www.patheos.com
Lee Strobel, Interview

Keith Mathison, "Our Ancient Foe," www.ligonier.org.
John Piper, "How to Deal with the Guilt of Sexual Failure for the Glory of Christ and His Global Cause," www.desiringgod.org

Afterward

I once heard a spiritual leader say, "If you want to be a great Christian, 1) read your Bible, 2) pray, and 3) tell other people about Jesus. Do these things every day for the rest of your life and you will grow to be a great Christian."

Three habits. That's simple, sound advice.

To be sure, we have introduced you to many more habits, disciplines, practices, relationships, and experiences than just three. But the truths you have learned in this discipleship guide are foundational principles that will serve you well for the rest of your life as a follower of Jesus. When you feel your love for Jesus and His Word waning, then you will likely find that it is because you failed to follow one or more of the principles we've held up in this material. Ask God for wisdom about which principles you need to reengage, review a section or two in this book, apply the truths to your life, and watch your love for and obedience to Jesus be rekindled.

But remember, the goal of discipleship is not external conformity to a set of rules and regulations of a religion. Neither is the goal of discipleship merely an intellectual adherence to what a group of people have defined as the correct doctrines.

The goal of discipleship is personal, radical transformation so that a person actually becomes conformed to the image of Jesus Christ. A disciple must actually begin to live the way Jesus would live if He were in that disciple's body. The reason this is possible is because He is actually inhabiting the body of every believer through the person of the Spirit of Christ. As a follower of Jesus yields more and more control to the Spirit, he or she will actually start living more and more like Christ.

Every spiritual practice, discipline, learning, relationship, and experience rightly followed must enable us to see, hear, and experience Jesus and His gospel more clearly. We dare not allow the disciplines, no matter how noble, to obstruct our view of Jesus. Instead, the best disciples are able to look through the disciplines to see Jesus better. When that happens, we change.

"And we all, with unveiled face, beholding the glory of the Lord, are being transformed into the same image of one degree of glory to another. For this comes from the Lord who is the Spirit" (2 Corinthians 3:18).

The goal of discipleship is not gaining information about Christ but growing in the imitation of Christ. As we look at Him more intently, we will love Him more immensely; and that, of course, will result in empowering us to live like Him more fully.

May you continue to apply the principles you've learned in *Living New: A Discipleship Journey to Grow in the Fruit of New Life* with the result that you'll grow to love Jesus so much that you will be enabled to Live New for His glory every day for the rest of your life.

Joining Jesus in His joy,

Chad Allen - Lead Pastor, Cuyahoga Valley Church
Rick Duncan - Founding Pastor, Cuyahoga Valley Church

ABOUT THE AUTHOR

Rick became a follower of Jesus as a child, but became earnest about his growth as a disciple when he was 21. Al Baker, a pastor who is now training church planters through the Presbyterian Evangelical Fellowship, was Rick's first intentional discipler as they roomed together on a baseball-oriented mission trip to Nicaragua, Guatemala, and Honduras. Tom Petersburg, staff member for Cru at Vanderbilt, and Frank "Pogo" Smith, sponsor of the Vandy Fellowship of Christian Athletes (FCA), were influential in Rick's development as a disciple. When he served with the FCA in Jacksonville, Florida, Bob Tebow, Jim Scroggins, and Ron Johnson were key influencers in his growth as a believer. In seminary, Chuck Steen of the Navigators, and fellow students John Rickenbacker and Steve Young helped keep the seminary experience from becoming a "cemetery" experience. Once Rick arrived in NE Ohio as a church planter, the State Missions director, Don Davidson, Cuyahoga Valley Church's sponsoring church pastor, Kenny Mahanes, and the Director of Missions for the Cleveland Hope Association, Dennis Betts, helped greatly with his spiritual formation.

For many years, Rick has been in pastors' forums here in NE Ohio where his growth in Christ has been greatly enhanced by leaders like Mike Misja, Joe Thompson, Tom Petersburg, Joe Abraham, Juri Amari, Paul Dalton, Randy Chestnut, Bob Mackey, Jim Weist, Bob Kuntz, George Mercardo, Jonathan Schaeffer, Garnett Slatton, and Chad Allen.

More recently, Rick has been challenged in his understanding of discipleship and how it works in the local church setting by Will Mancini and Jim Randall of Auxano. In addition, Mac Lake, founder of the Multiply Group and Senior Director for Church Planter Development with the North American Mission Board, has helped Rick think more clearly about leadership development in the local church as well as how adults learn best in 21st Century environments.

Made in the USA
San Bernardino, CA
28 August 2016